Sister Style

Sister Style

The Politics of Appearance for Black Women Political Elites

NADIA E. BROWN AND
DANIELLE CASAREZ LEMI

OXFORD
UNIVERSITY PRESS

OXFORD
UNIVERSITY PRESS

Oxford University Press is a department of the University of Oxford. It furthers
the University's objective of excellence in research, scholarship, and education
by publishing worldwide. Oxford is a registered trade mark of Oxford University
Press in the UK and certain other countries.

Published in the United States of America by Oxford University Press
198 Madison Avenue, New York, NY 10016, United States of America.

Library of Congress Cataloging-in-Publication Data
Names: Brown, Nadia E., author. | Lemi, Danielle Casarez, author.
Title: Sister style : the politics of appearance for black women political elites /
Nadia E. Brown, Danielle Casarez Lemi.
Other titles: Politics of appearance for black women political elites
Description: New York : Oxford University Press, 2021. |
Includes bibliographical references and index.
Identifiers: LCCN 2020044164 (print) | LCCN 2020044165 (ebook) |
ISBN 9780197540572 (hardback) | ISBN 9780197540589 (paperback) |
ISBN 9780197540602 (epub)
Subjects: LCSH: African American women—Political activity. |
African American women politicians. | Beauty, Personal—Political
aspects—United States. | Hairstyles—Social aspects—United States. |
Colorism—United States. | African Americans—Politics and government—21st century.
Classification: LCC E185.86 .B697448 2021 (print) | LCC E185.86 (ebook) |
DDC 305.48/896073—dc23
LC record available at https://lccn.loc.gov/2020044164
LC ebook record available at https://lccn.loc.gov/2020044165

DOI: 10.1093/oso/9780197540572.001.0001

1 3 5 7 9 8 6 4 2

Paperback printed by LSC Communications, United States of America
Hardback printed by Bridgeport National Bindery, Inc., United States of America

Dedicated to Nile, Nuri, and Neva
And for the Black womxn who we remember when we #SayHerName

Contents

Acknowledgments

Nadia E. Brown

This book has been a journey in self-love. The idea of this project started in 2009 when I first started to seriously think about going natural (after three failed attempts in college). However, I was advised not to go natural when I was on the academic job market because I did not want potential employers to view me as the "scary Black feminist." I followed that bad advice, and my decision to do so has haunted me ever since. During data collection for my first book, *Sisters in the Statehouse*, Black women legislators candidly shared their natural hair journeys with me and openly detailed the ways that their appearance influenced their political experiences. In fact, a majority of my interviews for that book would open up with legislators talking about some aspect of their appearance. Casual Black women's conversations in which we complimented one another on our hair, clothing, or make up would organically lead to a conversation about how their appearance has political implications. From there, the idea for this book project was born.

This book is several years in the making. I got married, had three kids in less than four years, switched institutions, and was involved in a car accident. Understandably, these incidents took me away from this project. Thankfully, Danielle Lemi agreed to join me in this vision and to co-author this book. She is a brilliant scholar, patient co-author, and steadfast ally. I am thankful for her friendship. Moreover, her expertise in sophisticated survey design and experiments has made this book richer. Danielle is a full and equal author and I am grateful for her work on this manuscript.

Likewise, I remain deeply grateful to Angela Chnapko for believing in this project and her steadfast commitment to seeing this in print. She was patient with me as I worked on this book in stages given my life circumstances. I am grateful and humbled by her commitment to this scholarship.

This manuscript benefited from the editorial assistance of Mili Jha and Abigail Bowen. The cover was designed by Acamy Schleikorn, a Black woman artist, who captured the essence of the women in our study. And this book was made stronger by the research assistance of Guillermo Caballero, Aiden Colburn, LaRae Crenshaw, Maricruz Osorio, India Lenear, Hanya Malik, Grace Reon, and Sono Shah.

I appreciate my many colleagues who have made this book possible. I am thankful for the support of the Butler Center at Purdue University for funding early parts of this project. Many thanks to my colleagues in African American studies for allowing me to teach courses on Black women's aesthetics as I honed this project. The leadership of Venetria Patton and Marlo David in this endeavor is unmatched. I am grateful to my colleagues in political science who read various drafts of this book, invited me give talks on my research, and made space for me to think through the ideas in these pages. I could not have completed this work with the academic support and friendship of Laurel Weldon, Valeria Sinclair-Chapman, Rosie, Clawson Pat Boling, and Molly Scudder and Jean Beaman (now at the University of California, Santa Barbara). Unmatched in her mentorship (and patience) is my former department head, Rosie Clawson. There are no words to express the amount of appreciation I have for Rosie. Indeed, it is difficult to adequately write about Rosie without tearing up. She is a force of nature who is always guided by principles, a sense of justice, and equity. She is a friend who is willing to tell it like it is even when it hurts, and is an advocate for her faculty. I have learned so much from Rosie. She has listened to me complain, wiped away tears, offered sage advice, connected me with influencers who would mold my career, co-hosted my first baby shower, and drunk margaritas with me. This book has been improved by my conversations with, and critiques from, Valeria Sinclair-Chapman, who is deeply rooted in the tradition of our great Black politics forebearers and who has reminded me that there is nothing new under the academic sun. Valeria is one of smartest people I know. I'm grateful to have a professional and personal relationship with this woman. We've opened up new doors together—as Black women political scientists—and as colleagues. I am thankful for what we built at Purdue, and believe that our legacy will tell the story of the power of what two Black women tenured professors can do to change a department with the support of leadership. My girls affectionately call her Auntie Val because of the relationship that I have with her. She's a colleague and a friend, an Academic Mama who has always been available to share parenting advice and scholarly tips. Rounding out the big three from Purdue's political science department was Laurel Weldon. I'm thankful for her vision, support, and belief in me since day one. Laurel—and Aaron Hoffman—are not only academic mentors but good friends who have offered excellent advice, provided opportunities for career advancement, and championed my growing family in numerous ways. Next, many thanks to Keith Shimko (and Chris Olofson), Molly Scudder, Kyle Haynes, Logan Strother, Tara Grillos, and Mark Tilton.

My time at Purdue University has been enriched by my chosen academic family. Words cannot express my appreciation and love for my graduate students: Guillermo Caballero, Jasmine Jackson, Michael Simrak, India Lenear, and Michael (MJ) Strawbridge. They are truly the best part of my academic life at Purdue. As I prepare to join the faculty at Georgetown University, I am most saddened to leave these students—as well as the other students that I recruited to the PhD program in political science at Purdue University. I remain excited for their futures and know that our bond is deeper than an institutional affiliation. Many thanks to the students in my spring 2020 Black Lady Classroom, who inspire me to be a better Black woman scholar. Our experience together has made me a better professor, mentor, and colleague. Thank you. Big ups to my students in African American studies and American studies at Purdue University. I am grateful for the interdisciplinary relationships that we were able to build and the resulting co-authored essays that were produced.

This book would have been impossible to produce without the guidance and foundation received from my colleagues and peers. Thank you for my sistah-scholars: Melina Abdullah, Lakeyta Bonnette, Khalilah Brown-Dean, Camille Burge, Niambi Carter, Pearl Dowe, Ashley Daniels, Natasha Duncan, Andra Gillespie, Christina Greer, Keneshia Grant, Megan Ming Francis, Zinga Fraser, Lorrie Frasure, Jenn M. Jackson, Kim Mealy, Taneisha Means, Jamila Michener, Shayla Nunally, Dianne Pinderhughes. Melanye Price, Jamil Scott, Christine Slaughter, Wendy Smooth, Tiffany Willoughby-Herard. I am grateful to Natasha Behl, Christina Bejarano, Cristina Beltran, Tabitha Bonilla, Ivy Cargile, Christian Dyogi Phillips, Magda Hinojosa, Mala Htun, Sophia Jordan Wallace, Nazita Lajevardi, Natalie Masuoka, Yalidy Matos, Jennifer Merolla, Zein Murib, Celeste Montoya, Maricruz Osorio, Stella Rouse and Kim Yi Dionne. I deeply appreciate Treva Lindsey, and Aria Halliday Danielle Phillips-Cunningham, for their friendship and interdisciplinary critiques of my work. I am indebted to the collegiality and support of my Women Also Know Stuff board members, the #PSSistahScholars crew, and the #MeTooPoliSci Collective. A special and heartfelt thank you to my National Conference of Black Political Scientists family. I am also appreciative of my fellow Bunchees and the Ralph Bunche Summer Institute program of the American Political Science Association. Thank you to Ray Block,

Jr., Christopher J. Clark, Bernard Fraga, Eric Gonzalez Juenke, Hakeem Jefferson, Dwaine Jengelley, Ravi Perry, Christopher Stout, Fernando Tormos-Aponte and for your steadfast support. A big thank you to the editorial team of *Politics, Groups and Identities*. I am thankful for my sorority sisters of Delta Sigma Theta Sorority, Inc., who supported this project in multiple meaningful ways. A special thank you goes to Tracy Y. Scott and the Black Women's PAC for graciously allowing Danielle and me to be a part of the organization as scholars.

None of this would be possible if were not for Jane Junn, my self-professed Academic Mama, and Alvin Tillery, my academic big brother. They have been my rock, a consistent source of support and the main guiding forces in my academic career. They molded me into a scholar, from my days as a graduate student at Rutgers University to my years on the tenure track and beyond. There will never be enough "thank yous" to adequately express my appreciation for them. Likewise, I am indebted to Sarah Allen Gershon, who is my "forever co-author." I am thankful for our academic partnership and our friendship.

Lastly, I am most grateful for my family. Thank you to the Browns: Joseph A. Brown, Nicholas and Cimberly Brown (along with Joseph C. Brown and Zoey E. Brown), Lindsey M. Brown and Thomas Martin, and Myra E. Brown. Thank you to the original Brown Girl, Janie Elizabeth Brown Barham, my paternal grandmother who passed in April 2020 before the completion of this book. Many thanks to the Hudson family. We are so excited to be moving closer to you as we return to the DMV. I am grateful for my cousin Carolyn James and her enduring belief in me. Thank you to my Auntie Barbara, Uncle Gilbert and Vernee Wilkinson for always being in my corner and praying for my family. I reserve my deepest gratitude for those who have loved me day in and day out, who helped to build me up, who cried and laughed with me, and who make me a better woman through their love and consistent support. Thank you to my mother, Nadine E. Medley, who selflessly moved to Indiana to help Brian and me take care our family in 2015 and has been with us ever since. She is the rock of our family. To Brian M. Lawrence, my partner: I am blessed each day to be your wife. Thank you for challenging me to be the best in all that I undertake. My efforts are strengthened by your love. I am grateful for B's unwavering belief in me—even when I do not believe in myself. I look forward to our future together and to growing into the fullness of our partnership. Throughout it all, I remain deeply grateful for the #BrownGirls: Nile, Nuri, and Neva. Being an Academic Mama has fundamentally transformed my identity as a scholar. My daughters have guided me to be a more intentional, thoughtful, and patient person. This book is for you. I hope that you see the beauty in your ebony skin and coiled hair. These are markers of your heritage, reminders that you are the hopes and dreams of our ancestors.

Danielle Casarez Lemi
This book has been a constant part of my daily life for about four years now. As a grad student writing about representation and getting ready to do elite interviews, I read Nadia's first book, *Sisters in the Statehouse.* I learned how to structure interviews and send interview invitations. I would later cold email Nadia asking for feedback, and Nadia graciously agreed to read my work and get on a call and give me feedback. I was a first-gen grad student from the California State University system in a doctoral program where women of color were neglected. I was just beginning to grasp my status as a woman of color in political science, and just beginning to realize that my experiences and frustration with the neglect are by design in our discipline. That Nadia was willing to give a random grad student such personal feedback meant so much to me. Nadia has influenced my work substantively and has been a model for staying true to myself as a scholar.

Over the years, we would meet in person, stay in touch, and learn that our research interests in intragroup diversity and representation were converging. This book has consisted of collecting a ton of original data, raising funds, learning Adobe Photoshop, dancing in Deep Ellum, and inviting ourselves to a corporate holiday party. As we dove into this book, I was finishing my doctorate and moving to Dallas, Texas, for a postdoctoral fellowship at the John G. Tower Center for Political Studies at Southern Methodist University. This book was a constant through my cross-country moves, job market trials, and ultimate career change. Over the course of this book, I have grown as a person and as a scholar. One of the biggest lessons from this project is my learning about interpretivism and work I wish I had read in graduate school. I was trained as a positivist, and during this project, I was trying to find my voice, learn how to publish, get exposure, and earn respect, all while trying to figure out what I wanted to do with my life since political science kept slamming the door in my face. Nadia was a patient co-author and friend when our dialogues showed how little I understood about interpretivism and what it meant to *fully* center Black women—without making cross-group comparisons—in this project. For that, I am grateful. Working on this project has been a true privilege.

So many people, many already mentioned, helped us push this forward. Chapter 4 would not have been possible without Tracy Scott and the Black Women's Political Action Committee of Texas (BW PAC). We are enormously grateful for Tracy's and the PAC's support of this project. Chapter 8 was made possible with the APSA Rita Mae Kelly fund and support from Pearl Dowe and Christina Bejarano. Gina Coorley and Sambhav Tripathi at Lucid also graciously helped us as I became frazzled fielding the second experiment. We thank Grace Reon for helping us proofread and check our second experiment before launching. Many thanks to Emily Beauliu, Niambi Carter, Christina Greer, and Christina Wolbrecht for their trust and permission for us to use their photos as we figured out how to design the second experiment. Earlier drafts of the first experiment of Chapter 7 benefited from feedback from the reviewers at *Journal of Race, Ethnicity, and Politics,* Amy Lerman and participants at the APSA 2018 meeting, participants at the APSA 2017 meeting, and participants at the 2018 Gender and Political Psychology conference. Chapter 6 was a massive data collection project, and we are thankful to Sono Shah, Maricruz Osorio, India Lenear, Guillermo Caballero, Hanya Malik, Aiden Colburn, LaRae Crenshaw, and Grace Reon for the scraping, the coding, and the searching they did to help us finish that chapter. The financial aspect of all of these moving parts was made easier with the help of Ray Rafidi at Southern Methodist University and Paige Pfeifer at Purdue University.

Another constant through my life over the last few years has been the support of Jim Hollifield and Luisa del Rosal at the Tower Center. I am grateful for the financial and moral support, and for the constant cheering both have given me as I worked to find my way in the discipline. At the Tower Center, I had the money I needed to support my work, the encouragement to keep going, and the time and autonomy to do whatever I wanted—exactly what early-career scholars need.

The final constant through all of this has been my parents. Throughout the ups and downs, my parents have stood by with love and patience. Everything I have been able to do is owed to them.

Sister Style

1

Introduction

> If I didn't define myself for myself, I would be crunched into other
> people's fantasies for me and eaten alive.
>
> —Audre Lorde

In a January 2020 interview with *The Root*, Representative Ayanna Pressley (D-MA) revealed that she suffered from alopecia areata and had lost her hair to the disease (Moulite 2020). Rep. Pressley, the first Black woman to represent Massachusetts in Congress, had garnered a significant amount of attention as a member of "the Squad" (McNulty 2019), a group of newly elected progressive politicians, and as one of the women elected during the 2018 Blue Wave (Fisher 2019). Rep. Pressley's political brand and signature style—her Senegalese twists—ignited conversations about representations of Black women political elites with Afro-textured hair (Branigin 2018). The Massachusetts Congresswoman told *The Root*,

> As a Black woman, the personal is political. My hair story is no exception.
> Sharing a very personal story today to create space for other. My twists have
> become such a synonymous and a conflated part of not only my personal
> identity and how I show up in the world, but my political brand. And that's
> why I think it's important that I'm transparent about this new normal and
> living with alopecia. (Moulite 2020)

In the interview, Rep. Pressley noted that Black girls and women had written affirming messages to her about her decision to wear her Afro-textured hair. Consequently, the decision to go public about her health condition was based on the fact that girls looked up her. Having been intentional in her decision to wear Senegalese twists as a transitional hairstyle, Rep. Pressley was prepared for people to believe her hair was a political statement. A transitional hairstyle is a protective style worn while moving from

Sister Style. Nadia E. Brown and Danielle Casarez Lemi, Oxford University Press (2021). © Oxford University Press.
DOI: 10.1093/oso/9780197540572.003.0001

chemically relaxed hair to natural hair (Ndichu and Upadhyaya 2019). She explained, "the reality is I'm Black. And I'm a Black woman. And I'm a Black woman in politics. Everything I do is political" (Moulite 2020). For Rep. Pressley, hair and her decision to forgo wigs to hide the alopecia is "about self-agency. It's about power. It's about acceptance" (Moulite 2020).

This book is about the everyday politicization of Black women's bodies and its ramifications for politics. Our focus is on Black women politicians and Black voters. Since President Donald Trump's election in 2016, there has been a renewed interest in intersectional approaches to voter behavior, particularly as scholars seek to explain why White women voted for Trump (Junn 2017). By contrast, Black women are the most reliable Democratic voters (Gillespie and Brown 2019). Preliminary exit poll data from the 2020 election suggests that 9 in 10 Black women reported support for the Biden/ Harris ticket. Indeed, it was Black women's organizing and voter turnout that delivered the presidency for Biden (Schmidt 2020). This pattern holds true for the previous presidential election as well. According to exit poll data, more than 90% of Black women voted for Hillary Clinton in 2016 and 96% voted for Barack Obama in 2012.[1] However, much attention—particularly in the Democratic Party—has been placed on turning Black women's high rates of political participation into electoral successes for those women as candidates (Robinson 2018).

Black women have won prominent elections and they comprise a sizable number of all women legislators. Despite these successes, however, they remain an underappreciated group in American politics. The Democratic Party and its allies are reluctant supporters of Black women, an idea that former DNC chair Donna Brazile, Yolanda Caraway, Leah Daughtry, and Minyon Moore (2018) reinforced in their latest memoir. Black women activists, politicians, and political strategists alike have urged the Democratic Party to support policies that benefit Black women as well as to support Black women candidates (Packnett 2017). Avis Jones DeWeever of the Black Women's Roundtable advised the Democrats to "water your own backyard" (Williams 2019) meaning that the party should do more to cultivate Black women candidates rather than attempting to woo back White male voters who are inconsistent Democratic supporters. Likewise, political activist Angela Davis touts the rationale for supporting Black women candidates:

Black women have had to develop a larger vision of our society than perhaps any other group. They have had to understand white men, white women, and black men. And they have had to understand themselves. When Black women win victories, it is a boost for virtually every segment of society. (Scott 2017)

Research supports Davis's claims. For example, Black women legislators are most likely to champion legislation that advances civil rights and women's rights (Brown and Banks 2014). Black women legislators are also especially attuned to how legislation that is seemingly beneficial to society as a whole may unintentionally harm Black women and all people of color (Orey et al. 2006).

After the 2016 election, Black women proved that they were "born for a time such as this," a quote from the Biblical Book of Esther that Stacey Abrams used in her Georgia gubernatorial primary victory speech in 2018 (Carr and Peeler-Allen 2018). As candidates, Black women were up to the task. In 2018, writer Luvvie Ajayi led a volunteer-run effort to create a database of Black women who would seek elected office. The website, Black Women in Politics, would go on to house information on over 600 Black women candidates for federal, state and local elections. Taking to heart Shirley Chisholm's oft-quoted saying, "If they don't give you a seat at the table, bring a folding chair," Black women mounted their own campaigns for public office in record-breaking numbers (Mohdin 2018), and many of them won their races. According to the Center for American Women in Politics, today Black women comprise about 17% to 18% of all women members of Congress and state legislators.[2] The significance of these victories indicates that Black women are a powerful voting bloc as well as viable candidates for political office.

In 2020, Black women candidates for Congress ran at record numbers. The Center for American Women and Politics notes that there were at least 130 Black women congressional candidates.[3] Black women, including multi-ethnic Black women who report having Black ancestry in combination with another race, comprise 20% of all women candidates for the House of Representatives and 21.7% of all women candidates for the Senate. Black women are seeking federal legislative office as both Democrats and Republicans. Furthermore, Black women candidates made national headlines. For instance, Cori Bush defeated 20-year incumbent Lacy Clay (D-MO) in a July 2020 primary to represent Missouri's 1st Congressional district. She handily won the general election is headed to Congress to join the more progressive branch of the Democratic party. And in the November 2020 election,

Candace Valenzuela narrowly lost her bid to become the first Afro-Latina in Texas's 24th Congressional district. And two Black women, Angela Stanton-King (R) and Georgia State Senator Nikema Williams (D) were candidates for Georgia's 5th Congressional district. Williams easily defeated Stanton-King for this open seat that was once held by Civil Rights icon Representative John Lewis (D), who died of cancer in July 2020. Other noticeable down ballot races where Black woman made historical inroads are Kim Jackson who became the first queer Georgia state senator and Michele Rayner-Goolsby who made history as the first openly Black queer woman elected to any position in Florida, she will serve in the state's House of Representatives. These women's successful elections demonstrate that the diversity among Black women candidates as well as their ability to win races (Brown and Gershon 2020).

The biggest electoral prize of all in 2020 goes to Kamala Harris for her successful candidacy as Vice President as part of the Biden/Harris ticket. This is a historic win. Harris, the second Black woman and first South Indian American senator in the nation's history, was tapped as the Democratic Party's vice presidential nominee after months of anticipation and speculation following Biden's announcement that his VP pick would be a woman. Black women activists, politicos, and citizens mobilized to demand a Black woman vice presidential nominee.[4] Indeed, the political moment was right for a Black woman—and a multi-ethnic Black woman—to be selected for the bottom of the ticket. As millions of protestors decried systemic racism and police brutality over the deaths of George Floyd, Breonna Taylor, Tony McCabe, Ahmaud Arbery, and Rayshard Brooks in 2020, Black Lives Matter activism seized the national stage. Similarly, the coronavirus panic and the lack of a cohesive response from federal government shone a national spotlight on the persistent racial inequities in the country. The anti–Asian Americans and xenophobic attacks stoked by fears and accusations that the virus originated from China also exacerbated hate crimes and led to an increase of hate crimes committed against this group. It is within this context that Kamala Harris emerged as the Democratic choice for vice president.

Indeed, Kamala Harris rose to this occasion and galvanized Americans, who cast more than 75 million votes for her and Biden. This was the most votes earned by any presidential ticket (North 2020). Americans convincingly showed their support for the Kamala Harris's historic bid for office. In recognition of this support, Harris directly thanked Americans for their support but also specifically called out Black women voters and acknowledged that Black women made this victory a reality. During her victory speech,

Kamala Harris stated "While I may be the first woman in this office, I will not the last, because every little girl watching tonight sees that this a country of possibilities" (Betancourt 2020).

Yet in still, Kamala Harris may have some possibilities available to her that other Black women candidates may not have because of her appearance. This multi-ethnic Black woman was once called the "best-looking attorney general in the country" by President Barack Obama (Lemi and Brown 2020). While Obama apologized for these gender-biased comments shortly after he said them in 2013, his comments underscores how people view Harris. Her competence as an attorney general, senator, and later the first woman of color vice presidential candidate for a major political party will be assessed in part on the basis of her record but also in the context of racialized-gendered beauty aesthetics. Like Black women political elites who have come before her, Harris will have to contend with ethno-racial and gendered stereotypes that will largely draw on her appearance and not her political accomplishments. At the time of writing, one focal point of public discourse is about Harris's identity and her connections to Black and Asian American voters given her multiracial background (e.g. Lemi 2020). In this study, we include Kamala Harris as a Black woman because she has written about herself as a Black woman (Harris 2019), and while some may perceive her dual backgrounds to be mutually exclusive, we do not believe her being Asian means she is not Black, nor do we believe that her being Black means she is not Asian.

Although their work "boost[s] virtually every segment of society" (Williams 2019), Black women politicians' bodies are deeply politicized in the United States, as Black women political figures consistently encounter inappropriate commentary on their bodies (Ford 2015). Often, this commentary is negative. For example, in 2011, Representative Jim Sensenbrenner (R-WI) criticized Michelle Obama's childhood obesity campaign, reportedly saying, ". . . Michelle Obama, her project is obesity. And look at her big butt."[5] In another instance, actress-comedian Roseanne Barr was fired from *Roseanne* in 2018 for likening Valerie Jarrett, former advisor to President Obama, to an ape.[6] Further, Congresswoman Cynthia McKinney made national headlines in 2006 when she was profiled by Capital Police as a visitor to Congress rather than a member of the national legislature. The Congresswoman had changed her hairstyle and suddenly became unrecognizable to Capital Police (Brown 2018). These examples demonstrate that the bodies of Black women political elites face a tremendous amount of scrutiny. Black women's bodies are perceived to be transgressive (Copeland 2010), out of place (Puwar 2004), defying norms (Shaw 2006), or grotesque (Kerchy 2005) in political spaces.

Furthermore, these actions and comments against Black women's bodies are reflective of the broader misogynoir in the United States that denies Black women bodily respect and autonomy in everyday life (Bailey 2018). The continuing manifestations and intrusions on their bodies today are legacies of Black women's historical lack of ownership of their bodies. To deny the racist, sexist, and patriarchal underpinnings that have created a culture in which Black women are both demeaned and fetishized on the basis of their physical appearances would be shortsighted. Black women are often simultaneously hypervisible and invisible, meaning that they are perceived as overly present and are yet ignored altogether, which either renders them as something with which they do not fully identify or erases other signifiers that they wish to adopt. Racialized difference and gendered performance simultaneously amplify racist and heteronormative politics at work (Story 2017). A historical examination shows that centuries of enslavement and colonialism has led to a defining/redefining the Black female body, and that colonialism is tied to racialized conceptualizations of gender and gendered notions of race (Story 2010).

Take for instance *Hudgins* v. *Wright* (1806) in which the Wrights, who were enslaved Americans, claimed that they were entitled freedom because they were descendants of a free American Indian woman. However, Hudgins their White enslaver contended that the Wrights were the descendents of an enslaved Black woman and an American Indiana man and thus, were not entitled to freedom. The Virginia High Court of Chanery concluded that because the Wrights were various shades that they were entitled to their freedom. The Virginia Supreme Court of Appeals granted the Wrights' their freedom, however, did not agree with the Chancellor's line of reasoning. Judge St. George Tucker draw on the physical characteristics of American Indians and people of African descendent to conclude that the phenotype present in generations of interracial descendants makes it difficult to conclude that the Wrights' appearances proved them not to be American Indian and thus, deserving of freedom. Indeed, Judge Tucker be decreed that "Nature has stampt upon the African and his descendants two characteristic marks, besides difference of complexion, which often remain visible long after the characteristic distinction of colour either disappears or becomes doubtful, a flat nose and woolly head of hair. The latter of these disappears the last of all" (Hudgins v. Wright, 11 VA 134). However, because the Wrights were determined not be Black and could not be enslaved, they were presumed free because of their pheno-type. Judge Tucker noted that "the witnesses concur in assigning to the hair of Hannah. . . the long, straight, black hair of the native aborigines of this country" (Hudgins v. Wright, 11 VA 139). Because Hannah Wright had long and straight hair, she was free. Phenotype, most notably hair and skin tone, were used to denote who was free and who could be enslaved. The phys-ical markers of women carried racial significance that marries ancestry and freedom. The centrality of race can be tied to one's appearance, even within a complicated and contested system of racial hierarchy that imparts meaning on this social phenomenon (Haney Lopez 1994). Indeed, generations of Wrights were able to forgo enslavement and racial subordination because they do not have distinct African features. Unlike Hannah and her family, Black women with African features have faced a uniquely racialized and gendered history in the United States because of the connections to their physical features and how social groups were formed and reified in America.

While rooted in histories of colonialism, imperialism, and slavery, discussions of Black women's bodies still contain agency and representation. For instance, soul and R&B singer Solange Knowles's fourth album contained a song entitled, "Don't Touch My Hair," in which she detailed the importance of Black women owning their own bodies. The song became an immediate anthem for Black women because, as one Black woman reviewer opined, it was a "beautiful reflection of how our locks are intertwined with our rich history and subsequently bear a special significance that goes beyond our outward appearances."[7]

To be sure, candidates for political office make strategic choices about how to present themselves to voters (e.g., McIlwain and Caliendo 2011). However, not all candidates have to weigh decisions about their self-presentation alongside stereotypical tropes, cultural norms that denigrate Blackness, and European beauty standards, in addition to the historical legacies of racism, colorism, sexism, and heteropatriarchy. As such, Black women candidates face unique pulls and pushes in presenting an acceptable image in the eyes of voters.

This is where our book begins. We tackle questions central to the politics of appearance for Black women politicians and the Black voters who evaluate them. We join positivist and interpretivist approaches and innovate with a multi-method investigation of the following questions: What are the origins of the contemporary focus on Black women's bodies in public life? How do Black women politicians make sense of the politics of appearance? Is there a phenotypic profile into which most Black women politicians fit? How do voters process the appearances of Black women candidates?

The Study of Black Women in Politics to Date

To answer these questions, we situate this book within two literatures: candidate evaluation and the politics of body, hair, and skin tone. These literatures traverse the subfields of political representation, gender and politics, and racial and ethnic politics.

Race, Gender, and Candidate Evaluation

There are distinct differences in how (mostly white) women and (mostly men) Black candidates have been evaluated by voters (Githens and Prestage 1977). Researchers have used experiments and surveys to demonstrate that voters believe that women politicians are more compassionate, more likely to prioritize family and women's issues, warmer, more equipped to deal with education issues, more liberal and Democratic, and more feminist than men (e.g., Alexander and Andersen 1993; Burrell 1994; Huddy and Terkildsen 1993; Kahn 1996; Koch 2000). On the other hand, men politicians are thought to be more intelligent, more conservative, stronger, and better suited to deal with issues of crime, defense, and foreign policy (Lawless 2004b). The public expresses more confidence in a male commander in chief, especially around issues of foreign policy (Deloitte and Touche 2000). Issue competency stereotypes may have more to do with the political socialization that implicitly teaches citizens that men are better at managing issues like crime and foreign affairs, or that they are more emotionally suited to politics (Huddy 1994; Sanbonmatsu 2003). These stereotypes about a candidate's personal traits shape voters' tendencies to vote for either a male or female candidate (Sanbonmatsu 2002; Lawless 2004a; Kahn 1996). Generally, women are more likely to support women candidates (Rosenthal 1995; Sanbonmatsu 2002). Support for women candidates is more prevalent among those who are more educated (Dolan 1996) and younger (McDermott 1998), and those who are sporadic church goers (Welch and Sigelman 1982). Additionally, ethnoracial minorities favor women in government at higher rates than their white counterparts (Dolan 1996). However, some research has demonstrated that gender has less of an effect on voter choice in real-world elections. Instead, a candidate's party identification and incumbency have the greatest influence on voter choice (Dolan 2004, 2014a; Sanbonmatsu 2003). Additionally, gender stereotypes may only be salient to the politically uninformed (Bauer 2015). Still, gendered stereotypes about political leadership are persistent (Due Billing and Alvesson 2000). Though enlightening, many of these gender-based studies have not assessed whether these issues apply to *Black* women.

Similar to the research on gender, scholars of Black politics have established that voters apply biases to Black candidates. Some have shown that Whites will purportedly vote for a qualified Black candidate (e.g., Schuman et al. 1997), and others have found that racial prejudice may not motivate Whites' vote choice (e.g., Citrin, Green, and Sears 1990). Certainly, Black politicians may be an exceptional "subtype" of Black people in the minds of White voters (Schneider and Bos 2011). Nevertheless, racial prejudice may affect evaluations of a Black candidate's personality and issue positions (Moskowitz and Stroh 1994). Black candidates' skin tone may be the deciding factor in Whites' willingness to vote for a Black candidate (Fiske and Taylor 1991; Ashmore and Del Boca 1981; Weaver 2012; Terkildsen 1993). The implicit bias toward lighter-skinned Blacks over darker-hued Blacks may have been present in Whites' preferences for Black candidates with differing skin tones (Citrin, Green, and Sears 1990). Like the women and politics literature, this body of work is instructive but limited in that it tends to neglect the study of Black *women* candidates.

Scholarship using an intersectional lens clarifies the politics of Black women candidates in particular (Smooth 2006). The literature suggests that Black women are not automatically doubly disadvantaged in American electoral politics because of their race and gender. Black women have developed a distinct Black female consciousness, which affects their political behavior and ideologies (Simien 2006). As such, Black women do not separate or rank their racial and gendered identities, and they instead form a new identity that represents the interlocking of their parts (Brown and Banks 2014; Hancock 2007; Simien 2006; Orey et al. 2006).

Studies have shown that Black women voters differ from Black men and White women voters in their evaluation of Black leaders and political phenomena (Burns, Schlozman, and Verba 2001; Gay and Tate 1998). Black women are the fiercest supporters of Black women candidates (Philpot and Walton, Jr. 2007), and Black women candidates can effectively mobilize Black voters, irrespective of gender (Philpot and Walton, Jr. 2007). Black women's support of Black women candidates may be due to a privileging of racial interests and identities over gendered interests and identities (Gay and Tate 1998; Mansbridge and Tate 1992). Other work shows that Black women candidates may be hurt by generalized perceptions of Black women as "assertive" (Hicks 2017, 21). In short, intersectional approaches imply that Black voter responses to Black women candidates may be distinct when compared to all-voter responses to White women candidates and Black men candidates. We have less of a scholarly understanding of how Black women are assessed in their own right, not in comparison to candidates of other identities. Our book speaks to this oversight by mitigating the undertheorizing of Black women political elites and their experiences as well as voters' evaluations of this group.

Black Women's Bodies

We now turn to scholarly assessments of the body. It is important to contextualize our study of Black women politicians within an interdisciplinary framework. These studies are the foundation for our empirical work, which, unlike traditional political science research, is informed by humanistic scholarship. Rather than taking an ahistorical approach to assessing how current sociopolitical events and present-day voters and candidates think about Black women's bodies, we draw heavily from scholars in history; women's, gender, and sexuality studies; and Black studies to ground our work.

The role of anti-Blackness and racism in reaction to Black bodies cannot be overstated. By defining Black women's acceptable aesthetics by race and contrasting Whiteness against Blackness in the American context, Black women are placed in a subjugated position. Consider Immanuel Kant's (1997) view that beauty is, in essence, the perfect realization of a human being. Or Noel Carroll's belief that non-beauty, or ugliness, is the pinnacle of imperfection. Indeed, Carroll suggests "the moral credentials of [an ethnic or racial] group . . . can be endorsed by means of an association with beauty, or it can be demeaned by being represented as . . . ugly" (2000, 38). The denigration of the Black body by Whites as non-beautiful or ugly thus reveals the role racism plays in people's view of attractiveness.

Feminist disability theory engages the politics of aesthetics to show how the (dis)abled female body defies social hierarchies and normalcy. The disabled body indicates imperfection and the lack of progress (Thomson 1997), whereas Kant defines perfection and progress as bodily beauty. Efforts to alter the female body—either through diet, exercise, cosmetics, and/or plastic surgery—are similar to attempts to fix or heal the disabled body. Both disabled and altered bodies are "cast as deviant and inferior" (Thomson 1997, 19). Bodies that are classified as physically disabled and diseased are unable to perform activities of daily living. Consequently, the physical limitations of bodies highlight the unnatural state that causes both physical and social isolation. Racism is a social ill (Nelson 2006) that, in turn, leads to perceptions of the Black body as "diseased" (Gilman 1985, 1). Black women's bodies, then, become a site of disturbance that takes on both the "outsider" and "disabled" status. As a result, the juxtaposition of Whiteness against Blackness to define "beauty" allows for devaluation of and discrimination against Black women's bodies.

Lorraine O'Grady, Black feminist artist and theorist, uses the mirror as a metaphor to understand how Black women's representational history is one of distorted images. She theorizes, "To name ourselves rather than be named we must first see ourselves. For some of us, this will not be easy. So long unmirrored we may have forgotten how we look" (O'Grady 1992, 14). Without a true reflection of themselves, Black women may misremember who they are and instead accept others' skewed interpretations of them (Carroll 2000). Black women's bodies are subject to stereotypical interpretations that have manifested in images meant to control Black women (Hill Collins 1990). Take, for example, the Mammy stereotype of a large or obese dark-skinned Black woman who finds pleasure in taking care of Whites. This asexual being is selfless in her performance of household labor for White families. Conversely, the Jezebel stereotype is a sexually wanton Black woman who uses her feminine wiles to seduce men. Her body is inherently unrapable, as Black women are deemed unchaste and lascivious. These two stereotypes are directly derived from Black women's bodies and, to a much lesser extent, from their actions.

The dominant White American culture has created these images of Black women's bodies, which in turn have impacted how Black women see themselves and each other (Harris-Perry 2011). Thus, Black feminist scholars have sought to reimagine the Black female body in an oppositional stance to the mainstream discourse. Black female beauty, in perceived contrast to Eurocentric beauty norms, has been both historically and culturally associated with deviance, sexuality, and being "unmirrored." Therefore, considering the Black female body to be "beautiful" is at once liberating and radical (Hobson 2003). Viewing Black women's bodies on a continuum between the past and the present necessitates that bodies are inscribed with historical meanings and an Afro-futurist cultural aesthetic.[8] In this book, we offer an analysis of the Black female body as a site for reclaiming agency and subjectivity.

Methodological Approach

Our innovative study is the first to systemically examine the political implications of Black women's phenotype. There are no other studies in political science or related social science fields to connect Black women's appearances to electoral politics. As such, we cannot draw from existing political science measures to gauge our research questions. Our project requires an interpretivist approach and in-depth qualitative methods not only because quantitative metrics have yet to be designed for this type of study but also because we seek to make meaning of the experiences of Black women political elites and their evaluations by voters. Our novel examination of Black women's appearances requires a new approach to assessing how political elites and voters view and interpret sociocultural phenomena.

In order to understand the politics of appearance for Black women candidates and elected officials, we employ a multi-method approach and blend epistemological orientations. A multi-method approach has two main advantages. First, it allows the researcher to tackle a question from multiple vantage points. Second, quantitative and qualitative methods complement each other to increase accuracy (Creswell and Clark 2017). Rather than only run regressions on large-scale data, and rather just collect data from a few cases, a multi-method approach allows the researcher to cover more ground underneath the research problem. Instead of simply drawing conclusions from large statistical associations without understanding why a relationship exists, or from a few cases without understanding whether a general relationship exists, multi-method research sheds light on both sides of an issue. Given the lack of political science research on Black women elites, and the even greater lack of intra-categorical research on Black women elites, this approach offers the most leverage for theorizing about the politics of appearance for Black women elites and will allow us to generate the most thorough data on this subject to date.

Because social science research methods cannot achieve absolute objectivity, we combine aspects of positivism and interpretivism. This requires that we explicitly demonstrate the underlying assumptions and the choice of analytical strategies used in this book. Understandably, we devote considerable attention to the trade-offs between these two epistemological frameworks. The meta-theoretical positions and assumptions of both positivism and interpretivism have shaped our approach to both theory and method. It is our belief that this approach provides a superior understanding and deeper explanation of the politics of Black women's appearance.

Positivism places value on experience in general. This philosophy of science is particularly concerned with observation and testing to better understand human behavior (Durkheim 1982). Conversely, interpretivism calls for subjective meaning. As such, this philosophy of science chiefly values concepts such as empathy and interpretation. Because nothing happens in society that is not formed by human beings, we are investigating the difference between social structures and human agency (Collier 1994; Spelman 1998). Indeed, social theory and reality are "causally interdependent" (Bhaskar 1989, 5), meaning that theory is a by-product of society and has consequences within it. The combination of positivism and interpretivism allows us to produce research that distinctly recognizes that social processes are entirely culturally, spatially, and historically specific.

Rather than relying on the positivist assumption that race/gender can be observed in meaningful ways for Black women candidates, the first chapters of the book use interpretivist methods to gain privileged access to knowledge, particularly that of Black women candidates themselves. To that end, we are able to provide descriptive analysis and offer an interpretation of these women's experiences. Perhaps what makes our study unique is its atypical paring of positivist and interpretivist methods in political science studies. Because interpretivism is a relatively new methodological approach, it is useful to introduce the epistemological paradigm (Travis 1999) and how it informs this book. In interpretivist studies, the researcher is herself an instrument of data collection (Denzin and Lincoln 2003). As a Black woman interpretivist researcher, one of this book's authors, Nadia Brown, is a raced-gendered insider but an outsider in terms of professional experiences (Brown 2012). This insider/outsider status shapes the access she had to participants, what was said during interviews and focus groups, and the context in which Black women candidates and elected officials shared their experiences. Her positionality is critical to understanding the process and the subjective traditions within Black women's culture. Nadia's identity status and that of the women in this study are important variables in this research endeavor (Baca Zinn 1979).

In the first section of this text, we use interpretivist frames within an ethnomethodological tradition to demonstrate how social actors come to know a phenomenon, come to recognize that phenomenon as common, and know how it carries out in the activities of Black women political elites. Here, priority is given to understanding meaning and intentionality and not causal explanations. As such, our interpretivist insights seek to understand the process through which Black women's appearances are subjectively constructed. To that end, we provide descriptive analysis and an interpretation of Black women's embodied experiences within American politics.

The latter half of the book centers positivist explanations for the salience of the politics of appearance to provide a wider explanation of this political phenomena. Rather than assuming a mutual incompatibility between positivist explanation and interpretivist understanding, we combine these philosophies of science to demonstrate the importance of observable characteristics—patterned forms of interaction among social processes and humans that may lead to causal outcomes (Clarke 2009). A feature of this book is its unusual marriage of positivist and interpretivist approaches to the knowledge-production process. This study brings together our individual substantive research agendas on race, gender, identity, and phenotype, and different epistemological orientations for a collaboration that will resonate with scholars across fields and different segments of society as a whole. As full and equal collaborators on this project, we have married our individual expertise to produce a rich and detailed account of how the bodies of Black women political elites impact electoral politics.

This Book Moving Forward

The common practice of using race or gender to evaluate Black women political elites fails to capture the dynamism of how bodily attributes influence perceptions of these candidates. In our work, we seek to make the connection that skin tone and hair texture, along with the historical legacies that shape the current cultural and political contexts in which Black women run for office, dictate voter preferences for some Black women candidates. To this end, we draw on the historical significance of hair and skin tone in the lives of Black women to study voter responses to Black women candidates who vary in phenotype.

Extant literature indicates that Black women lawmakers are keenly aware of (a) how their bodies and corporeal experiences are racialized and gendered, (b) the ways in which their bodies fall outside the hegemonic constructions of beauty and femininity, and (c) the impact of race/gender-based stereotypes on how colleagues and voters perceive them (Brown 2014). For Black women, hair and skin tone are deeply political. Yet, scholars have little understanding of how Black women's skin tone and hair texture affect their chances of winning elected office. Because of the raced-gendered constructions of beauty, Black women office seekers may face different challenges and opportunities in their self-presentation than Black men, White men, and White women. As such, we contend that Black women's appearance may impact voters' perceptions of them.

Like Rep. Pressley, we seek to show Black women as political actors who have agency in their styling choices and in establishing a political brand. They are not victims of Eurocentric beauty norms; rather, they are traversing and navigating a culture that has restrictive, one-size-fits-all beauty norms. We center the voices of Black women elected officials to illustrate the complexities of crafting a professional image as a politician. We weave together an interdisciplinary analysis on electoral politics to evaluate Black women political elites, which is often not done in traditional gender and politics or race and politics literature. We are not interested in comparing Black women elites to White women elites or to Black men. Throughout this book, intersectional theory guides us as we assess the differences in Black women politicians' own political narratives and Black voters' responses to them (Crenshaw 1989). In doing so, we take a deep dive into intersectional theory building. While the research to date tends to lump all Black women together, we argue that physical features, namely skin tone and hair texture or style, distinguish the real political experiences of Black women elected officials and the inferences Black voters make about them. By paying special attention to Black women political elites, we argue that there is not a one-size-fits-all model for women in politics.

In Chapter 2, we trace the historical development of the politics of Black women's appearances in the United States and touch on sociological, political, and legal forces that have built the political opportunity structure for Black women politicians. Through a case study of the Creating a Respectful and Open World for Natural Hair (CROWN) Act, we examine how New Jersey state lawmakers successfully passed legislation to end hair discrimination. In Chapter 3, we present one-on-one interviews with Black women political elites to examine Black women's appearances, specifically hair, as a political site. In Chapters 4 and 5, we talk directly to Black women elected officials and Black women voters through focus groups to continue theorizing the politics of appearance. In Chapter 6, we conduct a visual content analysis of Black women candidates' headshots to examine whether there is a "phenotypic archetype" of Black women candidates to which Black women are exposed. In Chapter 7, we conduct two experiments that assess how Black women's hair and skin tone affect how Black voters evaluate them. Though this chapter speaks to the literature on race and campaign strategies, our focus is on individuals' presentation of their racialized appearance (e.g., McIlwain and Caliendo 2011; Gillespie 2010). In Chapter 8, we examine the extent to which linked fate, or a sense of political connectedness with their group, is relevant to evaluations of Black women candidates who vary in skin tone and hairstyle. In Chapter 9, we discuss the implications of this book for the study of race, gender, and Black women in American politics.

Using an intersectional framework, we argue that dominant, Eurocentric, beauty standards influence the electoral chances of Black women in varied and distinct ways. Because of the raced-gendered constructions of beauty, Black women office seekers may face different challenges and opportunities in their self-presentation than Black men, White men, and White women. We thus move beyond telling a causal story about how a particular variable affects outcomes for Black women politicians. Rather, our intervention is a paradigmatic one: we are further developing how scholars should employ intersectional analysis—by focusing on intragroup diversity (McCall 2005)—while breaking new empirical ground in the study of race, gender, Black women, and representational politics.

As this chapter's epigraph by the incomparable Audre Lorde illustrates, Black women need the ability to shape their own narratives. Indeed, much of what we know about Black women voters and political elites is based on their evaluations by others. These women are assessed, measured, and weighed against other demographic groups, often White women and Black men, rather than examined as political actors in their own right who need no comparison group to validate their contributions to American politics. Because the dominant discourse on Black women in American politics is based on the perceptions of outsiders, Black women have, in Lorde's words, been "eaten alive" in the political science literature. By foregrounding the narratives of Black women voters and politicians, we show the powerful ways in which this group is shaping American politics.

2

Afro-Textured Hair and the CROWN Act

Do not remove the kinks from your hair, remove them from your brain.

—Marcus Garvey

In December 2018, Andrew Johnson, a Buena Regional High School wrestler in New Jersey, was forced to cut his dreadlocks, or locs, courtside 90 seconds before his match. The referee informed Johnson that he'd have to cut his locs off or forfeit the match. According to a rule that regulates wrestlers' hair, an athlete's hair must be covered if it is over a certain length. In reality, though, this rule is rarely enforced. Dressed in his wrestler's uniform and surrounded by White adults, Johnson stood motionless as his locs fell to the floor. Images of a White woman cutting Johnson's hair with scissors went viral. In response, the New Jersey Sports Division opened a Civil Rights Investigation and sidelined the referee who had delivered the ultimatum to Johnson. Though Johnson won the match, he would later refer to it as an empty victory.

This incident became the impetus for New Jersey's Creating a Respectful and Open World for Natural Hair (CROWN) Act. The legislation provides protection from discrimination based on hairstyles by extending statutory protection to hair texture and protective styles in the Fair Employment and Housing Act (FEHA) and state education codes. In other words, people with Afro-textured hair will enjoy equal rights under the law and be allowed to wear their hair in culturally appropriate ways. The CROWN Act was named and first introduced by California State Senator Holly J. Mitchell. It was approved by the governor of California in July 2019, and went into effect on January 1, 2020—the one-year anniversary of Johnson's infamous wrestling match. The CROWN Act campaign is led by the CROWN Coalition, a partnership founded by the skincare brand Dove, and the social and political

Sister Style. Nadia E. Brown and Danielle Casarez Lemi, Oxford University Press (2021). © Oxford University Press.
DOI: 10.1093/oso/9780197540572.003.0002

justice organizations the National Urban League, the Color of Change, and the Western Center on Law & Poverty. To date, New York, New Jersey, Maryland, Virginia, Colorado, California, Washington, and several municipalities in Maryland and Ohio have passed the CROWN Act, while 23 other states have filed or pre-filed this legislation. Only two states, Florida and West Virginia, have filed, but not passed, the CROWN Act. Furthermore, July 3, 2020, was declared National Crown Day to celebrate the day that the CROWN Act was signed into law.

Legislators who have led CROWN Act efforts in their states, city councils, and municipalities are overwhelmingly Black women; however, Black men, Latinx men and women, and White women and men have signed on as lead sponsors, too. In December 2019, U.S. Senator Cory Booker (D-NJ) and Representative Cedric Richmond (D-LA) introduced this legislation at the federal level. The bill passed by voice vote in the House on September 21, 2020. The federal bill had 63 co-sponsors. Nationwide, these bills enjoy co-sponsorship by a diverse group of legislators. The growing popularity of this legislation is largely driven by an increase in the number of social media posts, videos, and reporting of discriminatory and humiliating experiences that Black people—particularly children—have encountered around their hair. Whether being forced to cut their hair in order to compete in a high school sport, as in Johnson's case, or being dismissed from school because of their hairstyle, which happened in 2018 to 11-year-old Faith Fennidy of Christ the King Middle School in Terrytown Parish, Louisiana, many young people have been victims, and the widespread online reporting of these incidents has sparked public outcry and highlighted discriminatory hair policies. The CROWN Act is a response to de jure and de facto discrimination based on hairstyle and hair texture.

In this chapter, we demonstrate both the need for legislative remedies for those with naturally textured hair and the importance of having Black women lawmakers champion polices around Black hair. Here, we connect policy formulation to Black women lawmakers' personal experiences and that of their community to create legislation. Using the New Jersey CROWN Act, we draw from interviews with two prime sponsors of the bill to understand the legislative process of this law. We show that this "easy bill," to quote New Jersey State Senator Sandra B. Cunningham, became law because of the salience of the issue, because of its resonance with (mostly young) Black Americans, and because the country was already talking about hair-based discrimination. Yet, there are limitations to the "ease" of passing this kind of legislation. The prevalence of hair-based discrimination points to a need to create a dialogue around kinky or coiled hair and other African American hairstyle practices. Legislators were clear that while hair discrimination may not be an intended consequence of employment policies or dress codes, the discriminatory outcome of such policies suggests that non-Black people or those who care for Black hair may be unaware of how these policies perpetuate discrimination.

The chapter proceeds with a discussion of Black hair. We describe common Black hairstyles and hair care practices. Next, we draw from select national and international incidents where Black people have been subjected to discriminatory practices around natural hair. These incidents demonstrate a rationale for legislative action. We conducted elite interviews with two prime sponsors of the New Jersey state legislature, including one of the key leaders in the CROWN Coalition, and we provide an account of these interviews and the legislative process for this bill. Lastly, we conclude that policy matters and that having Black women lawmakers at the table provides invaluable representation for previously uncrystallized issues (Mansbridge 1999).

What Is Black Hair?

There is no chemical difference between hair that is considered Afro-textured and hair of other ethno-racial groups (Lee 2012); however, persons with Afro-textured hair are socially assigned to the racial category "Black," as hair texture is a "racial marker" (Sims et al. 2019; Mercer 2005). There are multiple types of Afro-textured hair, but Black people's hair is usually coarser in texture, more delicate, and tighter in curl pattern than that of other ethno-races of people. Black hair can vary in texture from extremely fine to coarse. The curl pattern can be straight, wavy, coiled, or kinky. Likewise, Afro-textured hair can be naturally blond or red and can range from various shades of brown to black. Afro-textured hair has been described as "wooly," "kinky," "nappy," or "spiraled."

All hair contains a cuticle (the outer layer), a cortex (the middle layer that consists of keratin, moisture, and melanin), and a medulla (the center of the hair shaft). These cuticle layers differ among ethnic groups. Afro-textured hair has seven to eleven layers, compared to White hair, which has four to seven layers, and Asian hair, which has eleven or more layers. The cuticle in curly hair does not lie flat, which creates a wave or curl contour. The cortex is the main bulk of hair. Afro-textured hair contains a para and an ortho cortex, both of which are easily damaged. The para cortex grows evenly while the ortho cortex fibers grow unevenly and at an uneven rate. The para cortex develops on the outside of the curl and the ortho is on the inside of the curl. This results in some strands that may be thicker or thinner than others. Lastly, the medulla is the central core of the hair and is present in the majority of hair types.

Hair characteristics are classified by type, texture, elasticity, porosity, density, and natural curl and shape. Hair type refers to the hair's curl pattern. Hair types range from straight, wavy, or curly, to coiled. Texture is the thickness of each individual strand of hair and is mainly measured by the size of the cortex, or the average diameter of a single strand of hair. Elasticity is the hair's ability to stretch and return to its natural state without breaking. Porosity is the hair's ability to absorb liquids. Density refers to the number of hairs per square inch of scalp. Curl pattern is genetically determined. The more bent or coiled the hair follicle is, the tighter the curl pattern. There are 32 different curl patterns. Many people have several different curl patterns on their head, as each section of hair may vary from the others. Most notably, the hairline, crown, nape, and temple areas typically have different curl patterns (Gittens 2002).

A tighter hair bond differentiates Afro-textured hair from other hair types, as the bond creates curlier hair (Morioka 2005). According to hairstylist Andre Walker (1997), there are four categories of hair types: (1) straight, (2) wavy, (3) curly, and (4) kinky. In addition, the letters A, B, and C refer to the degree of coil variation within each type category, though Walker only differentiated two additional sub-categories and did not include a C texture in his original formulation. Figure 2.1 presents the different hair types.

Types 3 and 4 are the most common texture types for Black hair. Those with Type 3 hair have S-shaped, bouncy, and well-defined curls that are dry and slightly rough. Within each texture type, there are three sub-classifications of curl patterns. 3A hair is springy, 3B can range from springy ringlet to corkscrew shape, and 3C hair is coarser and often wiry or frizzy. 3C hair is often difficult to straighten. Type 4 hair is kinky and characterized by its Z shape. 4A hair is extremely coiled and may have a mixture of an S and a Z shape. 4A may be both wiry and frizzy and have a fine texture. 4B hair has a prominent Z shape pattern and is often shorter, springy, and coarser. 4C hair is naturally drier and is characterized by strands that are densely packed together. While Afro-textured hair naturally produces more oils than White and Asian hair,

HAIR TYPES

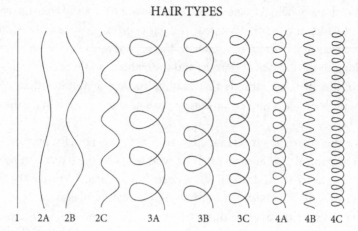

Figure 2.1 Hair Types

the tight curls of Black hair prevent the natural oils from spreading evenly along the hair from root to tip. Without this lubrication, hair becomes dry and brittle, which causes the hair to break or feel coarse to the touch. Kinky hair, or hair that is very tightly coiled, is more prone to breakage (Quaresma et al. 2015). As such, Afro-textured hair requires supplemental moisture because it naturally dries out as oil does not travel down the strands of the hair.

Curly and kinky hair textures are more vulnerable to drying out and breaking because the natural oils do not work their way down the hair shaft. Afro-textured hair is more fragile than other hair because it has less tensile strength and reaches its breaking point earlier than hair of other racial groups with less coiled or kinky hair. Lastly, Afro-textured hair experiences a phenomenon known as shrinkage, or the phenomenon that occurs when naturally coiled hair appears much shorter in length than when it is straightened. Shrinkage is most easily seen when the hair has been wet. The more tightly coiled the hair, the more shrinkage appears.

Black Hairstyles

Protective styles are commonly used to maintain and promote healthy Afro-textured hair. These styles require minimal daily upkeep and allow naturally dry hair to retain moisture. Because protective styles do not involve daily manipulation, these styles promote hair growth. Examples of protective styles include braids, two-strand twists, buns, wigs, head wraps, and weaves. Any style that protects the ends, which are the weakest and most fragile parts of Afro-textured hair, and can be worn for several days, is a protective style. An example of a Black woman styling Afro-textured hair in a protective style can been seen in the accompanying photo. Here, the stylist is two-strand twisting Afro-textured hair, which is a versatile style that can either be worn as a protective style or be taken out to provide a defined wavy pattern in loose natural hair.

Protective styles on natural hair may last from two weeks to two months, depending on the style and the wearer's hair texture. Hair in a protective style can be moisturized by spritzing it with a mixture of water and a light oil or applying a water-based leave-in conditioner. Afro-textured hair should be protected from coming into contact with harsh fabrics that absorb moisture—such as a cotton pillow case. Wrapping Afro-textured hair in a silk or satin covering at night will keep moisture in the hair and reduce breakage, tangles, frizz, and hair loss.

More than a style, braiding is an art form that has left an indelible mark on human history. For kinkier Afro-textured hair, braiding is more than a fashion statement. Braids protect natural hair from humidity and damage. The Himba people of Namibia starting braiding hair around 3500 BCE (Allen 2019). The origins of braids trace back to African culture, where a person's tribe, age, marital status, power, and religion could be identified from the pattern and style of their braids. Because braiding takes a considerable amount of time, people socialized during hair braiding and elders taught children how to braid. Thus, braiding was an intergenerational experience through which children learned how to create traditional styles. As cited in Allen (2019), Alysa Pace of Bomane Salon in Beverly Hills, CA notes that braided hairstyles have been popular in a variety of cultures across time and space. She dates cornrows as originating in Africa in 3500 BCE and then Afro box braids in Egypt in 3100 BCE. The halo braid was a staple in Greece around the first century CE, Native American pigtail braids in the fifth century, and the crown braid in Europe from 1066 to 1485. The staircase braid was popular in China from 1644 to 1912. With the advent of YouTube in 2005, braid tutorials became in vogue and gained renewed interest (Bey 2012; Perry 2020).

Examples of Afro-textured braided hairstyles may be seen in the accompanying photo. This image shows box braids with hair added to provide length and to extend the life of the style. These hair extensions are a protective style that gives hair a break from daily styling as well as adding length and the possibility for different hairstyling. For instance, Academy Award–winning actress Regina King wore purple box braids that she styled into a high and loose topknot at the LACMA Art+Film Gala in 2019. Pairing this style with a Gucci gown, King had one of the most acclaimed styles of 2019. For Regina King's summer 2019 appearances, the purple box braids were styled in several different ways that were widely praised by fashion critics and emulated by fashionistas around the world.

Locs are another protective hairstyle that dates back to Africa. This rope-like hairstyle is achieved by matting the hair. Priests of the Ethiopian Coptic religion in 500 BCE wore locs, and the first archaeological evidence of locs comes from East Africa. Indeed, a discovery of mummies revealed locs still intact (Trüeb 2017). Like braids, this hairstyle has been enjoyed by other ethno-racial groups. For example, the oldest scriptures of Hinduism document the Hindu god Shiva as wearing locs, or *jata* in Sanskrit (Trüeb 2017). Furthermore, other locked hairstyles have been found in civilizations ranging from Asia Minor, the Near East, the Caucasus, the East Mediterranean, and North Africa. African tribes such as the Maasai of Kenya have worn locs for eons. However, the modern popularity of locs is most readily associated with Jamaican and Rastafari culture. From the 1930s to 1950s, Rastafarians began to lock their hair in homage to their African identity and as a religious vow to mark their separation from Babylon, or wider society. While historians differ in their accounts of how locs settled in Jamaica during this time—either from East Indian slaves or from Kenyan Mau Mau warriors—this style denotes that the individual wearing it is a social outcast (Loc Artist 2016). Wearing locs, however, does not mean that one practices Rastafarianism.

Locs are a low-maintenance protective style. They can be braided, twisted, curled, or colored, worn in up-dos such as buns or rolls, and cut into a desired styled. This matted hairstyle cannot be combed. Black women celebrities such as Lauryn Hill, Zoë Kravitz, Whoopie Goldberg, Erykah Badu, India Arie, Lisa Bonet, and Zendaya have all worn locs. This style is also popular for men, and celebrities such as Lenny Kravitz, Lil Wayne, Chris Bosh, J. Cole, and Stevie Wonder have loc'd hair. Locs, seen in the accompanying photo, are ropelike strands that do not require much attention by the wearer. This style is ideal for those with Type 3 or 4 hair textures, as it will take longer for loose hair textures to fully lock. This style has become popular, most notably due to Bob Marley's music and cultural influence, but it has taken on a new cultural aesthetic since the 1970s with contemporary Black celebrities.

Afro-textured hair is versatile. It can be worn in a myriad of styles. Individuals with Afro-textured hair have the ability to change their style to as they deem fit—from long, straight weaves or wigs such as those worn by cast members of the Real House Wives of Atlanta to the short, cropped natural hairstyles worn by actress Lupita Nyong'o. Indeed, it's difficult to identify a Black woman celebrity with a signature hairstyle because looks and styles are ever changing. Even Angela Davis's iconic Afro hairstyle has been replaced with a gray coiffed twist-out style. And style icons Tracee Ellis Ross and Yara

Shahidi have been photographed in a variety of styles, ranging from Afros to head wraps. Black women political elites do not change their hair as often as celebrities, but they are also known to change their look as well. Take for instance, Representative Gwen Moore (D-WI), who started her career with straightened tresses but now wears sisterlocks. She has also worn braids and head wraps during her political career. See the Appendix for photos of hairstyles that are popular for those with Afro-textured hair.

Contextualizing Afro-textured Hair Today

Afro-textured hair has fascinated and intrigued many who are unfamiliar with this type of hair (Johnson 2013). When Afro-textured hair is in its natural state and free of chemicals, it often inspires fear and desire (Mokoena 2016). Misconceptions about Black hair—propagated by people of all ethnicities and races—include the idea that Afro-textured hair does not grow, that it is unmanageable, and that it is dirty. These myths stem from a history of White supremacy, colonialism, and imperialism that have been used to uphold stereotypes of Black inferiority (Mokena 2016).

Today's digital technology has led to the dissemination of information about Black hairstyles and the best products to use on Afro-textured hair, which has created renewed fascination with traditional protective styles.

Examples of celebrities and artists adopting these styles have sparked debates on cultural appropriation, Black hair, and authenticity. Take for example, the pop star Zendaya's 2015 Oscar red carpet appearance where she paired a Vivienne Westwood gown with faux locs. E!'s *Fashion Police* co-host, Giuliana Rancic, commented that Zendaya's hair must "smell like patchouli or weed" (Hoff 2015). Rancic had previously commented that Kylie Jenner's faux locs were edgy. Rancic's praising of a White woman for wearing the same style that she criticized on a Black woman reveals a racial disparity in the assessment of this traditionally Black hairstyle. White women celebrities such as Gwen Stefani, Lena Dunham, Kristen Stewart, Miley Cyrus, Juliette Lewis, and Paris Hilton have all worn cornrows and received considerable attention and backlash (Lambert 2020).

Still, for those with Afro-textured hair or those who care for people with Afro-textured hair, the Internet is a resource for learning how to maintain Afro-textured hair. Indeed, during the 2020 coronavirus pandemic, natural hairstylists such as Niani Barracks, who is based in Detroit, started online classes to teach braiding and basic styling techniques to maintain healthy hair (Perry 2020). Online natural hair care tutorials have become even more of a staple during the 2020 pandemic, when salons have been forced to stay closed.

The natural hair movement, which embraces the wearing of untreated tresses, has given rise to a new industry. "Naturalistas" or "naturals" are individuals with Afro-textured hair who feel at peace with their kinks and curls. YouTube and social media have become platforms for naturalistas to discuss their hair journey, offer hair care practices and tips, review products, and develop a community with other naturals (Bey 2011). Over a decade old, the natural hair movement has entered the mainstream. Online hair tutorials have helped those with Afro-textured hair become reacquainted with their untreated hair by explaining what products work best on certain hair textures, how to achieve specific styles, and how to maintain healthy hair. Indeed, natural hair care is a $2.5 billion industry in the United States alone (Schaverien 2019). Beyond providing information on hair care and maintenance, discussions on social media around natural hair frequently incorporate self-esteem and body image. This is important, as terms commonly used to describe Afro-textured hair, like "nappy," have traditionally had a negative connotation. By contrast, "kinky" is a positive reclamation of tightly coiled hair. The natural hair movement has helped those with coarser hair to embrace the tresses that they were born with (Bey 2011).

The burgeoning acceptance of natural hair is gaining representation in mainstream media. From films such as Netflix's *Nappily Ever After* and the global blockbuster *Black Panther* to the popularity of celebrities like Lupita Nyong'o and Janelle Monáe, who wear Afro-textured coiffured hairstyles, the media attention on Black women's natural hair has demonstrated a globally strong culture of challenging Eurocentric beauty norms. Rather than "managing" or straightening their hair, Black women with Afro-textured hair are embracing their natural curls or kinks (Schaverien 2019). The increased visibility of natural hair has been helpful in promoting self-acceptance among Black women and girls (Harrison 2018) even if some aspects of mainstream culture do not accept natural hair (Joseph-Salisbury and Connelly 2018). As the natural beauty phenomenon continues, Black women are more likely to wear their natural hair and to report that health is the ultimate beauty accessory (Schaverian 2019). Afrocentric beauty aesthetics have thus been embraced by Black women who are looking for a styled version of their natural tresses.

The Need for the CROWN Act

Title VI of the 1964 Civil Rights Act prohibits schools that receive public funding from discriminating on the basis of religious belief or race. However, students with Afro-textured hair are nonetheless suspended or barred from school activities because of their hairstyles. Videos and posts have spread on social media of students who have stood up for their natural hair in the face of these restrictive policies. Regrettably, examples of students who have encountered hair-based discrimination are numerous.

Take for instance, Ashanti Scott, a then 15-year-old cheerleader and a student at Butler Traditional High School in Louisville, Kentucky, who realized days before the school year started that a new policy that banned hairstyles mostly worn by Black students was set to go into effect. Scott, whose mother, Attica Scott, is a Kentucky state legislator, saw the 2016 policy as a personal attack "on me, and who I am and my culture, my upbringing" (Roberts et al. 2016). Ashanti Scott is now a McConnell Scholar Class of 2023 student at the University of Louisville, where she studies political science. In a tweet, Attica Scott noted that the school's policy banned dreadlocks, twists, Afros that are longer than two inches, and "cornrolls"—the policy misspelled "cornrows" (Roberts et al., 2016). The tweet and the policy received national attention. In response, the school amended its policy to note that "hair must be well-groomed, well-kept and at a reasonable length" (Ettinger 2020).

Another example of a Black teenaged girl who took to social media to denounce restrictive hair policies is Tayjha Deleveaux, who, while attending C.R. Walker Senior High School in The Bahamas, was threatened with suspension for wearing an "afropuff" hairstyle that was deemed "untidy" and "unruly" (BBC Trending 2016). To be sure, this international incident is not subject to US federal laws. But Deleveaux's experiences demonstrate the global reach of denigrating Afro-textured hairstyles. The school's principal, T. Nicola Mckay (who is also Black), said that she disallowed hair that "looks like it would not have been combed for days" (BBC Trending 2016). In response, Deleveaux's mother posted her daughter's photo on Facebook and Twitter with the hashtags #SupportThePuff and #ISupportThePuff, which encourage others to post their own photos of natural hairstyles. In their social media response, the Bahamian Ministry of Education vowed to review the policy but ultimately stood in support of the school's administration. The Deleveaux example showcases intra-racial conflicts over natural hair. Deleveaux was dismayed that "another Black woman thinks that a Black girl cannot wear her hair in its natural state" (Ettinger 2020).

By contrast, in January 2020, DeAndre Arnold, a student at Barbers Hill high school in Mont Belvieu, Texas, was told he could not participate in his graduation ceremony because of his hairstyle. The teen was advised that he would need to cut his locs if he wanted to walk in the ceremony with his class. Arnold's case received national attention when Matthew Cherry, writer and director of the short film *Hair Love* and its producer, actress Gabrielle Union, invited the 18-year-old to attend the February 2020 Oscars ceremony. Union posted a video on social media to support Arnold, in which she said, "When we heard about your story, and you just wanting to wear your hair the way you want, at school, and all this scrutiny that you faced and how unwavering you have been in standing up for yourself, we know that we had to get involved" (Feldman 2020). *Hair Love* won the 2020 Academy Award for the Best Animated Short Film and is also a *New York Times* Best Seller picture book that depicts the relationship of an African American father who does his daughter's hair in advance of her mother arriving home from a trip. The story promotes hair love for Afro-textured haired and Black children.

While examples of children like Johnson, Fennidy, Scott, Deleveaux, and Arnold reveal a distressing pattern of schools' dress codes banning natural hair, this is not a new phenomenon. Policies restricting Afro-textured hair worn in its natural state and anti-Black sentiments have been in place since Africans set foot in the New World (Randle 2015). For example, in the 1800s, in cities with free Creole women of color, like New Orleans, laws were implemented that required women to wear a tignon—a scarf or handkerchief—over their heads to signify that they were part of the slave class, regardless of their status. These free Creole women of color often wore elaborate hairstyles that drew attention from Whites and attracted White men (Randle 2015). In the early decades of the twentieth century, Madam C.J. Walker, the first Black woman millionaire, made her fortune on selling Black hair care techniques. She also popularized the hair-straightening comb, which perpetuated the belief that having straight hair would lead to social acceptance and social and economic advancement of Black women (Rooks 1996). However, as an entrepreneur, Madam C.J. Walker provided opportunities for other Black women to use the beauty industry to achieve economic independence and self-sufficiency.

Today's natural hair movement has its roots in the first wave of natural hair that emerged in the 1960s. While some Black people have always embraced natural hair, the style of unprocessed Afro-textured hair gained prominence in the 1960s during Black nationalist movements (Thompson 2014). Take, for example, Angela Davis's iconic Afro that serves as a sign of Black power and rebellion against Euro-American beauty standards (Davis 1994). The convergence of pop culture, the civil rights movement, and the rise of "Black is Beautiful" sentiments led to declarations of self-love and a sense of shared connection with Black communities. Indeed, a 1972 survey of Black St. Louis teens noted that 90% of men and 40% of women wore their hair naturally (Goering 1972).

While the 1980s and 1990s saw an increase of Black women sporting relaxed and pressed hair, the 2000s brought a renewed interest in Afro-textured hair. Indeed, the beauty-industry-informed popular culture depictions of Black women wearing straightened styles were paramount (Mayes 1997), although there were exceptions in media depictions of Black women, like Janet Jackson wearing braids in the film *Poetic Justice*. As previously noted, much of the increase in wearing natural hair and embracing Afro-textured hair in the twenty-first century is due to the prevalence of social media. YouTube and other social media platforms have disseminated information about natural hair and have changed the cultural understanding of it. The global research firm Mintel reports that between 2012 and 2017, sales of perm relaxers dropped by 36.6% (Mitchell 2019). Indeed, this 2019 report found that 79% of consumers wore a natural hairstyle in 2017 and that maintaining healthy hair was a priority in their decision to do so (Mitchell 2019). While relaxer sales have dropped, the Black hair care market is steadily growing, with sales of other products soaring. Mintel estimated that Black consumer spending on natural hair care products would reach $473 million in 2017 (Mitchell 2019). The current natural hair movement is about more than hair; it also signifies a healthy lifestyle that encourages individuals to be their authentic selves. Naturalistas frequent natural hair expos, festivals, and Black-owned business that use all natural and vegan products.

Though the Civil Rights Act of 1964 banned employment discrimination, the idea that this law would be used to provide those with Afro-textured hair with equal access to public workplaces was not considered at the time of the bill's passage. The first natural hair discrimination case, *Jenkins v. Blue Cross Mutual Hospital Insurance*, occurred in 1976 when the U.S. Court of Appeals for the Seventh Circuit upheld that workers were allowed to wear Afros under Title VII of the Civil Rights Act. In a reversal of the decision against natural Afro-textured hair, *Rogers v. American Airlines* upheld that the airline could ban its employees from wearing braids because this style can be easily changed and is not specifically tied to race, and as such, it did not fall under the protection of Title VII. The American Airlines ruling established the standing legal precedent. In 2006, the Equal Employment Opportunity Commission (EEOC) developed its Compliance Manual on Race and Color Discrimination, which protects "against employment discrimination based on a person's physical characteristics associated with race, such as a person's color, hair, facial features, height and weight" (Griffin 2019). In practice, this means that an employer cannot discriminate against an employee who wears an Afro, but it can request that the employee wears a well-groomed Afro. These policies, however, still leave room for judicial interpretation of whether natural hairstyles are protected by law as a racial characteristic (Griffin 2019).

In 2014, the Pentagon issued updated grooming policies that prohibited natural hairstyles such as dreadlocks, twists, and double ponytails that were favored by Black women in the U.S. Army. The Congressional Black Caucus (CBC) intervened and sent a letter to then-Secretary of Defense Chuck Hagel. The chair of the CBC, Marcia Fudge (D-OH), declared that the army's new policies "were biased and racially insensitive" (Grigsby Bates 2014). In response, Hagel altered the hair policy and sent a letter to members of Congress to note that the military requirements must be "reflective of our diverse force" (Grigsby Bates 2014). The navy followed suit in 2017 with a policy that would now allow braided styles and locs.

In short, hair discrimination has become a civil rights issue. The growing natural movement of the 2000s has given rise to a generation of Black Americans who desire to wear their Afro-textured hair and who expect schools and employers to readily allow them to do so. Legislators now take up this issue as constituents turn to social media to document forms of hair discrimination. In what follows, we report findings from our interviews with New Jersey state legislators who sponsored the bill, to provide insight into the legislative process.

Data and Method

Semi-structured interviews with New Jersey state legislators Senator Sandra B. Cunningham and Assemblywoman Angela V. McKnight were conducted in April 2020 via Zoom web conferencing software. Both Cunningham and McKnight were primary sponsors of the New Jersey CROWN Act. Other primary sponsors of this legislation included Senators Nia H. Gill and Shirley K. Turner and Assembly members Verlina Reynolds-Jackson, Shanique Speight, and Britnee Timberlake, who are all Democratic Black women. The bill's other sponsors include Linda Carter, Nilsa Cruz-Perez, Vin Gopal, Jamal Holley, Valerie Vainieri Huttle, Mila Jasey, Gabby Mosquera, Annette Quijano, Ron Rice, Teresa Ruiz, Troy Singleton, Shavonda Sumter, and Cleopatra Tucker. These non-primary sponsors are all Democrats, but they come from varying ethno-racial groups and include men lawmakers. We contacted all 20 of the bill sponsors but were only able to gain interviews with Cunningham and McKnight. We sent three follow-up invitations to the five other primary sponsors of this bill. We believe that the 2020 coronavirus pandemic negatively impacted our ability to speak with the legislators.

We selected semi-structured interviews for this research due to the conversational nature of this method, as it allowed for us to explore a set of issues in a nondirective form. Semi-structured interviews, a common qualitative method (Kitchin and Tate 2000), are informal in tone and allow for an open response in participants' own words, rather than eliciting a "yes" or "no" type of answer. As a social interaction, semi-structured interviews do not contain hard and fast rules (Valentine 2005), as each conversation will be unique.

Semi-structured interviews are useful for facilitating discussions around politics, knowledge, power, identity, and subjectivity because they rely on greater reflexivity within the research process (Longhurst 2005). In investigating complex behaviors and experiences with lawmaking, semi-structured interviews allowed us to examine each legislator's political decision-making and its influence on legislative agenda setting. Therefore, our semi-structured interviews allowed us partial insight into what elected officials do and think.

We focused our attention on the New Jersey State Legislature. Legislative districts in the New Jersey General Assembly are multi-member districts, which means that electoral districts send at least two members to a legislative chamber. Only 10 states have at least one legislative chamber that elects officials from multi-member districts. In New Jersey, two representatives are elected from each district. In the Democratic and Republican primary elections, only the top two candidates move forward to general election and are declared the winners.[1] In 2017, all 80 seats of the New Jersey General Assembly were up for election. Assembly members are elected to two-year terms and senators hold four-year terms. Similarly, elections for all 40 seats of the New Jersey State Senate were held in 2017. New Jersey currently has a Democratic state government trifecta, meaning that one political party holds the governor's office and has majorities in both legislative bodies.

First elected to the New Jersey State Senate via a special election in October 2007, Senator Sandra B. Cunningham represents District 31. She currently serves as the state senate deputy majority leader and serves on the following committees: Budget and Appropriations (vice chair), Higher Education (chair), and Education. She consistently won re-election, with huge margins over her political competitors in 2011, 2013, and 2017.[2] Sen. Cunningham holds a BA in liberal arts from Bloomfield College and is a graduate of New York University School of Continuing Education's Finance, Law and Taxation program. She previously served as the executive director of the Sandra and Glenn D. Cunningham Foundation, is a former executive director of the Hudson County Bar Association, and is the deputy director of the Metropolitan Ecumenical Ministry.[3] Also representing District 31, Assemblywoman Angela V. McKnight was elected in 2016. She serves on the following committees: Women and Children, Homeland Security and State Preparedness (chair), and Aging and Senior Services.[4] Asw. McKnight is the Founder and CEO of AngelaCARES, Inc., and holds a BS in business management from the University of Phoenix.

The first set of questions used in semi-structured interviews are often factual or descriptive. We asked McKnight and Cunningham more thought-provoking questions toward the end of the interview, leaving room for the discussion to unfold in a conversational manner that enabled the legislators to explore issues that they felt were important but were not previously discussed. While we used a predetermined set of questions to guide the conversation, the legislators had the leeway to respond with an angle that best suited them.

Each semi-structured interview was recorded and transcribed. We also took notes during the interview. The general tone of the conversation was documented; we highlighted key themes that arose and noted things that surprised the interviewees or items that needed additional follow-up. Taking notes in this way is a form of data analysis (Kitchin and Tate 2000). Once the interviews were transcribed, we identified other themes and organized the written narratives into relevant chunks of text.

In the following section, we present the analysis of our semi-structured interviews with Cunningham and McKnight. We show that these women successfully shepherded the CROWN Act to passage because of an overwhelming level of support from both constituents and lawmakers. Both parties recognized that the bill was necessary given the national spotlight of Andrew Johnson's forced ringside haircut in 2018, and given their own lived experiences with having Afro-textured hair. We argue that having Black women in policymaking positions enables different kinds of conversations to come to the forefront that ordinarily would not happen if such individuals were not in elected positions.

Passing the New Jersey CROWN Act—Perspectives from Prime Sponsors of the Bill

When asked about the impetus behind sponsoring the CROWN Act, McKnight gushed: "[I]t's one of my pride and joys." She is immensely proud of this bill and is featured on the CROWN Coalition's website as the prime sponsor of the New Jersey legislation. The assemblywoman credited the Andrew Johnson story as the lightning rod that led her to pursue legislative action around hair discrimination, noting,

The wrestler, Andrew Johnson, was forced to cut his hair. So, I was watching it on the news and when I saw that, I was devastated. This poor man either has to forgo his fight or forgo his dreads, something that he had grown for years. So, I had a moment. I was like, "Wait a minute, you're an assemblyperson. You could do something about this."

This realization that she could do something about hair discrimination led McKnight to work with her staff to develop legislation. While she was working on this legislation, she became aware of the CROWN Act and its status in the New York and California statehouses. She recalled,

Now, unbeknownst to myself, I had no idea that the CROWN Act was taking place in New York and California. No idea. I did it because of Andrew Johnson. That's why I sponsored the bill. And then we . . . they found out about me and then we connected. Connected with the CROWN Coalition, connected with Dove. And they were like, "Oh, we are already doing this. We are doing this in California, we're doing it in New York and we would love to help you do this." And, I was like, "Fine!" So, that's how it happened. It didn't happen because they sought me. I told [them about] Andrew Johnson, and that "I want to do something." Not knowing 500 miles away they were already working . . . and across the bridge they were already working. So, we formed a team and we went out and advocated more and more for this.

This account of events was similar to Sandra B. Cunningham's articulation of the origins of the bill. She reiterated the role that McKnight played in bringing this legislation to the New Jersey statehouse. Cunningham noted that she got involved in the CROWN Act for one specific reason: "because at the time that this came to us . . . Dove actually came to us and asked for help and other people came, [and] brought this to my attention. Well, my co-sponsor, our assemblywoman, is also on the legislation. She talked to people that she knew." Cunningham also acknowledged that Andrew Johnson was the impetus behind the bill. The state senator referred to the inspiration of "a little boy in New Jersey who . . . suddenly, couldn't play at the top of [his] sports league because one of the guys decide[d], who had always been wearing his hair in dreadlocks." The national fallout from Johnson's haircut went viral and caused lawmakers and constituents alike to discuss hair discrimination.

Unlike Cunningham, McKnight shared a personal reason for sponsoring the CROWN Act: her own experiences with Afro-textured hair. Without prompting, she shared her natural hair journey:

So, back in 2011, I went natural. I was in the corporate world and I did the big chop. And, when I went to work, you know, some people stared at me, you know, a little funny like, "Oh, yeah, your hair looks nice." Because I got tired of all the perms, I got tired of trying to find the right salon, I was like, "I'm done. I'm done with the perms. I am done with all this." So, I did the big chop. And maybe, within six months, I started wearing protective styles because I didn't feel comfortable in my own skin. And it had to do with how people looked at me and I didn't want to deal with that and then I was just wearing protective styles, protective styles. Now, just last year, January of last year, I decided that I was just going to wear my hair natural, no matter what. Mostly twists outs. So, for over a year now, I haven't put any type of protective style in my hair. I've been wearing my hair natural for over a year.

The "big chop" the assemblywoman refers to here is the act of cutting off all of her chemically relaxed hair (what she references as "perms") to leave only the natural Afro-textured hair. This is contrary to transitioning from relaxed hair to one's naturally textured hair, which requires one to grow one's hair out after ceasing to chemically relax it. Because the big chop is a fast and largely irreversible way to go natural, many women experience some anxiety around their natural texture or the shape of their head as a short haircut reveals an aspect of one's body that has been unseen for a long period of time (Williams 2014). Additionally, because the hair is cut short, there are limited styling options. The assemblywoman noted that she felt less comfortable in her skin six months after the big chop, which left her wanting to add hair via protective styles, such as crochet braids. Her mind focused on the ramifications of wearing her natural hair as a member of the New Jersey state legislature. Although she was initially concerned, McKnight found that her colleagues were largely unconcerned with her hair. She stated,

[G]oing down to the Statehouse, you know, people look. . . . Going down to the Statehouse and typically there is more men down there, more Caucasians, and some colleagues would look at my hair and try to figure out, like "What in the world? Like, what's going on?" Because before, I would wear my protective styles. I would have my curls shaped. I went with my braids. And some people were like, "Oh, that's nice, how did you get your hair like that?" That's the famous question, right? [laughter] But, now, over a year, I've been wearing my hair naturally, and I wear my Afro, I wear my twists, I wear my pin-up styles and I'm good because right now,

I feel comfortable in my skin so I don't care what people say. Before I used to care about how people would react to me, but now I am like, "Wait a minute, this is my body. This is my body. As long as I feel comfortable, as long as I am proud, I don't care what anyone says." So, girl, I'll be going to the Statehouse in my Afro, this is some wildflower in my hair.

For McKnight, discomfort about wearing her natural hair after the big chop was steadily replaced by confidence in her own skin. She now takes pride and ownership over her naturally coarse hair and unabashedly wears an Afro in the halls of the state legislature and often accessorizes with a flower. While this look may be something that is new to legislative chambers, McKnight is unapologetic about her Afro-textured hair. Her own hair journey, coming to love and embrace the texture of her hair, led her to want to support Andrew Johnson and others like him who are on the receiving end of hair discrimination. She noted that this journey was a process—one of radical self-love and acceptance. McKnight was candid in her sharing of the steps she took to embrace her 4C hair: "I look in the mirror and say 'I'm beautiful.' Those affirmations, affirmations help me on a daily basis. I say 'I am strong. I am beautiful. I am pretty. My hair makes me. My skin is the color that my Lord has given to me.' So, it took me some time." The process of learning to accept and affirm one's beauty is widely acknowledged in today's naturalista movement (Williams 2014). Black women are learning to eschew dominant Eurocentric beauty ideals that denigrate Blackness. These daily affirmations helped the assemblywoman feel comfortable in her skin and love her hair.

Even with this new appreciation of her body, McKnight is cognizant that her styling choices may cause some to question her effectiveness as a lawmaker. She stated,

So, I had to take time to myself to say, "Don't worry about how people look at you because you're going to be looked at any type of way." First of all, I'm Black. Second of all, I'm a woman. Third of all, I am an elected official. Those three titles, sometimes they don't mix. Down in Trenton, I think there's about 14? No, 24 of us women—not Black women. And then it's about 7 or 8 . . . 8 of us that are Black. And there's 120 legislators between the Assembly and the Senate. So, about 9 of us are Black women out of 120. That is . . . you know, you have to find your place. I know I am very outspoken; I am very professional and they know I'll come in here with a bow in my hair, I'm coming in with an Afro, I'm coming in with some twists and that's just who I am. And I walk confidently, so I don't have a problem with anyone commenting on me, "You know, you need to tie your hair down." I wish that one would. I'm gonna look like, "Seriously?" [laughter]

As McKnight noted, having natural hair does not impede her from doing her job or being a professional. Instead, she has a heightened sense of awareness of how hair discrimination affects people and how Afro-textured hair is regarded in society. She understands the necessity of this legislation because she lived with insecurities around her natural hair texture. These experiences enable her to advocate for people like Andrew Johnson. Although as a Black woman she is in the minority of legislators in terms of ethno-race and gender, being a minority does not stop her from legislating effectively.

While Sen. Cunningham did not share her personal hair journey during the semi-structured interview, she acknowledged the oversized role of hair in Black communities, observing, "I mean, quite honestly, in the Black community hair has always been an issue. That's a fact, it's always been an issue." She recognized that hair is a frequent topic of conversation for people of African descent, and stated that people always want to know about it:

"What kind of hair do they have? Do they have long hair? Do they have short hair? Is their hair going to be straight here?" So that is something that African Americans have been concerned with for a very, very long time, so we're kind of accustomed to it, to some degree. And as I said, hair has always been an issue and on some level in the African American community, so therefore I think there's always been some questions and some feelings attached to those questions of feeling not accepted depending on which end of the rope you will happen to be at.

This observation played out in the legislative listening sessions that Sen. Cunningham and Asw. McKnight held around the CROWN Act. The lawmakers held events at St. Peter's University and Rutgers University to listen to constituents' concerns about the bill. These sessions helped to inform Cunningham about the importance of this legislation. She explained,

We brought people together, young people at St. Peter's University here in Jersey City. And one at Rutgers University and one at St. Peter's. And it was a very nice turnout. We invited young people to come and talk about this issue. We had a nice turnout for both events. But it was interesting hearing what experiences people had, um, young women primarily. So, um, it was very . . . it was a good experience, and it gave us an opportunity to talk about it and when you realize that these things will . . . have been going on for a long time. But it was interesting talking to young people who, um, had experiences with relatives about their hair. Or, um, didn't know the history or wondered why it was such a big deal or why they were treated differently as a result of it.

These legislative listening sessions helped provide perspective on why hair matters so much in Black communities and how some young people have had negative experiences around their Afro-textured hair. Cunningham believed that it was important for constituents to come together and share their own stories of how having Afro-textured hair impacted their experiences. One example that stood out in the state senator's mind was a dialogue among a particular group of students who were concerned about employment prospects. She shared,

And, I think there were a group of pre-med students who were there, and, um, they were concerned. There was some conversation about how they would be treated. They were going to medical school and wanted to talk about how their hair would play a role in this—or wouldn't play a role—in it. Um, so I mean, this is something that's been going on for a long time.

The students were grateful for the opportunity to voice their concerns around the CROWN Act with their elected officials. They welcomed the chance to talk about their experiences with hair discrimination and why this bill was essential. Cunningham added,

But from the beginning, it kind of took off, um, very quickly. And when something . . . a piece of legislation moves that quickly, then you know that there is a reason for it. And people just wanted an opportunity to come and to talk about their experience, talk about their hair and experiences that other people had. But certainly, they were very excited about the possibility of change. Um, and that's what this bill did. It just offered the opportunity for a change.

Similarly, Asw. McKnight found that her constituents appreciated the opportunity to speak with her about the importance of this bill. She heard from constituents when she "started getting all this press. People, predominately Black women, were like, 'Yes, thank you so much. Thank you! Thank you!'" Furthermore, the assemblywoman learned that many constituents were unaware of the legislative process and that she could create a bill that would end hair discrimination. McKnight noted that Black women who approached her about the bill were "intrigued. They said, 'Wow! You can make that happen?' Because think about it. Before I became an assemblyperson, I really wasn't into politics. So now, I educate my constituents on what a legislator does." McKnight opined that many people are unaware of how public policy is made. She also noted that many are unaware that what legislators do in the statehouse has the ability to impact citizens' day-to-day life. This is why she holds legislative listening sessions, speaks with constituents about the community's issues, and asks constituents for feedback on her bills. Regarding the CROWN Act, McKnight expressed that she received overwhelmingly positive feedback, noting, "Constituents came up to me and said, 'Wow, I can wear my hair like I want to?' I said, "Yes, as soon as the Governor signs this bill, you can. And if you get discriminated against because of your hair, you can file charges against them. My constituent base was very, very happy."

While the overall response to the bill was positive, McKnight noted there were some detractors. She referred to "naysayers" who are always going to have something negative to say: "I tell people that if they still talk about Jesus, then who am I? Think about it. Just me, a little person. They still talk about Jesus." She provided an example of negative feedback that she received stating that "the naysayers are like, 'Why is it that you got to do this?' 'Why do you have to make this into a law?' Or, 'Do you need to do another type of law?' 'There are bigger issues in the State of New Jersey that she should be worried about.'" However, both she and Sen. Cunningham remained unwavering in their support of the CROWN Act. McKnight retorted to the naysayers,

> I can work on multiple things at one time. And just because it is not important to you, it doesn't mean that it is not important to someone else. I can work on hair [discrimination], I can work on animals, I can work on the environment, I can work on helping small businesses, I can work on helping disabled people. I can do the law. Not everything will affect you, but everything will affect someone. So, that's how they got it. And that's what I told my constituents, the naysayers. Sometimes I just move around them. Sometimes I just move away because you can't please everybody.

In the end, it was easy to "move around" the naysayers because as Sen. Cunningham reiterated multiple times during the interview, this was not a difficult bill. It was easy to build consensus among her colleagues that the CROWN Act should be become law in New Jersey.

Sen. Cunningham shared that she would have supported this bill even if she was not a Black woman. She believed that the Andrew Johnson incident and the legislative listening events helped her colleagues to see the necessity of this bill. The state senator reflected on why this was the case:

> I think that they [NJ state legislators] understood it more than I thought that they did. And I'll say that because it was not a difficult bill. I imagined that it might be more difficult to get support for, and I was wrong. It was not that difficult to get support for. There were Caucasian older gentlemen in the legislature who were aware of issues that people had and talked about it. My colleagues saw the community's need [for this bill and] respond to it. . . . So I wasn't quite sure how it would . . . how long it would take it and it how would go. But I think people realized that this was something that was important and heard the stories and maybe had some experiences. So, it caught on quickly.

Asw. McKnight credits the bill's passage to helping her colleagues— both men and women, Democrats and Republicans—understand why hair discrimination is harmful. She also explained that legislators, just like constituents, have to be informed about an issue. Furthermore, legislators must look beyond their own personal experiences to see how an issue may impact a social group that is not their own. McKnight detailed the process she used to usher this bill through the New Jersey statehouse:

> So, the Republicans and the Democrats, whether they were women or men, they actually agreed with this bill because of the story that goes behind the bill and why it is so important. With anything, with any piece of legislation, you have to educate your fellow legislators. Just like you have to educate me because I don't know everything. So, with my stories, with my testimony, with the constituents who came to testify for this bill, with the amount of news coverage, this is a wave that's happening. They understood. And I had no problems with my fellow assembly people. It passed unanimously. So, it's all about education. It's all about education.

Sen. Cunningham reiterated her colleague's assertation that this bill, like all others, requires that legislators provide their colleagues with information and a compelling reason to support legislation. When asked if this bill could be passed in other states and about the success of the CROWN Coalition in other states, Cunningham was a bit reluctant. She responded,

> Perhaps not. Um perhaps not, because the culture, the experiences of the community may or may not be similar. It was easier here because Black, White, Hispanic, and other ethnic people [are here]. You know, Muslims, too. There were so many different cultures that had similar experiences. And because we're in a very diverse and a densely populated area it increases the opportunity for running into someone who had a similar experience with hair discrimination. So, um, where depending upon how large the, um, diversity is, I think that would play a role. I would think it would not be as easy as it was in New Jersey . . . I don't know. But here in New Jersey, I didn't' have pushback on this bill. Not at all.

Sen. Cunningham offered advice for other states that are interested in joining the CROWN Coalition. She recommended that state legislators talk with their constituents about hair discrimination and that they "watch *Hair Love*, that little video. That was adorable. Watch the video and say 'Does this look familiar to anyone here?' I think that would be a start, everyone has different needs. So, you have to address who lives in your community." Further addressing legislators, she added , "You never know unless you ask if it's a problem. And if this isn't a problem, let me know what your problem is. Legislators need to hear stories, that's how you find out."

Similarly, Asw. McKnight agreed that legislators from other states need to start talking to their constituent base: "You have to start talking, having people sign petitions. Having people come to the statehouse and committee hearings. Talk to your fellow legislators. Try to get the CROWN Coalition behind you, because we're out here. They are waiting for fellow legislators to contact them and say, 'Hey, this is what I want to do. Can you help?'" In end, the assemblywoman recommended that other legislators find their support system and recommended that the CROWN Coalition could be that support system. She also tied the goals of the CROWN Coalition to other Black women's experiences with their Afro-textured hair. She said that, culturally, Black women understand hair discrimination:

So, if you are an African American, you know, for years, we have been dis-criminated against. And sometimes we discriminate against each other with our hair. "Girl, you need to put something on your hair." Right? Because that's how we were taught. Our mom and our grandmother, you know, it's been taught that our hair is not beautiful, our hair is ugly, we need to straighten it like the Eurocentric [beauty ideals]. But now, we are in the 2000s, 2020 where people have embraced their natural hair and it's beautiful. So, go ahead and find those naysayers whether they are African Americans or others and educate them. Because, again, what grows out of our heads is what grows out of our head. We can't stop that. And what grows out of my head doesn't make my brain any different. Whatever is in my brain is in my brain.

In reminding Black women that rebuking Eurocentric beauty ideals is ac-ceptable, McKnight also lauded the progress of the natural hair movement. She quoted Frederick Douglass, who, in his 1857 speech in Canandaigua, New York, said, "If there is no struggle, there is no progress. . . . Power concedes nothing without a demand"[5] to express the elation she feels for how far Black women have come in embracing their hair and pushing society to do so as well. Furthermore, she was heartened that Senator Cory Booker (D-NJ) introduced the CROWN Act in Congress. She stated, "I've been in con-tact with [Sen. Booker's] office and he took my legislation and said, 'I'm going to do this,' and I said, 'You good, Senator.' So, he did. He introduced it."

At the end of her interview, Sen. Cunningham shared that she is pleased that this bill is titled the CROWN Act. She elaborated:

> I just love that it's called the CROWN Act. I like the idea of the crown. We teach young girls all the time here that they are queens. And, I like that. I think that sends a positive and a pleasant note just hearing those words. The CROWN Act. It suddenly makes people think, "What is that?" You know, interest. So, I think that that's exciting. I think that helps to bring some of the drama that's needed for it to glow. And I think it's something that should continue. And hopefully other states will start to do it.

This optimism was shared by Asw. McKnight. Both these New Jersey state legislators are pleased with the passage of this legislation and even more thrilled about the possibility of other states passing similar laws. They believe that this bill has the power not only to change the experiences of those with

Afro-textured hair, but also to offer young Black women and girls an opportunity to embrace their full selves. They see this bill as a positive declaration
of Black self-love and an affirmation of Afrocentric features.

Discussion and Conclusion

The purpose of this chapter was to demonstrate the differences in Afro-
textured hair and why people with Afro-textured hair require different maintenance and styling practices that often require considerable time, effort, and
money. Indeed, all hair is not the same. In laying the foundation for the re-
mainder of this book, we have demonstrated that these differences also require a political intervention to address how the broader society responds to
Afro-textured hair.

Even in an era of natural hair, those with Afro-textured hair have experienced discriminatory incidents because of their styling choices. Social media
has exposed the prevalence of injustice and bias against those with natural
hair. Unlike previous periods, the advent of technology to build and sustain communities around natural hair care have helped to usher in a generation of naturalistas who prefer natural hair over Euro-American standards
of beauty. This new technology has made having Afro-textured hair more
mainstream and acceptable. Take, for example, routine features in popular
women's magazines such as *Cosmopolitan* and *Elle* that feature hair braiding
and other protective styles. Still, those who do not often come into contact
with Afro-textured hair have little understanding of what it takes to maintain
and grow this type of hair.

As exemplified by the narratives of Sen. Sandra B. Cunningham and Asw.
Angela V. McKnight, combatting hair discrimination requires legislative
oversight. The New Jersey state lawmakers expressed the need for the bill and
offered insight into how other states might enact their own legislation. Their
role as Black women legislators, while perhaps not essential, was useful in
advancing the CROWN Act, as they were familiar with Black hair culture
and hair discriminatory practices. The legislators also showcased the importance of listening to constituents, particularly younger women, who advocate for change in the status quo. These young naturalistas are taking to social
media to expose injustices against those with Afro-textured hair. This movement has pushed older generations of Black people to prioritize issues that
matter to this generation.

In sum, state and local elected officials have been at the frontlines of responding to viral accounts of hair discrimination, as California, New York, and New Jersey were the first states to pass the CROWN Act. The federal government has been slower to respond. Less diverse states may trail behind these states in passing this legislation, as Sen. Cunningham notes, because legislators may be less familiar with incidents of hair discrimination. Still, this type of legislation exposes the legal complications of enforcing laws against race-based discrimination. The CROWN Act declares that hair discrimination is a form of bias against Afro-textured hair, which commonly belongs to people of African descent, to demonstrate that forms of racism not previously included in the Civil Rights Act of 1964 continue to play a role in post-Obama America.

In this chapter, we discussed the reasons for, and the logic of, legislation to protect against hair discrimination. The next chapter analyzes one-on-one interviews with Black women candidates and elected officials to uncover their perceptions of the impact of their styling choices on their political experiences. We explore how this group of political elites believes that their appearance is understood by voters and constituents. This perception is key, because as we learned in this chapter, Afro-textured hair and race-based biases are political. As such, Black women political elites' perceptions of how their bodies are read by others is an indicator of inequality in their political experiences. We carry this thread through the remaining chapters in this book to demonstrate that the politics of appearance have consequential meanings for Black women political elites.

3

What Black Women Political Elites Look Like Matters

> It's not about my hair. . . . It's just been a treat and an honor to be able
> to be my full authentic self on this campaign.
>
> —Lauren Underwood (D-IL)

In 2018, Lauren Underwood, a 32-year-old nurse, made history by becoming
the youngest Black congresswoman ever elected. Representing Illinois's 14th
congressional district, she ran on a platform of expanding healthcare to, and
preserving access for, those with pre-existing conditions. She beat out six
White men to win the Democratic primary in March 2017, and she unseated
the White male Republican incumbent. With African Americans making up
only 3% of her district, Rep. Underwood told *Good Morning America* that
she "didn't want to surrender to the pressure of conforming to certain beauty
standards" (Scott et al. 2018). Rather, she wears her Afro-textured hair in a
close-cropped style, as she "takes pride in having an image that is authentic to
who she is" (Scott et al. 2018). Rep. Underwood credited her political success
to people getting to know her rather than judging her on the appearance of
her hair.

Bringing her full and authentic self into her campaign meant that as
she entered office, she was free to wear twist outs and to style her Afro in
ways that were pleasing to her alone. While she sought to represent a constituency that largely did not share her racial background, she felt little
angst about presenting herself with her natural Afro-textured hair. As a
Millennial—a member of the cohort born between 1981 and 1996 (Dimock
2019)—Underwood is similar to her peers who have embraced the natural
hair movement. Her experiences may be unique because of her district, age,
policy stances, or perhaps her hair texture. Nevertheless, political scientists
have yet to unpack how Black women's hair affects their political experiences.

Sister Style. Nadia E. Brown and Danielle Casarez Lemi, Oxford University Press (2021). © Oxford University Press.
DOI: 10.1093/oso/9780197540572.003.0003

Rather than assuming that Black women have a single political experience because they share the same ethno-racial identity, we interrogate the ways that a Black woman politician's hair may factor into how she sees herself on the campaign trail and how voters perceive her.

In this chapter, we explore the politics of appearance for Black women's hair. We use personal interviews with political elites who vary by generation, geographic location, partisanship, motherhood status, and office-holding status to offer a fuller picture of the ways that Black women's hair remains a political issue. Centering Black women political elites themselves in our study gives us unique entry into understanding how the myriad perceptions of Black women's hair—that have often been framed negatively—becomes an issue for electoral politics.

While hair matters for all the women in the study, it does so in varying ways and to varying intensities. Our methodological intervention of looking only at Black women offers a more nuanced understanding of the uniqueness and differences *among* members of this group, a group that is often presented as highly uniform, monolithic, and unvaried. We find that the symbolic meaning of hair and the choices around self-presentation of political elites reflect a deeply personal and fluid understanding of gender and race in American politics. In sum, this chapter builds on the preceding, theoretical chapter to empirically demonstrate how hair is an enduring aspect of how Black women political elites navigate electoral politics.

Afro-Textured Hair: Black Women and Aesthetics

Colorism and hair texture preferences have consequences that impact Black women's lives in meaningful ways. Importantly, skin tone, hair texture, and the combination of the two have distinct meanings. For women, hairstyle is a malleable marker that communicates race (Sims et al. 2019). Beginning conversations about Black women's bodily aesthetics, namely their hair practices, with a discussion of enslavement in North America often leads to reductive scholarly understandings of Black women's bodies as devoid of self-care and humanity. However, it may be necessary to belabor hair practices during this historical period to contextualize why hair and skin tone remain such important factors in the lives of Black women. Intra- and interracial ideas about Black women's beauty practices have existed since the onset of enslaved African women on this continent. Black aesthetics, under the inhumane conditions of slavery, were part of the grooming practices of enslaved Black women, for both health and convenience (Blackwelder 2003). Many bondswomen braided or used head wraps to protect their coils from sun damage. They used products like kerosene, butter goose grease, lye, and coffee, to clean, dye, or straighten their hair. Many of these products and methods left enslaved Black women with permanent hair loss. White enslavers would also punish bondswomen by shaving their heads as way to eradicate their sense of self, beauty, and culture (White and White 1995).

Beginning in the period directly following enslavement and continuing into the New Negro movement in the 1920s, Black Americans used the politics of adornment to signal their status and demonstrate their place in the newly changed American society (Lindsey 2017). Beauty culture and the politics of appearance for Black women were used as powerful tools to combat the prevailing (and often contradictory) stereotypes of Black women in the Jim Crow era of the late nineteenth and early twentieth centuries. Through the archetypes of the Mammy, Jezebel, and Sapphire, prevailing stereotypes[1] of Black women as lascivious, savage, lazy, vulgar, matronly, and unconcerned with their appearance abounded (Terborg-Penn and Harley 1978). Black women created new models of Black aesthetics by altering, adorning, and maintaining their physical appearance (Baldwin 2007), and their bodies thus became physical sites to challenge ideas about race, gender, sexuality, class, and labor. Bodily aesthetics, particularly Black women's beauty culture, were used to shed vestiges of enslavement and as a way to assert personal autonomy (Lindsey 2017).

Black women's expanded options for self-expression and transformative bodily aesthetics within this period dovetailed with greater demands for a challenge to White cultural hegemony and Black sexism. African American women's hair was a frequent topic of conversation in racial uplift circles advertisements, and editorial pages within Black-owned papers (Lindsey 2017). Take, for example, this 1910 quote from the *Washington Bee* in which Black businessman and journalist Calvin Chase wrote,

> We say straighten your hair ladies, beautify yourselves, make those aggravating, reclusive, elusive, shrinking kinks long flowing tresses . . . even if it takes every ounce of hair straightening preparation that can be manufactured . . . even God, who discriminated against our women on this hair

proposition, knows that straight hair beautifies a woman. (Calvin Chase, *Washington Bee*, March 15, 1910, cited in Lindsey 2017)

While positions like Chase's were paramount, there were others—held particularly by Black women themselves—that contributed to an alternative discourse around Black women's beauty and bodily aesthetics (Gill 2010). These women pushed back against this centered Black male gaze and articulated their own hairstyling choices and preferences (Lindsey 2017).

In future generations, Black people would more publicly embrace a beauty culture that was less beholden to White corporeal tastes. Lester (2000) claims that it was not until the twentieth century that Black people were more fully able to resist the image of White beauty and choose primarily Afrocentric bodily aesthetics. The Black Power movements of the 1960s and 1970s emphasized that hair was both important and political. The Afro challenged hegemonic beauty norms that devalued natural Black features. Indeed, Blackness became an attribute, and "Black is Beautiful" became a popular saying and movement that acknowledged self-determination while also uplifting Black women's self-esteem (Mercer 2005). We are currently living in a resurgence of the "Black is Beautiful" moment in which more women have decided to stop chemically processing their hair to "go natural." Black women, many of whom may not have seen their hair in its unprocessed state in years, are finding ways to embrace it, and at the same time learning how to love and accept themselves (Bey 2011). Indeed, video artist and filmmaker Zina Saro-Wiwa (2012) notes that racial consciousness is a necessary first step that a Black woman must take before going natural. Because Black hair and Black bodies have remained a site of political contestation throughout American history and within the American imagination, wearing natural hair today is a radical expression of self-acceptance—an evolution of Black political expression.

Given this history, we view Black beauty culture holistically to understand the sustained salience of hair in Black communities. For Black women, hair is not just hair. The combination of skin tone and hair texture produce a unique set of cultural meanings in Black communities (Shebly Rosette and Dumas 2007). Hair texture is laden with value distinctions, such that hair can alter the significance attached to skin tone—making a lighter-skinned Black woman "Blacker" or a darker-skinned Black woman more "assimilated" into Whiteness. Generations of racial mixing have produced variations of Black hair textures—from coiled to kinky, wavy, curly, and straight (Spellers 2002,

2003; Sellers 2003). Kinkier hair requires a considerable amount of oil to prevent breakage and grows slower than straighter hair, which requires less oil and grows longer (Sims 1982). Because most Black women have kinkier hair, they do not have the texture or the length to conform to American beauty standards (Robinson 2011). Conversely, kinkier hair allows more diversity in hairstyles because it is the most versatile (Spellers 2003). It can be "twisted, locked, braided, weaved, curled, dyed, fried and laid to the side" (Spellers 2003, 235). Although kinkier hair may be more flexible with respect to styling options, its linkage to African heritage makes it undesirable. Black hair hierarchies determine "good" and "bad" hair valuations. Good hair is the absence of kink while bad hair has prominent kink. Good hair is considered far more attractive, is soft to the touch, manageable, has the ability to grow long, and requires minimal intervention to be considered beautiful, whereas bad hair is short, course, brittle, and more slow-growing (Robinson 2011; Craig 2006). Black women's appearance, based on hair texture and skin tone, is on a beauty continuum that ranges from "privilege and opportunity to discrimination and social isolation" (Robinson-Moore 2008, 81). Hair texture variation impacts Black women's racial experiences and mediates the severity of discrimination that they may face (Treviño, Harris, and Wallace 2008).

Studies have shown that Americans prefer Black women with smooth hair rather than natural hair (Rudman and McLean 2016; Woolford, et al. 2016). Hair serves as a marker not only for racial identification but also for beauty (Robinson 2011). Indeed, tightly coiled hair texture is uniquely tied to Blackness, meaning that Afro-descended peoples have more tightly coiled hair than others. This type of hair texture has been a marker of racial identity (Banks 2000) and is linked to beauty norms that denigrate Blackness (Craig 2006).

Because American beauty standards are tied to race, Black women often experience a disadvantage that is unique to their race and gender identity. For example, using experiments and images of Black women with various hairstyles and White women with straight hair, Opie and Phillips (2015) found that straight hair was associated with higher perceptions of professionalism (Study 1), and that even Black respondents viewed Black women with unstraightened hair as having "inappropriate" and/or "problematic" looks for "corporate America" (Study 2). Furthermore, there are noticeable intra-group gendered differences in views of how Black women should wear their hair. Rudman and McLean (2016) found that Black men preferred Black women celebrities such as Janet Jackson, Viola Davis, and Solange Knowles to have smooth hair. However, Black women did not express a preference and said that they liked the celebrities with both natural and straight styles. In a national survey that assessed views of Black women's natural hair, McGill Johnson et al. (2017) found that Black women with natural hair were more supportive of women with textured hair than any other demographic group. The findings also indicated that Millennial naturalistas have more positive attitudes toward textured hair than all other women. However, McGill Johnson and colleagues found that while Black women celebrate natural hair, they also perceive a high level of social stigma against Afro-textured hair. This study confirmed a "hair paradox": Black women have positive explicit attitudes toward natural hair, but because of social pressures, they have an implicit bias against textured hair (McGill Johnson et al., 2017, 13). Black women's perception of beauty and their desire to conform to Euro-American standards of beauty have serious impacts on this population. Indeed, many women in McGill Johnson and colleagues' survey noted that they have significant anxiety related to their hair and hair maintenance.

Thus, on the one hand, Black voters may take pride in seeing a candidate with dark skin and who wears Afro-textured hair, but on the other hand, they may favor a candidate with a straightened hairstyle. The "hair paradox" may be more complicated for Black women with political aspirations. Voters may assess these women via a complicated set of criteria that is informed by the voters' generational cohort, ideals of respectability, and or professional norms that may or may not incorporate Euro-American beauty standards. These attitudinal puzzles animate our inquiry into the politics of appearance for Black women politicians.

Respectability Politics and Black Women Candidates' Hair Choices

Black women's hair and hairstyle choices are a salient political issue because of the cultural, symbolic, and economic meaning attached to Black hair. Hair is linked to symbolic meanings that are classed and gendered (Gill 2010), and it has social meanings that are often obscured in discussions of personal choice and self-expression. The ways that race and gender interact with certain privileges and social norms for Black women have most often been explored through concepts such as respectability politics, which holds that Black women are evaluated by the extent to which their actions, style choices, and lifestyles adhere to Whiteness (Higginbotham 1992; Hine 1997; Hobson 2003; Cooper 2017). The tight coils and kinks of some Black hair have been negatively viewed as a curse, both within and outside of Africana communities (Lindsey 2017; Candelario 2007). It is within this context that we may understand perceptions of Black women's appearances, particularly regarding their hair.

One aspect of respectability politics is the policing of Black women, by other Black women, urging them to comport to the social values and norms of the middle to upper-class White women and society. Rather than challenging the dominant values of the mainstream culture, appearance, and behavior, this form of respectability politics reassigns blame from the oppressors to the oppressed. Respectability is a social and political process. The suggestion that Black hairstyles are merely a form of expressing individual identity is deeply misguided and lacking in a sociohistorical understanding of the centrality of hair in both the lives of Black women and American culture (Mercer 2005). Along with Black music, food, and culture, hair is a central component of Africana life.

For example, during the Reconstruction Era (1863–1877) and early Jim Crow, Black clubwomen—women who belonged to race-based social improvement organizations—endorsed White Victorian norms in attempts to uplift the Black race (Higginbotham 1993). They organized at the local, state, and federal levels throughout the nineteenth century to improve the social welfare of Black communities (Lerner 1974). The politics of respectability that informed such organizations, a Black middle-class ideology that was born at the turn of the twentieth century, sought to manage Black people's behavior in order to lift the race from dismal conditions (Harris 2014). Black elites like W.E.B. Du Bois , who conceived the concept of the "talented tenth," and improvement organizations like the National Association of Colored Women's Clubs, whose motto was "Lift As We Climb," sought to prove to White America that Blacks were deserving of full citizenship and equal rights. The talented tenth referred to a segment of African Americans who had access to education and economic resources who would then uses their social position to uplift the race (Du Bois 1903). However, this claim was based on the ideal of ridding the untalented nine-tenths of their poor habits, customs, and social behaviors (Harris 2014). These Black elites attempted to outperform White upper-middle-class culture as a way to demonstrate their humanity and show that the racist/sexist sentiments toward them were unfounded. By behaving in a culturally accepted manner, Black clubwomen sought to challenge the prevailing stereotypes of them by simply acting more Victorian than Whites.

This was a strategic political decision, to be sure. While their values were deeply rooted in conservative class and sexual politics, Black clubwomen attempted to craft a distinct gendered space for Black men and women. In doing so, clubwomen such as Nannie Barrier Williams, Mary Church Terrell, and Lucy Craft Laney used the Black female body as a site for social construction within an embodied discourse (Cooper 2017). In other words, the Black female body became the main tool in articulating, policing, theorizing, and advancing respectability politics. Ideas about and gender and race are to this day mapped onto Black women's bodies, as well as what it means to properly perform racialized gender.

In the modern era, respectability politics has an outsized role in Black politics. Ideals of self-correction and care are consistently seen as effective strategies for advancing the Black poor. The politics of respectability are embraced by Black America so much that Frederick Harris notes that it "operates as common sense in most quarters of Black America" (2014, 34). This common knowledge has even led to terms once associated with poor, segregated neighborhoods now being used to refer to unacceptable behavior. For example, the term "ghetto" has been appropriated to refer to Black people who behave in socially unacceptable ways regardless of their social class or where they live.

Harris aptly points out that during the Obama's first term he favored policies that would help everyone rather than targeted social politics that would benefit poor Black and Brown communities (Harris 2012). Obama's lack of interest in using policy to lift socioeconomically and politically marginalized Black people was underscored by his My Brother's Keeper initiative, which encouraged Blacks to take personal responsibility. This initiative and its rollout drew criticism from Black feminists who argued that Black women and girls also need targeted and urgent action that did not center respectability politics.[2] This role of respectability politics within electoral politics is undertheorized[3] and there is even less attention paid to how respectability manifests itself in the political experiences of Black women.

Turning our attention to electoral politics, we argue that Black women's hair has political ramifications. Johnson Carew (2012, 2016) and Brown (2014) have shown that Black women political elites are evaluated differently than their race or gender counterparts because of their appearance. Intersectional experiences and stereotypes drive not only Black women's political experiences, but evaluations of them by voters and constituents. Humanities scholars and sociologists have been on the forefront of examining the ways that hair texture and styles matter in the lives of Black women. Political scientists, however, are late to study the political impact of Black women's hair, which, to date, is little known. Much of what we do know is limited in scope and breadth, and moreover, is restricted to narrow definitions of politics. Using hair as a political site, we examine the multilayered and intersecting ways that Black women's hair is simultaneously raced, gendered, classed, aged, used to communicate personal self, and viewed as a geographic marker. We center the experiences of Black women political elites to better understand their perspectives on the politics of appearance. This unique intervention places Black women at the epicenter of the discussion rather than merely examining them as subjects of other's perceptions and or stereotypes. Hearing directly from these women provides them with agency to shape scholarly understandings of the politics of appearance for Black women. Ultimately, this study enables readers to have a deeper and more detailed understanding of how hair matters for Black women political elites.

Data and Method

This chapter draws on elite interviews with Black women candidates for political office and elected officials. Qualitative research methods are instrumental to this study because, as Hawkesworth (2003, 532) notes, quantitative techniques "devised to reveal uniformities of behavior are by design insensitive to difference, treating anything that deviates from the norm as an outlier or anomaly." In addition, standard social science research methods that are intended to limit the role of race or gender by simply "controlling" for these variables are at odds with efforts to elucidate the multifaceted relationship between race and gender. For these reasons, we use qualitative methods to examine the nuances of how Black women's hair affects their candidacies.

Between 2014 and 2017, twenty one-on-one, in-depth, semi-structured and open-ended in person interviews were conducted with Black women in Maryland, the District of Columbia, Virginia, Illinois, and Missouri. These states were selected because we had access to this population through existing professional relationships with these candidates and lawmakers from previous academic research projects. Interviews lasted 45–90 minutes and were recorded. These interviews were transcribed and organized into themes. All the women in the study were asked, "Please tell me about how you decided to wear your hair." and, "Do you think that your hair plays a role in politics, broadly defined?" These questions serve as the basis for the analysis of this chapter.[4]

Interpretivist approaches were used to code the data because this analytical approach is better suited to explore the hidden reasons behind complex intersectional sociopolitical processes. Interpretivist researchers are trained to see, analyze, and interpret a complex set of perspectives that are informed by sociopolitical phenomena, as well as to reconcile the differences among the participants and social norms. Interpretivist approaches require the researcher to take her own personal biases and the access granted to research participants seriously due to shared raced/gendered identity (Brown 2012). Taking personal positionality seriously also requires that the researcher build and sustain trust with research participants. The researcher must be mindful of actions, words, or misconceptions that may hinder full trust. A lack of trust between the two parties will result in a less than honest self-representation on the part of the participants and in biased conclusions on the part of the researcher. As such, Nadia diligently worked to maintain a relationship with nearly all of the Black women political elites in this study and invited them to view several aspects of the data analysis and writing process.

We then coded the transcripts using an open-ended method by identifying quotes for the analysis that were more deeply based on a set of broad codes. We then performed a more fine-grained analysis on the highlighted quotes and developed a list of secondary themes that were more detailed than the original coding scheme. From there, we thematically organized quotes by the Black women political elites to reveal overlapping and divergent narratives.

How Hair Matters, in Black Women's Own Voices

In what follows, we present the narratives of Black women political elites to better understand the politics of appearance by focusing on hair using six major themes: (1) straight hair as respectable hair; (2) natural hair as not always a political statement; (3) generational differences; (4) straight hair as campaign hair;

(5) natural hair as political empowerment; and (6) head wrap. Basing our analysis within the social context of race/gender in America and within the structures of electoral politics, we critically assess the experiences and views of Black women political elites regarding the salience of hair as an intersectional project. By providing a thick description of these women's narratives, we provide deeper insight into how the politics of appearance is fluid, contextual, and largely based on sociopolitical factors that are deeply embedded in the symbolic meanings of Black women's hair both inside and outside of formal politics. The women are identified by pseudonyms to provide some anonymity to their narratives.

Straight Hair as Respectable Hair

Several of the women in the study explicitly noted that Black constituents and communities view having straight hair as the gold standard for Black women political elites. However, they pushed back against this view in nuanced and dynamic ways. Oftentimes, they did this covertly, such as only straightening their hair with heat for campaign events or while in session. Others indicated that while they knew the expectations of having straight hair, their personal styling decisions were not swayed by those expectations. Instead, they opted to have a more conservative look given their profession or personal taste. Some shared that they were aware of societal tropes pertaining to Black women, and that they used personal styling as a way to counteract these stereotypical images. While the strategies and internal calculations informing each woman's personal decision about how to wear her hair varied, the calculation of respectability politics within electoral politics was a common theme across participants.

For example, consider the narrative of Darlene Hobbs, who was a candidate for a seat in the Illinois House of Representatives when we first spoke in the winter of 2014. Hobbs is a Republican who has run unsuccessfully several times to represent majority-minority districts in the Chicagoland area. When asked about her hair choices, Hobbs described her hair as often pulled back in a bun because she does not have the resources to pay a beautician for the routine maintenance of chemically relaxed hair. For Hobbs, her conservative political values were reflected in her personal styling decisions. However, because she was unable to afford regular hair appoints, the reality of her personal style was largely dictated by financial concerns. Her analysis of how possible constituents viewed her hair reveals the way that White co-partisans make inferences about Black women political elites based on their hair. Hobbs commented,

> Republicans don't know what's going on with my hair. African American voters, I know they look at what a person looks like. And I say that because I've been there, I know. As far as Republicans, I know that they will look, but I don't think that it is more of an emphasis as much as African American Democrats. They [Republicans] may wonder how much I'm spending and whose money I'm spending. But I don't think that the focus [on my hair] would be more critical as it is on the Democratic side. I'm sure you know what I mean [reference to Nadia, as a Black woman]. We were raised that we should look our best and be our best. And if we're going to be representing people, that is what is expected. To look our best and to be our best. It's expensive and time consuming. The others [Whites] might not have to. But you can't please everybody.

Here, Hobbs juxtaposes how Black and White voters, and by consequence, Democrats and Republicans (e.g., Mason and Wronski 2018), view "looking and being one's best." Hobbs's comments reify norms of respectability, which may give her inroads with Republicans, but she is aware of how appearance matters among Blacks and how Black women should navigate societal norms. Hobbs's understanding of Black voters and their perceived values of propriety and morality are reflected in respectability politics as they relate to Black women's appearances. She is not contesting racism and sexism nor the societal structures that re-create these oppressions, and thus different bodily norms for Black women. Rather, she is highlighting the differences between Black voters, whom she sees as Democrats, and Republicans, whom she identifies as White voters.

Unlike Hobbs, Delegate Assata Blaine campaigns in and is elected to serve a majority-minority constituency. While it would seem that Blaine would have more flexibility in her personal style, she still prefers a conservative look. At the time of our interview, Blaine was in the midst of an unsuccessful bid to be Maryland's attorney general. At the time, she represented a suburban Washington, D.C. district in the Maryland House of Delegates. Blaine is a member of Generation X (the cohort born between 1965 and 1980, Dimock 2019), is darker-skinned, and wears her hair in a straight, close, cropped cut. For Delegate Blaine, the politics of appearance has distinct electoral consequences for candidates. She noted, "How you decide to present yourself matters. Because we know that voters, you could be saying all the right things, but they can't get past what you look like, the dress you have on, how you combed your hair. How you present yourself matters." To further elucidate this point, Blaine shared,

I'm pretty conservative, and I think that most voters, regardless of whether I'm a woman or a man, I think most voters feel more comfortable with people who [present themselves in a more conservative matter]. So yes, a more conservative look. Plus, I'm a lawyer. We don't go into courtrooms with rock star hair or anything like that.

Delegate Blaine's presentation style is coupled with her own personal and professional preferences that lean conservative, as well as her assessment of what voters prefer. She believes that non-conservative self-presentation of candidates serves as noise that interrupts how voters perceive candidate's messages.

Unlike Blaine and Hobbs, who were seeking to represent majority-minority communities, school board member Christi Brownell ran for election in in a small town in Indiana that has an overwhelmingly White population. Also dissimilar to Blaine and Hobbs, Brownell does not have straightened hair. Brownell served on the school board from the mid-1980s through the early 1990s, while her daughters were in school. Her medium-hued brown skin and small, yet perfectly round Afro are features that others in the majority-White community do not have. Brownell received pushback on her personal styling decisions from other Black women, and she asserted the possibility of some voters ascribing negative stereotypes to her solely because of her race, gender, and natural hair. Additionally, she mentioned that respectability politics played a role in initial reactions to her decision to stop chemically relaxing her hair. She recalled,

When I went natural, I got flack from old ladies and church sistas. [They'd ask,] "Why are you wearing your hair nappy like that?" This was back in 1971. The sisters in the church were the ones that gave me the most grief. These ladies, they were into the creamy crack. They didn't want no naps on their heads. And [thought] that we shouldn't either. And when I talk about the church sisters, I'm talking about the old ones, the ones that helped raise me. So, they were the ones sucking through their teeth and whatnot. But my peers were different. Oh yea, we were all wearing, letting our hair grow out. . . . But I was quick to say [to the church sisters], "Why are you wearing your hair like that?" Because I don't think we need to adhere to European standards of beauty.

That Brownell embraced her natural hair and questioned European beauty standards was a by-product of the time. As Tanisha Ford (2017) argues, Black women used their hair and personal style as a form of resistance during the Black Power era (late 1960s to early 1970s) and beyond. By celebrating her identity through natural hair, Brownell pushed her church sisters to re-think beauty culture as a symbol of both gender and political liberation. The Black church and Black church women in particular were the location where Evelyn Higginbotham (1993) theorized the politics of respectability. The women in this space elevated the Black church into a social and political in-stitution during the Progressive era. The legacies of these women's conserva-tive body politics have present-day ramifications. Therefore, as an heir to this liturgic and cultural movement, Brownell's initial decision to go natural in the early 1970s was made with a full awareness that this hairstyle might have political repercussions.

Lastly, Missouri State Senator Joya Muhammad, who represents a district in St. Louis, decided to straighten her naturally kinky-curly hair while on the campaign trail. She connected her personal aesthetic to going mainstream so that voters could pay full attention to her policies rather than her appear-ance. Muhammad also connected her appearance to legacies of racism and gender-based discrimination which dictated that Black women needed to look more Eurocentric to be considered beautiful. She noted,

A lot of African Americans are not confident in their own skin. And they want to be accepted. So, they change their dialect when they are around non–African Americans. Their posture, their hair. They allow for people, not all Black folks, but many, allow for people to define who they are versus them defining themselves. This is troubling. Because what was defined as "beauty" within the African American community, with the first 50 elected officials, you had to almost look like a White person.

For Sen. Muhammad, beauty norms for Black women are part and parcel of racialized/gendered stereotyping. Black women's self-presentation is viewed through a lens of otherness, and in order to be fully heard and ac-knowledged as a viable candidate, a Black woman running for office must conform to Eurocentric beauty norms—even if she is running in a majority Black district.

Natural Hair Is NOT Always a Political Statement

Contrary to the ways in which Black women's natural hair has been framed in both the public discourse and academic scholarship, Maryland House of Delegates member Ada Appleton forcefully rebuked the idea that she was making a political statement by wearing her natural hair in campaign literature. Delegate Appleton is a darker-skinned, divorced mother of five and a member of Generation X. At the time of our interview, she was a newly elected delegate, but she had been active in state and local politics for nearly 10 years. She is a graduate of an HBCU (Historically Black Colleges and Universities) in Virginia, and she later went on to earn a law degree and be admitted to the bar. Appleton spoke openly about the tenacious policing of Black women's bodies, often by other Black women, which she herself has experienced. She was, for example, told by older Black women to straighten her hair to be seen as a viable candidate for office. Over time, she grew a thick skin in response to such attempts to control her body, and she recognized that some of these women were advising her out of a place of personal hurt, shame, and low self-esteem. However, Appleton did not internalize their disdain for natural hair as an indictment of her personal decision to wear braids. When asked to further explain the kinds of dirty looks and questions she received by older Black women because of her decision to campaign with natural hair, Appleton shared a story of similar conversations in inappropriate places about her hair:

> It wasn't just [around] kitchen tables, [instead] it was me walking down the hall at my job and like three [Black] women yoking me up, like "Come here. I need to talk to you." And I'm like "Yes." They were like, literally "You can't run for office with your hair all over your head like that." And I was like, "What? What do you mean?"

Delegate Appleton seemed to be appalled that her Black women colleagues were asking her about her hair choices and condemning her decision to wear natural hair on the campaign trail. Rather than internalizing these admonitions, then-candidate Appleton turned the question around to ask, Why not? Appleton resisted the that there was something wrong with running for the state legislature with natural hair. How effective this tactic was or if the other women changed their opinions of either Appleton or natural hair as a result of these conversations is unknown.

Perhaps it was easier for Appleton to confront these women and ignore their criticisms of her natural hair because she views hairstyle as a personal choice. In recounting her decision-making process about how to self-present while in the state legislature, Appleton commented,

> This is a blow dryer, you need it [laughs]. It was serious business [the decision to remain natural on the campaign trail]. But, I saw how I did after a blowout. There was a little resistance, but then, it's one of the things that you have to make a decision. Is this a battle that I really want to fight? Right? And for me, my natural hair, ummm . . . it's not necessary, it's not a political statement. You know, to a certain extent, like this is just my hair.

In sum, Appleton was told that she looked more polished with straightened hair. So, she decided to blow dry her hair straight.

> You could see how, after I started blowing my hair out, how people would come up to me. They'd say, "Oh, you look so nice. You look so polished." The word "polished" was often used. You look so much more professional. Ummm, because you know, you could really tell that I have a law degree because I have a blowout [laughs].

While Appleton laughed about these encounters post-election, she reported feeling frustrated about the judgment passed on her for her choice of hairstyle. Rather sarcastically, she questioned how people's views of her qualifications changed almost immediately when she straightened her hair.

Delegate Appleton's narrative demonstrates two key points. First, natural hairstyle choices are not viewed by all Black women as political or as deeply connected to personal identity. Second, straight hair remains the gold standard for Black women political elites in the eyes of voters. While the candidate herself may hold a sense of indifference about her natural hair and preferred hairstyle, voters do not. These two points will be reflected in the other narratives of Black women candidates and elected officials.

Generational Differences

Preferred hairstyle and self-presentation choices varied by age cohort. Those who came of age during the 1960s often share similar ideas of what the acceptable professional looks are or should be for Black women political elites (Brown 2014). Lawmakers of the Baby Boomer generation (those born between 1946 and 1964, Dimock 2019) in this study were less likely to view their natural hair as a political issue. These women made the decision to go natural not because it was en vogue; rather, they did it for lifestyle, financial, or health reasons. Going through menopause and/or dealing with years of damaged hair from chemical relaxers led these women to embrace short, natural styles.

Bonita Mumford is an outspoken Missouri state legislator who gave a phone interview in 2014. Born in 1952, Representative Mumford served in the Missouri state legislature from 2013 to 2017, where she represented parts of Kansas City. She lost a 2016 Democratic primary race to a Black man representative who was a longtime resident of Kansas City. When asked directly about the politics of appearance for Black women politicians, Rep. Mumford expressed a self-assuredness in her hair. She noted that her hair had been thinning and that she had therefore elected to wear it closely cropped to her scalp. "Changing my hair is . . . a piece [that] I'm not going to be able to change. Matter of fact, I just went to the barbershop yesterday. This is me and I'm not trying to change this for the world." Mumford expressed that her hair does not impact the ways that her constituents view her: "My voters know me and the majority of voters . . . they are ok with it." Mumford also shared that keeping her natural hair cut very low enabled her to spend more time on other things. For example, she enjoys buying shoes and has a large collection of footwear. Whereas hair may have been a focal point for some constituents, for Mumford, shoes are her signature statement of self-expression. Indeed, Rep. Mumford made sure that Nadia understood that thinning hair and her consequently close-cropped style has not diminished her sense of fashion.

Similar to Rep. Mumford, school board member Christi Brownell noted that her age plays a large role in how she currently wears her hair. Part of the Boomer cohort, Brownell explained, "I first had my hair in a natural style in high school. That was just the style at the time. It never dawned on me that it could be a problem." When asked how to describe how she looks, Brownell said, "I'm a caramel-colored African American woman with a short natural.

I would not call it a natural. Not an Afro." Like Blaine and Hobbs, Brownell wanted her campaign material to be timeless. She reflected, "I just wanted the pictures to be a classic. That was my only concern." Having natural hair for her was part of her classic look. Brownell opined,

> There is no way that I would have changed my hair or put the creamy crack in it. It wasn't going to happen. I was who I was. Vote for me or leave it. . . . They knew that I was gregarious, friendly. They knew that I was clean, I never smelled bad. I mean, they knew "She was articulate." I know that I looked respectable.

When asked more directly why she preferred to refer to her hairstyle as "a natural, not an Afro," and connected this terminology to being respectable, Brownell explained that she saw a difference in how a Black woman classifies her hairstyle and the way she carries herself: "I'm trying to be comfortable, help people be comfortable with me. And um . . . calling it an Afro would make some people uncomfortable. Yeah, I think so. So, you don't know what kind of an impact your words are going to have."

These statements reflect Brownell's self-assuredness as well as her trepidations about her selected hairstyle. She is confident that her short natural is not a defining characteristic for how others define her, but she is concerned that some voters may have believed that she was not respectable enough to garner their vote. It is also telling that Brownell described the possibility of some voters ascribing negative stereotypes to her solely because of her race, gender, and natural hair. This stereotype of natural hair included misconceptions that it smelled or that it did not need to be cleaned often. This ignorance of how natural hair is maintained and styled plays into respectability politics that prioritize European beauty standards by falling back on tropes associate Blackness with negative associations. Additionally, she mentioned that respectability politics played a role in initial reactions to her decision to stop chemically relaxing her hair.

Though Brownell went natural in the 1970s as a reflection of the racial consciousness and pride of the era, she largely remained natural over the coming decades. She did, however, chemically process her hair several times, to get it either straight or wavy. The decision to return to being natural was largely economic. Brownell shared, I let the guy [beautician] put the stuff [chemicals to alter kinky hair] in my hair. And I liked what I looked like. And I kept it up for a while. After I did a couple of touch ups, I said, 'I'm through with this.'

It was costing me money! I went back to being natural." Since then, she has worn her hair "mostly natural," and recalls, "I think I did have the extensions for a bit. I also went to locs after that."

Regardless of her hairstyle choices, Brownell reaffirmed her opinion that voters assess candidates on their overall appearance. She commented:

> I have a feeling that the way you dress and present yourself is more telling than the way you wear your hair. You don't want anything garish or too ethnic. I've got a couple of African dresses in my closet. I don't wear that when I'm campaigning. I just tried to make sure that I presented myself in a professional manner. And that's it. I think that's the most important thing.

This comment is closely related to Delegate Blaine's discussion of conservativism and the importance of modest dressing for Black women political elites. Brownell's observation demonstrates that hairstyle may take a backseat to the overall package of a candidate's self-presentation if other aspects, such as dress, are more ethnic. For these Black woman candidates, the idea of looking ethnic as signaled by their hair choices demonstrates a sense of otherness that may be outside the mainstream. This may give certain voters pause. Here, the candidates note that they are conscious of how they present themselves to voters and that they therefore moderate their appearance to be less Afrocentric.

Campaign Hair = Straight Hair

Several of the Black women political elites in this study were natural prior to their campaigns. Others remained natural, but used wigs or straightened their hair with heat for their promotional materials.

Lindsey Blackburn ran an unsuccessful 2014 campaign to unseat the prosecuting attorney for St. Louis County, Missouri. The incumbent had held the seat for 20 years when challenged by Blackburn, who is a lifelong resident of St. Louis and a graduate of the University of Missouri's Law School. Blackburn was a municipal judge and served as an elected committeeperson in her town. She is a tall, slender, brown-skinned, married mother of four. The interview with Lindsey Blackburn was conducted a month before the election, in her grandmother's kitchen as she was balancing helping her eldest daughter with homework, approving the final designs of her campaign leaflets, and preparing a shopping list for a quick run to the local grocery store to pick up dinner items. In the midst of all this multitasking, Blackburn forcefully articulated her belief that her natural hair would intimidate the county's White population. She said,

> I can't win this race solely on the African American vote. I felt like my twists would intimidate the White population because I think they see that and think you are a militant person. And I am not. So, I relaxed it. And I'm still not happy about that.

The decision for Blackburn to chemically straighten her hair was made in consultation with her political strategists. She and her self-described peer-mentor, a Black man who would later defeat the long-serving St. Louis County prosecuting attorney in 2018—would often discuss her hairstyle choices and the double standard for Black men and women candidates. This was another point of contention for Blackburn, who lamented the fact that natural hair would be perceived negatively for Black women candidates. In response to these conversations and others with local political strategists, she decided to chemically straighten her hair. She commented,

> I was told that I needed to keep it up during the campaign. So, a bob has been it. I admit it, I need to have an appointment for a cut and some color. . . . I'm going back natural after the election. My husband prefers my hair straight and long. I find it to be boring. I think it makes me look older. Even as professional as I am, there's still something about me. I still like something a little fun. . . . When I think of professional, I think of at least clean and put together. Could I have pulled it off with my natural hair? You know, I would like to think I could have. But, I'm also in Missouri.

Blackwell also noted that Black women in Missouri, specifically the St. Louis area, have a harder time convincing voters that they are qualified candidates. She finds that many Missourians hold deeply rooted stereotypes and misconceptions about Black women's ability to lead even when they hold the same credentials as their White or male challengers. Hairstyle may help to either reaffirm some of these stereotypes or assuage concerns for some voters.

Unlike Lindsey Blackwell, Delegate Appleton never chemically straightened her hair, but she chose to wear protective styles with added hair as a way to achieve the desired "professional look." Much of the decision to wear these protective styles was predicated on the fact that they were just easier to manage during the intensity of a campaign season. Appleton noted,

> I got braids. Crochet braids, which I love. But the braids were of a basically straight but wavy style. I got those for ease and also because you know that we're up late and working late and then having to get up early. [I liked] not having to worry about doing my hair because you know [having] natural hair can be a job—picking out products and getting up and wetting it every morning. So, I got braids and then a lot of people, because of my braids, you know, if you get crochet braids these days, they look a lot like a wig or weave. Then there were people who liked it. They said it was a good look. Like, they were basically like "oh, you finally jumped on the wig train. Good for you."

Some people who interacted with Appleton during her campaign preferred her to have a braided protective style that looked like a wig or weave. However, their preference for straight hair, even if it was not her own hair, was not a major issue or concern for Appleton. She described others' preferences about her hair as not being a major factor in her decision about how to wear her hair:

> It's never ummm . . . that much on my conscious. I'm Black and I'm proud. It's more like, this is my hair. . . . But the respectability politics is very real. And it's very interesting. For example, I had an interview [that I posted] on Facebook and I thought about my hair. There was a moment where I was like "do I straighten my hair? Am I going to be able to like, go home and blow it out?" Because I never actually did a professional interview or done like a really public appearance with my hair not straight. You know and even, I'm from the Midwest. So, like, my mother's, you know from the Midwest, but she [was] raised, ummm, her folks are from Mississippi. So, when she sees me, it's a constant, like "What are you going to do [with] your hair today?"

Appleton's reference to her mother's preference for straight hair respectability politics as a by-product of her mother's generation and of being raised in Mississippi indicates that Appleton is well aware of how Black women's bodies are policed. Appleton reveals here that, for her, hair texture is contro-versial not only in a professional setting, but within her own family as well. She also stated that, as the mother of five daughters, she works hard to instill self-acceptance and love within her girls, with a focus on dispelling the myths of "good" and "bad" hair and features. She wants all of her girls to "embrace their beauty, not to be envious" of others. This broader reflection on respecta-bility politics leads Delegate Appleton to note that the process of challenging these norms of denigrating African phenotypes begins at home.

Natural Hair as Political Empowerment

St. Louis City Alderman Deborah Fabron wore her natural hair in a close-shaven cut during the day of our interview. When asked about her chosen hair selection, the, slender, brown-skinned, Generation X alderman politely laughed as she discussed her close-cropped, natural, strawberry blond hair. She noted that her father owned one of St. Louis's most popular barbershops, and that he had encouraged young Deborah to go to barber school when she decided not to finish her undergraduate degree in the early 1990s. Her father's barbershop was a place where Black men and other members of the community would gather to discuss politics, and her father would eventually run for office and serve in local government. This environment was where young Deborah Fabron sharpened her barbering skills and cut her political teeth. However, she still relaxed her hair at the time. It was not until years later that she decided to stop chemically straightening her hair. In fact, she cut her hair and went natural for the first time as an elected official. Fabron stated,

> [N]ow this is the first time I have had natural hair. . . . it's interesting, the people here at the board when I first started going natural. Some didn't know what to say. Then others were like, "Oh, I like that on you." Then there were White women who actually said, "I understand, Black women don't want to . . . have perms anymore."

These interactions seem rather positive and accepting of Alderman Fabron's decision not to relax her hair. Her colleagues on the council demon-strated support for her hair choices, and even the White women members of the St. Louis City Council offered Fabron verbal support and complimented her on this new style. These pleasant interactions with her colleagues are a refreshing change from how the other women in this study—as well as in the extant literature—have documented their transition phase from processed to natural hair within a professional environment.

Perhaps Black women's hair is not a topic of denigrating conversation in the St. Louis City Council because the city has a history of fostering pioneers in the Black hair care industry. Both Madam C.J. Walker and Annie Turnbo Malone called the city home and revolutionized Black women's hair care in the late 1800s. Walker and Malone were businesswomen who specialized in developing and marketing hair care products for Black women. These entrepreneurial women were among the first Black millionaires and believed deeply in philanthropy, sharing much of their wealth with underserved St. Louis–area Blacks. To this day, the city acknowledges the legacies of these women. It is in this spirit that some Whites in St. Louis may appreciate and recognize Black women's hair care regimes and styles.

To be clear, not all Whites in the city shared positive affirmations of Alderman Fabron's new natural hair. She recalled an experience with a White woman at her church who admonished her for this hairstyle. "There was a Caucasian lady that came up to me in church and just shook her head and said, '[expletive].' And I just said, 'This is what God gave me.'" Thankfully, this woman's response was a rare encounter for Fabron. As rude and disrespectful—particularly in church—as this interaction was, the Alderman has received far more favorable responses to her hair than negative ones.

As a barber, Fabron is able to frequently change her hairstyle. She encouraged Nadia to look at the annual council pictures during her tenure in the chamber to get a better sense of how she routinely changes her hair. "I have never had the same hairstyle, she noted. "So, you'll look, you'll see it down, you'll see it short, you'll see it colored. You'll see my pictures are different." When asked about the impact of changing her hair so frequently in a professional setting that does not value the versatility of Black women's hair, Fabron responded,

> It has been different down here, when you change your look. The corporate [environment] is a little different. And I think sometimes when I show up on the scene, some of them are like, "Oh, I didn't expect that." But then, when I talk, they're okay.

According to Fabron, the St. Louis City aldermen are accepting of her hair, even if they are a little taken aback by the new styles. She has not found her hair choices to be an issue for her legislative work in this environment. When asked if her appearance impacts how voters perceive her, Fabron mused, "I don't think it matters to my constituents. But I do get a lot of, 'Oh, I like your hair.' And 'Wow, you're kind of like me'" from Black women in her ward. She is proud that her constituents know her and like her. Some of that connection is based on her hair. For example, Fabron shared that "retired, senior citizen Black women love it. Now some of them don't. . . . But they like it, they love it. Now I get a lot of White men that will say, 'I like your hair better the other way.' And I say, 'Well, if you want to pay to get it done, then no problem. But for now, this is it.'" In previous research, Brown (2014) found that constituents may offer inconsequential opinions of Black women lawmakers' hair, but Fabron's narrative is different. Here, she notes that her hairstyling choices are a point of engagement with some constituents. These conversations do not necessarily turn into conversations about politics or policy, but they demonstrate that her constituents feel comfortable enough with her to engage in personal conversations about her hair. This may be a form of political empowerment for her constituents, as a heightened level of comfort with one's elected representatives may lead to increased attentiveness to political affairs (Bobo and Gilliam 1990). However, more research is necessary to make a definitive claim in this regard. It is also noteworthy that both Black and White residents in Aldermen Fabron's ward feel empowered to engage with her around hairstyle.

Head Wrap

Missouri State Senator Joya Muhammad has an atypical narrative about the politics of hair for Black women lawmakers. Unlike her colleagues, she often wears a hijab, the head covering, or head wrap, worn in public by some Muslim women. Muhammad converted to Islam as a young adult and changed her name from Jessica Williamson. The medium-build, brown-skinned lawmaker is often viewed as a controversial figure in Missouri politics for several reasons. First, Sen. Muhammad was active in the 2014 Ferguson unrest and was arrested for her protest-related activities. She also failed to stand during the Pledge of Allegiance in September 2016, in solidarity with former San Francisco 49ers quarterback Colin Kaepernick, who took a knee to protest police brutality and racial injustices. Sen. Muhammad has had a long and vocal presence in Missouri politics, often championing the needs and desires of economically marginalized Blacks in the St. Louis area.

When we met for this interview, Sen. Muhammad offered to walk Nadia through the process of her decision to wear a head wrap and then to stop wrapping her hair. She stated,

> I just got tired of that look. And I decided that I just wanted to go into a more mainstream look. Which, it's unfortunate, but people, when I had my hair wrap on versus it being off, even the women in the capital and like the lobbyists approach me differently. They would be like, "Girl, come here! Your hair looks so good!" and "You should let your beautiful hair flow." They had this perception of how I should look. That didn't bother me. So, I decided, and my hair started breaking out at the back because of the head wraps.

Once she stopped wearing the head wraps, Sen. Muhammad enjoyed a variety of hairstyles. Her decision to stop wrapping her hair was partially because the hair around her face and neck started to fall out due to the friction of the fabric rubbing against the hair. In spite of the rational to stop wearing the head wraps out of concern for the health of her hair, she was concerned that the different hairstyles, not the head wraps, would disorient voters and colleagues. To further elucidate this point, she said,

> I don't think you should change looks. I feel like once you put one image or one look out there, that's what you want to resonate in the minds of people when they think about you. I don't want to put a picture with my curly red hair and [then] have a picture with black straight hair. It's just too many images that messes up how people perceive you. . . . Your image is non-verbal. You are talking to people even when you are not talking. And they are going to listen to you, not literally listen to you, but listen to you and pay attention to you based on your appearance. They prejudge you way before you open your mouth. So, you have to have this mainstream image so to speak. . . . I took off my head wrap not for people to accept me though. But for people to be a little more comfortable and for me to be able to get, well, when I took the head wrap off, I was more approachable. When I had the head wrap on, people were afraid to approach me because they felt [that]

I was too militant. People said, "Ahh, she took her head wrap off because she's around these White folks now! [laughs] I get it from both sides: "Ahh, she's gone and assimilated."

Having a consistent and nonthreatening image was important to Sen. Muhammad, although her primary reason for not wearing the head wrap was to curtail the damage to her hair. The constant rubbing of the fabric around the most sensitive and fragile areas of her head led to her hair thinning out around her hairline. To be clear, she did not appreciate her colleagues and voters attributing this decision to her trying to either assimilate into mainstream White culture or signal that she was a Black radical. Muhammad's decision to wear a hijab was based on her religious practices, and the decision to stop wearing a hijab was based on both pragmatic reasons about the health of her hair and the desire for others to feel comfortable around her.

While others in the study shared that they were pro-Black or at least unashamed of being Black, Sen. Muhammad was the only woman in our sample to directly discuss Black people who may be anti-Black. She acknowledged that one can be of African descent and feel uncomfortable in one's own skin—a legacy of racism and colorism. The fear of not being accepted because of one's race has been extensively studied in other disciplines. While this subject is not the focus of this chapter, Senator Muhammad's comments beg the question of how race, gender, self-presentation, and self-acceptance are manifested in legislative settings. Muhammad alleges that some of her Black colleagues are uncomfortable because of their race, and others are learning to fully embrace racial markers. Understandably, the legacies of racism and society's anti-Black belief systems make it difficult to change social hierarchies that place Blacks on the bottom (Masouka and Junn 2013). Institutions are made up of people who re-enact societal norms, and as such, these practices and beliefs become ingrained within the statehouse. The need to challenge anti-Blackness and the host of stereotypes that surround Black women (Hill Collins 2000) is therefore ever-present.

Discussion and Conclusion

This chapter has demonstrated that Black women political elites do not view the politics of appearance uniformly. Through the six themes presented in this chapter, we see that this group of women desires to present a professional image that is often seen as conservative, but that they come to their hairstyle decisions in a myriad of distinct ways. Even among these differences, however, we find significant similarities and conclude that hair, both texture and style, has consequences for Black women political elites. This diverse sample—in terms of region, generational cohort, partisanship, and elected office sought or held—allowed us to present a more holistic picture of the salience of hair for Black women policymakers and candidates. This chapter signals that there may have been some shifts in our understanding of Black women's hair within electoral politics.

The Black women political elites in this study present a varied but consistent discussion of how their hair matters in the context of electoral politics. They uniformly agree that Black women should present themselves as professionals. However, there is no one "professional look" that these women politicians find to be best suited to their personal needs and how they desire to look. These women understand that straight hair is and has been the gold standard for Black women political elites, yet some of them are actively challenging that narrative. The desire to present oneself as professional is complicated, and a more detailed look at how Black women political elites are making these decisions is necessary.

The self-presentations of political elites are carefully constructed identities that reflect social and cultural norms. They either directly or indirectly provide viewers with a glimpse of the politicians' personalities, political ideologies, and sense of self. These images, in sum, communicate more than personal style and can be used as a political heuristic. For Black women, gender stereotyping creates a unique tension. Women's beauty regimes that alter a female candidate's or lawmaker's outward appearance can create an inaccurate physical representation of the woman (Hancock and Toma 2009). The dual processes of racing-gendering (Hawkesworth 2003) and women's beauty norms may lead Black women candidates to alter their self-presentations in order to appear more feminine, with softer, racially distinct features. Because hair, both in texture and style, is a political heuristic, Black women candidates may forgo Afro-centric styles in order to achieve their political goals in a field dominated by White men.

The women we interviewed credit respectability politics as playing a large role in their hairstyles and how others perceive them. The acknowledgment of respectability politics is more than a tacit understanding of the policing of Black women's bodies, as it shows an engagement with (dis)respectability in ways that are organic for each woman in this study. By centering Black women political elites as agents, we offer scholars the opportunity to more fully grapple with how this population self-defines and engages with controlling tropes.

Black women political elites have to "walk a fine line" (Carroll 1994) in crafting a professional image. The act of balancing racialized/gendered stereotypes and one's self-presentation is often a difficult negotiation for Black women candidates and elected officials. Yet, this issue is often seen as frivolous or trivial in mainstream discussions of candidates and is not discussed in political science literature. Black communities, and Black women in particular, routinely share the challenges surrounding their personal appearances on the campaign trail or within legislative bodies. The narratives of the women in this chapter demonstrate that Black women political elites are concerned with respectability politics. Some may argue that this is an overly exaggerated concern given today's more liberal sexual and gender politics. However, the Black women candidates and elected officials in this research show that Black communities in particular remain deeply committed to respectability politics, and Black women political elites display their adherence to respectability norms through their hairstyle choices. The demonstration of respectable styling and grooming choices signal a resistance to the three prevailing race/gendered stereotypes that continue to stigmatize this group. In turn, Black women political elites are conscious of these community norms and historical stereotypes, and of their current role in dictating Black women's sociopolitical positioning.

These findings should push scholars to think more holistically about how women's bodies impact their sense of self, the opinions of voters, and the persistent stereotypes that are communicated about Black women, particularly because of their hair choices. In this chapter, we have shown that Black women political elites are not passive subjects; rather, they are active in shaping how they are perceived by others. They also make specific choices that best suit their daily lives and hair care needs. By foregrounding the narratives of Black women candidates, in which they self-describe the ways that hair impacts their decisions as candidates, we have allowed them space to dictate their own experiences. Rather than being "eaten alive" by mainstream narratives and respectability politics, Black women candidates in this study have articulated how they strategically engage with the politics of appearance.

In the next chapter, we explore these topics with Black women political elites within a group setting We find that concerns of respectability and generation are constant frames that influence how these women navigate the political terrain. The interviews in this chapter, and the epigraph from Rep. Lauren Underwood, demonstrate that Black women have varying personal experiences with the politics of appearance. In the following group conversation, we examine a deeper relational understanding of how Black women are socialized to present themselves as political candidates and elected officials.

4

Candid Conversations: Black Women Political Elites and Appearances

I need to see my own beauty and to continue to be reminded that I am enough, that I am worthy of love without effort, that I am beautiful, that the texture of my hair and that the shape of my curves, the size of my lips, the color of my skin, and the feelings that I have are all worthy and okay.

—Tracee Ellis Ross

We need to reshape our own perception of how we view ourselves. We have to step up as women and take the lead.

—Beyoncé

In 2018, 17 Black women were elected to judgeships in Harris County, Texas, bringing the total number of Black women judges in the county to 19. These 19 Black women judges have been an inspiration to Black girls, and they exemplify Black Girl Magic—a movement that celebrates Black women and girls' accomplishments (Halliday and Brown 2018; Schneider 2019). Following her historic win, Judge Cassandra Holleman told NPR, "I've had parents that tell me that their daughter took the picture that we had and they framed it, and it's actually on their wall in the bedroom" (Schneider 2019). The imagery of Black women finding electoral success in large numbers has excited communities well beyond Harris County. The national attention paid to these Black women judges demonstrates that Black women can be lauded just as much for their electoral success as for their roles as voters who deliver key elections to Democrats. Holleman's electoral victory brought the courts of Harris County, which has a population of over four million people and is 13% Black, closer to descriptively representing the county's constituents.

Sister Style. Nadia E. Brown and Danielle Casarez Lemi, Oxford University Press (2021). © Oxford University Press.
DOI: 10.1093/oso/9780197540572.003.0004

This chapter's discussion takes place in Texas. Here, we expand upon the previous chapter's findings and use the focus group method to examine how Black women elites view the politics of appearance when talking in a room full of other Black women elites who are largely from Texas and who gathered to attend the Black Women's Political Action Committee 2nd Annual Summit in 2019 in Dallas, Texas. Although leadership is often treated as an individual phenomenon, with legislators' individual experiences and characteristics shaping outcomes (e.g., Krcemaric et al. 2020), the reality is that leadership and policymaking occur in group settings rife with complex interpersonal dynamics (e.g., Caldeira et al. 1988; Caldeira and Patterson 1987; Arnold et al. 2000; Tyson 2016). For instance, using organizational theory to analyze legislative bodies as workplaces, Tyson (2016, 145–46) showed that the legislature is a micro-aggressive environment for legislators of color. Research on Latinx/Latina legislators suggests that Latinas tend to view themselves as more collaborative than Latinx legislators (Fraga et al. 2006). Multiple studies show that the substantive representation of marginalized groups is more likely when multiple marginalized groups hold seats in the legislature (e.g., Minta and Sinclair-Chapman 2013; Minta and Brown 2014; Minta 2019).

Within legislative bodies, physical appearances are salient to legislators. For example, in Brown (2014, 302), Black women state legislators in Maryland discussed each other's appearances, with one legislator believing that her skin tone was the reason a senior colleague did not support her bills. In Lemi (2018, 735), one legislator described himself as a "dark-skinned person" while other legislators wondered why an apparently White person, who identified as both Black and White, sought the endorsement of the Legislative Black Caucus as he ran for a state representative seat. These examples show that leadership and representation occur not just on an individual level but on a highly interpersonal, group level as well. We therefore expand here on the discussion in the previous chapter and dive deeper into the politics of appearance by incorporating a group element via the focus group.

In Chapter 3, we described the generational differences we found in how the way Black women political elites think about their appearance influences their political experiences. Building upon this finding, in this chapter we systematically explore generational attitudes toward Black women's appearances through our focus group with participants in the Black Women's Political Action Committee's 2nd annual summit. This thematic frame was organically discussed by the focus group participants, and it mirrors the findings from the one-on-one interview with other Black women political elites.

Generational Differences

Adding another vector to our intersectional analysis of Black women elites' appearance is our discussion of generational differences. Taking generational cohort as a salient political identity, we draw on previous studies that demonstrated differences among cohorts of Black politicians (Gillespie 2010; Brown 2014; Williams 2001). Unlike these studies, which largely explore policy differences, this chapter examines how generational differences lead to Black women candidates' varying experiences with their appearances.

Individuals develop specific political orientations based on their experiences with the political system (Almond and Verba 1965). The formative years, from childhood to adulthood, are the period when people develop values that are shaped by their socioeconomic conditions. In turn, people develop different political orientations based on the socioeconomic conditions that occurred when they came of age. Different generations have distinct political leanings that were informed by their early cultural and political experiences.

Much of the scholarly discussion of generational differences in political science centers around vote choice and partisanship (Fisher 2018, 2020). There are generational differences in partisanship (Abramson 1976), basic values (Abramson and Inglehart 1987; Inglehart 1977), and electoral behavior (Butler and Stokes 1969). For example, members of the Greatest Generation, born between 1901 and 1927, are the country's oldest citizens. They tend to have a lasting belief in government activism and to display support for the Democratic Party (Miller 1992). The Silent Generation, those born between 1928 and 1945, are most likely to attend religious services, are more conservative, and are more likely to support the Republican Party (Fisher 2020). Next, Baby Boomers, born between 1946 and 1964, are more liberal than their predecessors, they still tend to be conservative and become increasing so with age (Fisher 2018). Generation X, those born between 1965 and 1980, have a more personal view of politics and display an individualistic orientation toward politics (Putnam 2000). Millennials, or those born between 1981 and 1996, hold more liberal ideas and generally vote for Democratic candidates.

Lastly, new research has found that members of Generation Z, those born between 1997 and 2012, hold similar policy preferences to Millennials and that they have embraced liberal attitudes (DeSante and Watts Smith 2020; Rouse and Ross 2018). However, these descriptions are not hard and fast. Some cohorts may share common generational outlooks with others on a particular set of political values (Mannheim 1972). In sum, the generation in which an individual comes of political age is a crucial determinant in that individual's political identity.

In general, Baby Boomers and members of the Silent Generation lean to the ideological right of the American population. In contrast, Millennials are decidedly to the left of center in American politics. This finding holds consistent with older studies that have found that younger cohorts are more liberal on feminist issues, for example, than are older generations (Rouse and Ross 2018, Sapiro 1980; Gurin 1985). The starkest contrast in policy position and vote choice are between Boomers/Silents and Millennials (Fisher 2018). This research, however, pays little attention to racialized differences among generational cohorts. Indeed, most of the literature centers the experiences of White Americans, as the surveys used to explicate the cohorts' policy preferences do not have large or representative samples of ethno-racial minorities.

Unlike previous cohorts of Americans, Millennials are considerably more ethno-racially diverse than older generations due to increase immigration and higher birthrates within minoritized communities. This generational cohort opines that Blacks are treated less fairly than Whites (Parker et al. 2019). These differences in racial attitudes may lead Millennials to support different ideals about Black women's roles in society than those held by older cohorts. Likewise, DeSante and Watts Smith (2020) find that younger Whites have lower levels of racial resentment and are least likely to advance old-fashioned anti-Black racism. Yet, this finding is a by-product of an outdated model, the racial resentment scale, that does not account for changing racial norms and colorblindness ideals. These norms ushered in the Age of Obama, which prioritized racial egalitarianism (Hochschild, Weaver, and Burch 2012), a view that insisted skin color was not a significant social marker. The Millennial generation is believed to be the most racially tolerant cohort in the nation's history (Pew Research Center 2010). Because White Millennials have been socialized not to "see" race or acknowledge racial differences (Bonilla-Silva 2014), they avoid explicitly discussing race to ensure political correctness (Jackson 2008). In turn, the historical processes and psychosocial norms of

White Millennials have led them to appear less prejudiced on the racial resentment scale in comparison to older cohorts.

Nevertheless, Millennials' political attitudes are notable for their diversity, and paying attention to only White Millennials paints an incomplete picture. There are significant differences between the policy attitudes of White and ethno-racial minority Millennials. Indeed, Rouse and Ross (2018) demonstrate that minority Millennials hold economic attitudes that are similar to older cohorts of their same ethno-racial group, a finding that is distinct from the results for White Millennials. For instance, ethno-racial minority Millennials support an increase in the minimum wage, government forgiveness of student loan debt, slow changes to Social Security, expanded immigration rights, the legalization of marijuana, and stronger gun control policies.

Furthermore, these studies do not offer insights into how generational cohorts think of Black women's roles in society. Our work stands in stark contrast to these studies, as we do not compare attitudes of Black Millennials to their White counterparts. While it is important to note that Black and White views on political ideology, policy preferences, and partisanship are underpinned by different factors (Hajnel and Lee 2011), we have yet to examine how these generational differences play out for Black women in particular. A comparative lens between Black and White opinions is unnecessary to understand Black women's experiences and political behavior. Holding Whites as the comparison group misconstrues Black women's political socialization on their own terms. Such comparative research assesses Black women's beliefs as being similar or dissimilar to ideological patterns present among generational cohorts and provides a flawed view of what animates Black women's politics. Our study assesses variation across age cohorts of Black women political elites to demonstrate differences in their political behavior and experiences. In short, talking with Black women political elites themselves reveals how this group displays generational differences on their own terms and in their own voices.

The Focus Group

We used the focus group method to examine the relational dynamics of conversations about appearance among Black women political elites. The focus group method complements individual interview methods in that a focus group is a conversation among similar individuals and thus encourages candidness (Krueger and Casey 2014). For example, one study found that, relative to individual interviews, focus groups encouraged participants to discuss "sensitive" topics more frequently (Guest et al. 2017, 704). By using the focus group method, we facilitated Black women elites' discussion with other Black women elites of personal experiences that they might not share with an individual researcher alone sitting with a recorder.

Another purpose of the focus group is to observe the group dynamic that emerges in the conversation—a dynamic that does not exist between a single participant and researcher (Smithson 2000; Onwuegbuzie et al. 2009; Montell 1999). As we discussed above, leadership is a group endeavor. By using the focus group, we were able to observe how Black women elites interact with each other, how they describe their experiences, and how they respond to others' experiences. Our individual interviews suggested that there is a generational aspect to how Black women elites view the politics of appearance and their styling decisions. The focus group allowed us to observe these dynamics in real time among participants who vary in age cohort. In short, the focus group was an ideal method to build upon what we found in the individual interviews.

The Black Women's Political Action Committee of Texas

We partnered with the Black Women's Political Action Committee of Texas (BWPAC TX), an organization dedicated to supporting Black women's paths to political office. We first met the BWPAC TX in November 2018, when we served as panelists at the BWPAC TX's 1st Annual Policy, Politics, and Donor Summit in Austin, Texas. The coordinator of the BWPAC TX expressed an interest in collaborating with us, and we kept in touch. Partnering with an organization that serves the population we were studying had several advantages. First, we sought to center the voices of Black women elites and Black women generally as producers of knowledge. As we discussed earlier, researchers often use communities of color as objects of study rather than active creators of knowledge. In political science, a dominant approach involves viewing people of color as "deviants" via theories constructed from the White American experience (Masuoka and Junn 2013). Partnering with a community-serving organization like the BWPAC TX ensures that our research is community-engaged, with a symbiotic relationship between academic researchers and the community participating in the research (Kantamneni et al. 2019, 65). By focusing on collaboration, we aimed for an ethical way of conducting community-based research (Mikesell et al. 2013, Table 2) and data collection (Montell 1999, 57). This approach is appropriate, as this book is driven by the narratives of Black women elites and meant for Black women interested in running for office. Second, we continue to advance a culturally sensitive approach, in which the cultural knowledge of Black women specifically is placed at the center of inquiry (Tillman 2002). In partnering with the BWPAC TX, we follow best practices for culturally sensitive research by building relationships with community members outside of academia (Tilman 2002, 6). Put simply, we worked with an organization that had a vast network of experts we sought to learn from: Black women elites.

Third, working with the BWPAC TX allowed us to observe in-depth a diverse set of perspectives about "shared cultural knowledge" (Tillman 2002, 4). The BWPAC TX's network consists of a range of elected officials at different levels of office, community organizers in different parts of the state, and practitioners operating in different spaces. The BWPAC TX's network is also diverse in terms of age cohort. Partnering with the BWPAC TX thus allowed us to observe how a group of individuals with a shared baseline of knowledge interpreted, used, and shared that knowledge with others from their own individual contexts.

Working with a Texas-based organization was also ideal for this project. Texas has a population of about 27 million people, and African Americans comprise 13% of the general population.[1] Texas is also home to key historical Black women figures. For example, Houston-based Congresswoman Barbara Jordan represented Texas's 18th congressional district.[2] Jordan held a number of firsts: first Black elected official post-Reconstruction, first Texan Black woman in Congress, and first Southern Black woman in Congress.[3] In 2018, Black women led the way in supporting Beto O'Rourke's challenge to Ted Cruz for the U.S. Senate[4] and in supporting Lupe Valdez, who stood to be the first Latina and lesbian governor of Texas.[5,6] As previously noted, that year, Harris County also elected 19 Black women judges.[7] Dallas set the backdrop for our conversation. The city is home to over one million people, and at least 25% of the population is African American.[8] Taken together, these factors produced a context that was highly appropriate for our questions. To our knowledge, this was the first focus group of its kind. As representation scholars know, getting on elites' calendars is notoriously difficult, and we were graciously afforded a unique opportunity to observe local elites engaging in this conversation together.

Our focus group took place on November 9, 2019, during the BW PAC TX's 2nd Annual Policy, Politics, and Donor Summit, a yearly event designed to fundraise for the BWPAC TX, discuss political issues relevant to Black women, and create the infrastructure to support Black women's candidacies. The 2019 event was held at The Riveter, a woman-owned workspace cooperative. To recruit our sample, we worked with the coordinator of the BWPAC TX to invite focus group participants with a survey link placed on the event registration website, and the coordinator of the BWPAC TX reached out personally to individuals who she thought might be interested. Our target participants were Black women who have run for office and Black women who were considering running for office, and we were also open to people who had worked on campaigns. In partnering with the BWPAC TX, we worked closely with the coordinator of the BWPAC TX to approve recruitment language, publicize the focus group, and recruit participants.

The focus group consisted of 12 participants. The Black women political elites in our study were from a variety of backgrounds. They ranged in age from their early thirties to their early seventies. The women either currently held or were seeking elected positions. The vast majority had a legal background and many were former military. Our participants primarily identified as Democrats. Indeed, two women were currently serving as chairs and three others held previous leadership positions in their local chapter of the Democratic Party. Three women in our focus group sought to represent their communities in the U.S. House of Representatives, while three others ran for their state legislature. One woman in our study launched an unsuccessful bid for lieutenant governor of her state, and another attempted to represent her state in the U.S. Senate. Only one of the women in our study was an appointed judge, whereas the other judges had either won a seat on the bench or were seeking one in their local county. As current candidates, some of our participants sought to hold judgeships on their local family court, mental illness court, county probate court, and district court.

After obtaining informed consent and permission to record the conversation, we opened the focus group with brief introductions. We asked questions similar to those posed in the individual interviews—namely about participants' visions of ideal Black women leaders, participants' paths to office, and participants' styling decisions. The entire focus group lasted 1 hour and 49 minutes. The focus group was held as a breakout session within the BW PAC TX 2nd annual summit. After the conclusion of the focus group, participants returned to a day of workshops and speakers. Danielle and Nadia did not formally participate in this summit and instead joined solely as researchers.

In what follows, we present the narratives of the focus group participants to demonstrate that the politics of appearance is a major concern for Black women political elites. We identify women with pseudonyms to protect some confidential aspects of our focus group. Focusing on three themes—professional appearance, hair, and makeup—we show that there are distinct generational differences in how Black women political elites both think about and display their personal style. There are deep contestations around what it means to look like a Black woman political elite, much of which centers around the politics of respectability (Brown, forthcoming).

Black Women Political Elites and the Discussion of Appearance

The focus group discussion began with the women describing traits or characteristics of Black women politicians. We asked the participants to call out descriptors of attributes as an open-ended warm-up exercise. Their responses uniformly demonstrate an empowering sense of Black womanhood that is a direct challenge to multiple jeopardy (King 1988), a theory that casts Black women as being disadvantaged at nearly every turn because of racism or sexism. Instead, our participants used the following words to describe Black women political elites: confident, prepared, humble, trustworthy, initiator, open-minded, leader, relatable, listener, visionary, knowledgeable, willing to sacrifice, reader, hardworking, experienced, thick skinned, focused, motivated, servant, ethical, and confident. Indeed, these nouns and adjectives may describe anyone who seeks political office. But for Black women, such descriptors often fail to align with popular misconceptions of Black womanhood. The prevailing stereotypes of Black women (Harris-Perry 2013; Terbog-Penn and Harley 1978) demonstrate that Black women themselves have a difficult time seeing themselves outside of the controlling images that society imposed upon them.

The women in our study actively challenged these stereotypes. For example, Marie, a Baby Boomer who currently serves on a local city council, stated, "Black women are courageous [and] are uninhibited by what others think, know what to do and [are] not afraid of the consequences." Stella, a Baby Boomer who recently lost an election to unseat a Republican congressman in her district, is considering running again for this seat. She quickly asserted that "women bring something different, things that men don't bring. We're nurturing, caretakers. Women run households and jobs. So, we need to encourage more Black women to run for office."

This opening exercise was useful in framing how the women view and generalize about their cadre. Leadership is a group endeavor. They see themselves and each other as leaders—capable and strong—and their perspective set the stage for our conversation. Their comments came from a place of empowerment rather than marginalization. The women in our focus group discussed both their strengths and weaknesses in ways that collectively demonstrated that Black women political elites are unique. In what follows, we thematically present how Black women candidates and elected officials think about the politics of their appearance.

Professional Appearance

The most vocal discussion in our focus group was about professional appearance. The participants broached this subject with attention to hair, makeup, styling choices, and clothes. They used this time to counsel one another on acceptable makeup and styles, as well as to police the choices of Millennials in the group. This was a dynamic conversation that happened organically. Indeed, Nadia and Danielle were largely silent during this conversation, and the focus group participants took control of the discussion. This harmonious dialogue underscores the usefulness of this research method. The women's conversation naturally ebbed and flowed around topics that they were most interested in as a collective, while also touching on the major thematic points that the authors were the most interested in uncovering.

The most senior woman in the room began the discussion by asserting, "The first thing is to have self-love." Rubina is a member of the Silent Generation and is a long-serving judge in her county. She said that she begins each day by "looking in the mirror and being happy with me. I have a positive conversation with myself, a pep talk. I compliment myself first thing in the morning. I say, 'Your hair is beautiful and your skin is flawless' to myself when I look in the mirror." Many of the women laughed while Rubina described how she talks to herself. They watched as Rubina held up an imaginary mirror, posed, smiled, and pretended to groom herself. This lighthearted entry into a conversation about professionalism and appearance surely helped many women to feel comfortable opening up.

In response to Rubina's antics, Paula exclaimed, "Nice! I love that. But, I'm running in North Texas. I like to be a little extra. I like glitter and nice things. I was told that I need to wear a blue dress and heels. Basically, I was told to try to look like a White woman. But, that's not me. I like to wear color on my lips, to have popping nail colors. I am happy with what I see." Paula also shared that she enjoys hot-pink lipstick, false eyelashes, brightly manicured acrylic nails, and glitter eyeshadow. For her, wearing a drab blue dress and subtle makeup was antithetical to what made her feel most like herself. She equated this look to a "traditional White woman politician" and referenced Hillary Clinton's pantsuits as an example.

In response, other participants echoed that they were told by political strategists, well-intentioned family members and friends, as well as some elected officials that they needed to alter their look in order to be seen as professional. Tabatha, a former member of the U.S. armed forces who ran for lieutenant governor in a southern state in 2018, shared that she was told to change her hair color. During our focus group, Tabatha wore a long blond weave. She noted that some people have expressed issues with her hair color. Likewise, Stella said that she was advised to "tone down [her] wardrobe." Also a retired member of the armed forces, Stella attended the focus group in a full black crinoline shirt, a red sequined blouse, and a black fringed shawl with a number of political buttons attached to it. In fact, Stella, Tabatha, and Paula may have been the most elaborately dressed members of the focus group. As these three political elites shared comments on how they have been perceived, Michelle validated their experiences while simultaneously advising that professional attire was more modest than what had previously been described:

> . . . [Y]ou have to be comfortable. If you are trying to mimic something other than what you are, that will not work. I am a lawyer. There are ways that you should dress at a law firm. So, I was comfortable doing that. When I was campaigning, I was told that you should look like a judge at all times. I translated that into professional attire. I have two kids. So, I typically wear jeans, a campaign T-shirt like the one I'm wearing today, a sweater or

a sports coat. I always keep a blazer in my car—even when I'm attending one of my kids' events. You have to have that when you are running. That's professional.

Michelle's vision of professional attire is both a personal and an occupational choice. As revealed by the comments of other lawyers in this book, Black women political elites from this professional background have a more conservative outlook on what it means to dress like a candidate for political office. In one word, Rubina summarized Michelle's advice: "simplify."

In turn, Adele laid bare the challenges of crafting a professional look as a Black woman political elite. Adele, a Baby Boomer, has served on her city's council for a number of years and holds a prominent leadership position in her county's Democratic Party. She said, "We carry so much on our shoulders. Building relationships with people is key. Some little old lady will tell you to come here, meaning no disrespect and say, 'I can see your cleavage from across the room.' You have to listen to her." Adele gave this example as a way of showcasing the importance of heeding the advice of elders, because oftentimes the elders are a group of dedicated voters who will be instrumental in a Black woman's election and/or re-election. Pivoting to the elephant in the room —professional image and youthful modes of personal expression—Adele said, "There is talk about people in this group. I hear it. People have said, 'She's stuck up, thinks that she's too cute.' That's the conversation. It is a conversation that some voters will listen to. That's the narrative. You have to understand that when you talk to people at a park or a civic organization, you need to be aware of how you look." This comment brought to a head the growing uncomfortablity between the younger and older women in the focus group.

At this point in our conversation, the Millennial political elites began to shift noticeably in their chairs as the conversation became more uncomfortable for them. In response to Adele, Paula emphasized her professionalism, sharing that she campaigns in "a Target dress. That fits my district. Target has affordable, professional dresses that have a little flair." Yet Paula also pushed back, stating that these Target dresses were more of her style and fit into her constrained budget. Carly, another Millennial, shared that she wears festive holiday sweaters to her city council meetings during the Christmas season as a way to liven her up appearance. As this conversation unfolded, the Baby Boomers in the room continued to challenge Millennials' chosen sense of style, which they considered lacking in sufficient professionalism. In response, Carly said,

Work and professionalism work in tandem. I work in the art world. For me, jeans are the norm. But I get it, you have to play the game. For council meetings, I dress up. For the campaign, it is different. Now that I'm on the job [having been elected to the county council], things are different. I'm still in my thirties, my constituents are not. They can see that I'm respectful in the position. As a Millennial, I want to change the culture. I had a job that you had to wear pantyhose. I didn't want that position. That is indicative of culture. Anyway, now that I'm elected to the council, I think that it's easier to introduce things and change the culture from the inside. We can change things once you are an elected official.

Carly's narrative demonstrates her willingness to "play the game" as a candidate to demonstrate to the older members in her district that she was worthy of their votes. But now that she is in office, she feels she can dress how she prefers and will let her voting record speak for itself.

In an attempt to ease some of the tension in the room, Sophia, a Generation X city council member, laughed and added the light-hearted comment, "Everyone wears jeans and tennis shoes in council meetings." Still, she quickly followed up with a more intense articulation of being a Black woman city council member in a majority White municipality. Sofia shared,

I was called uppity because I don't wear jeans and tennis shoes. I serve in a small town, we're 80% White. They don't want me there. In fact, they brought due process charges against me and tried to recall me. It doesn't matter what I wear. My mayor wears tennis shoes. They still see me as Black [Rubina chimes in to add a salient factor: "A Black *woman*"] and it doesn't matter what I wear.

For Sophia, who remained largely quiet during our focus group, professional attire could not insulate her from racist and sexist attacks on her legitimacy as a duly elected member of her city council. She noted that her appearance does not matter; her race and gender are the primary reasons for her marginality on the city council and not her styling choices.

The women in our focus group indicated a variety of strategies to present a professional image as political elites. Their approaches were mostly consistent with their personal choices, but all noted that styling choices were decisions that were often fraught with internal or external tensions. The recurring source of tension in the room remained the choices of Millennial women compared to those of Baby Boomers, who seemed to push back at the professional images of the younger generation.

Hair

Our focus group participants wore a variety of hairstyles, but the majority wore straightened hair. Corinne, a member of Generation X, is currently a long-serving member of her city council and was the only woman who wore braids at the time of our focus group. Corinne commented, "I got my braids because they are low maintenance. Before that, I used to wear really nice and expensive wigs. I had to make sure that my braids are professional and neat. People will always comment on how neat my hair is. It's always neat." Corinne later shared that she does not pay much attention to her looks, nor does she attempt to change her style to fit into what others have defined as a professional image for Black political elites. Because she is a successful city council member and leader of her local Democratic Party, Corinne rarely faces challengers, and at this point in her political career, her constituents have become more like family. In fact, Corinne shared that she does not stay up on election nights to watch the returns. She is comfortable that she will have an electoral victory and does not spend her scarce time considering how others think that she should dress.

Contrasting sharply with Corinne's experiences, Paula was mounting her first campaign at the time our focus group, and as a Millennial and part of the naturalista movement, she stated, "My reality is that I cannot run in North Texas with blue hair. It's about how you present yourself." At this point in the discussion, Paula began to cry. As her emotions started to overcome her, she recounted her experiences on the campaign trail and the below-the-belt tactics of her opponent. She continued, "I'm running against a White woman who targeted people of color. That's what's happening to me now. I'm a Black woman with two kids. I can't pretend that I'm not. I have my hair braided back, my Afro braided back. It's underneath this wig. I'm doing this because I'm trying to get elected, because I'm trying to get someone out of office that is targeting people of color." Michelle interrupted Paula while another focus group participant consoled her. Michelle commented, "We cannot do what a White woman or man does." Cora, a Baby Boomer who is a judge, cosigned Michelle's comment, declaring, "It is institutional racism. We are resilient people. Black women are the most resilient. That's the extra layer." Turning to

Paula, Cora added, "Stay focused, girl. We got it, girl." Paula notes here that Black women have to twice as good as White or male candidates to be seen as electable. That "extra layer" refers to the adage that Black Americans have to work twice as hard to get half as far as their White counterparts (Wise 2009).

Another Millennial, Kesia, who was running for a judge position in North Dallas, added that these attacks against Black women candidates come from racists. Kesia explained that while she has not experienced these types of attacks, she has seen them happen to other Black women. She cited the experience of her friend, who was also running for a judgeship, as an example. Kesia commented that hair is part of what people use to discredit Black women candidates: "The whole issue was a big thing. North of Downtown Dallas, the natural thing may not go over too well. Campaign people are saying that you need to do something different with your hair. South of Downtown, being natural is seen as being more authentic and being a 'real Black woman.'" For Kesia, having natural hair is either an asset or liability, depending on where one is running. Here, she is suggesting that a Black woman candidate should know her district and select a hairstyle based on constituent preferences.

Similarly, Adele opined that a Black woman candidate's hair should be embraced and that constituents will deal with it. She circled back around to Paula to offer this advice:

> If I have my Afro, I would say that 'I like my hair' and use it as an ice breaker. I'd own it. I'd explain it. This is who I am. I like my hair this color, too. Then, I'd use my hair as an opportunity to say that I love this about myself and that you should, too. But, you have to know your voting pool. You want to be sure to listen to them and what they are saying, especially when it comes out of kindness.

While Paula was not necessarily looking for advice on how to wear her hair in response to her emotional retelling of the campaign challenges that she faced with natural hair, she seemed to embrace Adele's recommendation of owning her look.

Perhaps because the majority of women in the room had straightened hair, this topic was not of particular appeal. In some ways, our discussion on hair alone was muted because of cultural attitudes around acceptable hair for Black women. For example, when asked about her appearance, Stella aptly chided Nadia: "I'm a Southern girl, I went to charm school. In the South you already know what to wear, what to look like, and what is appropriate for certain events." While this Baby Boomer's comment may be related to her generational approach to how a Black woman should appear, it also reveals regional differences. In particular, Stella's comment shows how Southern culture colors the undercurrent of conversations about Black women's appearances. This discussion may have taken a different turn if the focus group was held in another region of the country.

Makeup

An unexpected topic arose when the conversation in our focus group shifted to makeup. The participants shared differing opinions about how to present themselves, but as before, there was a noticeable generational divide. At the close of our focus group, Corinne posed a question to her fellow Black women political elites. She asked about wearing makeup by sharing that she does not wear any, does not know how to apply it, and would rather not deal with makeup. The women were largely supportive of Corinne's decision not to wear makeup since she does not feel comfortable wearing it. However, this question sparked a larger discussion about what the various women in the group do regarding makeup, and why makeup plays a role in their candidacies. For instance, Adele shared that it is not a good idea to campaign door-to-door in heavy makeup. "If you're going on a block walk with a lot of foundation, it's not a smart decision. You should do something simple that you can maintain." The women nodded in agreement. Our participants unanimously found Adele's advice to be sage wisdom and acknowledged the veracity of her statement. Michelle added, "Less is better. Certainly, if I'm on TV, I will ask for a makeup artist. But, I tell the artist that I want to look like myself. I want something natural looking." Several of our participants nodded in agreement, as they seemed to prefer a more natural look. Indeed, the majority of the women in our focus group wore natural-looking makeup.

However, Paula disagreed. In response to Michelle's statement, Paula quipped, "I don't want to be casket sharp. But, as a Millennial, I like to beat my face. I like Smash Box. I spend time on YouTube looking at makeup tutorials. I even did a video, a makeup tutorial of my own. Now, when I'm campaigning, I tone down the hot pinks, greens and glitter. But I like those things—I like experimenting with makeup. I do it because it's fun. And I like to do it." Paula laughed after her statement and only made eye contact with

Nadia and Danielle, who are also Millennials and who each wore bright colored lip stick during the focus group. We provided nonverbal communication to express that we understood and validated Paula's appreciation of makeup. However, speaking as though Paula did not share her love for makeup, Adele quickly interjected that is it is important to "invest in the right products." She implored her fellow political elites to "please match up your foundation. You need to make sure that you are put together."

Carly, another Millennial, directed her response to both Adele and Paula, making eye contact with each woman as she addressed her approach to makeup. Carly affirmed that makeup is important, noting,

> Look, I grew up in a space where I could not put on makeup. So, in my campaign I believe that the product is you. Politics is about appearance. Being aware of it is important. Having lip color is my thing. Well, because our city council records our meetings. The visuals are bad. The video looks like a hostage video because of the bad quality. I'll wear an orange or red lip color. I want to pop. These are colors that Black women look good in. I want to look better in these awful quality videos. But I also don't want to come across as an older elected official. I'm happy to be a Millennial. I wear color when [older elected officials] do not.

Perhaps striking the middle ground between Adele and Paula, Carly demonstrated how one can use makeup to differentiate oneself as an elected official. The women in our focus group nodded as an acknowledgment of Carly's point and took her contribution to the conversation seriously.

In response, the older women chimed in with slight affirmations of Paula and Carly's points. Rubina added that she always "keeps pressed powder around. Look, we shine. [laughs] So, I keep lipstick and pressed powder." Millie, another Baby Boomer who is a judge in Southeast Texas, jokingly added, "At this age you get hot flashes! Yes, pressed powder."

The creation of a space for the women to discuss their makeup practices and tips was an unintentional boon of the focus group. We did not anticipate this conversation about makeup, nor did we anticipate how younger Black women might differ from their older counterparts in their styling decisions. Again, this is a benefit of using a focus group to learn more about the politics of appearance for Black women political elites. The organic nature of this conversation led to an unexpected conversation about how Black women style themselves to appeal to a political audience.

Discussion and Conclusion

Like Tracee Ellis Ross and Beyoncé in the quotes that form this chapter's epigraph, the Black women political elites in our study demonstrate that they feel they are enough. They are leaders who are beautiful. The women in our focus group epitomize these opening quotes and collectively live these sentiments. Through the three broad themes of professionalism, hair, and makeup, we see that Black women political elites pay attention to their appearance in deeply raced-gendered ways. A growing generational divide is also apparent in how these women choose to present themselves to voters and constituents. All of the women in our study were cognizant that their appearance is an important aspect of their political lives and experiences. Yet, their styling decisions were shaped by personal, and sometimes strategic, considerations.

We also found that the Black women political elites in our focus group were committed to one another's success. Even when they disagreed, the women addressed each other's differences constructively. They offered support, advice, and affirming glances or touches to one another during our focus group. While some participants had relationships with one another prior to the focus group, many did not. This bond of sisterhood, rooted in a belief in the collective attributes of Black women political elites, contributed to creating a unique space for the women to discuss the challenges and opportunities of running for or serving in office.

To be sure, our study has limitations. Our focus group represents a snapshot in time and is not generalizable to all Black women who are running for political office. However, the findings are consistent with other themes we have found elsewhere in our conversations with Black women political elites. We also anticipate that our findings might be different if we engaged with Black women office seekers from a different geographical location. Additionally, because we uncovered experiences that were unique to Millennials, we believe that our findings have a generational dynamic that could be better explored in focus groups that target specific generational cohorts. We contend that our limited, but powerful, findings may serve as an indication of a change in Black politics as Millennials replace older Black representatives. What is deemed acceptable may change as younger Black women seek office with natural hair, colorful makeup, and flashier appearances. Lastly, because our focus group was larger than expected, several women did not have the opportunity to speak, while others spoke at length. We imagine that if we had had the opportunity to conduct two smaller focus groups with the BWPAC

TX participants, we might have had a more robust conversation among a greater number of candidates and elected officials.

Furthermore, our work echoes the findings of Cathy Cohen's (2010) foundational work on Black youth, in which she provides a counter-narrative to generational differences among Black Americans by centering the voices of the youth. While the members of Cohen's youth population do not fall uniformly within the Millennial age cohort, they do present similarities with those who were born between 1980 and 1996. The moral panic of older generations that Cohen describes—a concern that Black youth have embraced a pathological ethos—places attention on the behavior of (poor) Blacks rather than on the structural and institutional factors that constrain their political choices. Like respectability politics, Cohen observes, racist and misogynist framing that polices the bodies and behavior of young Black women is couched in worries about public presentation. As Cohen notes, "Some Black people with some privilege and access are concerned that they (we) will be confused with 'too many young Black Americans' who they think 'threaten the progress of respectable Black people who are trying to do the right things" (2010, 38). This perspective relates to our focus group findings, in that the older Black women political elites viewed their Millennial counterparts as breaking with agreed-on norms of respectable presentation. The older women in study seemed to assert that the younger women's personal styling choices will reflect negatively on them. Younger Blacks who challenge dominant norms are viewed as deviant, and thus they should be regulated by older and elite Blacks.

All the participants in our study agreed that Black woman political elites should carry themselves in a dignified manner. They differed, however, on what that looks like in practice. They all believed that their humanity and equal status as Americans were conveyed through their styling choices. In adopting this perspective, the women in our study conceded to the hegemonic values of White society, even when they embraced aesthetic aspects of Black womanhood as a source of pride and self-presentation. In essence, they are practicing a form of respectability politics that historian Evelyn Brooks-Higginbotham (1992) theorized as a subversive practice that allowed Blacks to act as Americans regardless of their racial background.

Yet, there remains a generational difference in how Black women political elites think about respectable self-presentation. Perhaps this stylistic divide is parallel to other age cohort puzzles among Black Americans. For instance, Cohen (2010, 44) finds that a super majority of older Blacks believe that younger Blacks have more opportunities than older generations did. Yet, the Black youth are viewed by their elders as deviant and lacking in self-control, and as failing to take advantage of these increased opportunities. This disconnect between access and perceived lack of results leads some older Blacks to decry the deficiencies of Black youth while ignoring the structural conditions that inform their behavior. A Black middle-class understanding of the American value structure, even within a post–civil rights and post-Obama era, holds that marginal members within Black communities should be policed. Black young women fall within the category of marginality, and they are thus policed into conforming to an acceptable ideal of Blackness. Data from the Black Youth Project confirm what our Millennial participants noted: that "most Black people over 40 do not respect young Black people" (Cohen 2010, 49).

In sum, our findings mirror theoretical expectations that the politics of appearance are a salient factor for Black women political elites. Our study is the first to conduct focus groups with Black women candidates and elected officials, and as such, it gives a voice to an often neglected population. Here, we have shown that when given the opportunity to speak as a collective, Black women express affirming sentiments about other Black women's appearances, but they also push back on less traditional methods of self-expression. In other chapters, we demonstrate that this pushback may be indicative of the politics of respectability and community policing. It is important to note that Black women political elites freely used the focus groups, a closed space among similarly situated women, to discuss the politics of appearance and how it impacts their political experiences.

Diverging from centering the voices of Black women political elites, Chapter 5 continues the appraisal of the politics of appearance for Black women candidates and elected officials by asking Black women voters how they assess Black women candidates. We use a focus group with members of Delta Sigma Theta Sorority, Inc., to learn more about what highly civically engaged women think about Black women candidates and their appearances. We draw from a conversation with Black sorority members to learn more about the salience of respectability politics and generational differences in how voters assess Black women candidates.

5

Sisterly Discussions about Black Women Candidates

I thank you, Delta Sigma Theta Sorority, for standing up for Attorney General Loretta Lynch of the United States and for coming today with a national agenda: equal pay for equal work, sustaining the Affordable Care Act, educational reform for college school funding.

Mr. Speaker, please join me and the three other Members of Congress of Delta Sigma Theta Sorority, for saluting them for being on the Hill today, and to my Columbus Alumnae Chapter, and Delta Kappa, where I was made.

—Rep. Joyce Beatty (D-OH)

In honor of Women's History Month, Representative Joyce Beatty (D-OH) addressed her colleagues on the House floor to recognize the Delta Sigma Theta Sorority, Inc. As a member of this Black Greek Letter Organization (BGLO), Rep. Beatty also acknowledged her three sorority sisters who were serving in Congress in 2016. Today, there are six Delta women who serve in the 116th Congress,[1] following in the footsteps of their sorority sister Representative Shirley Chisholm (D-NY), who, in 1968, became the first Black woman elected to Congress. Of the 22 Black women in the 116th Congress, 15 are members of BGLOs—primarily members of Delta Sigma Theta and Alpha Kappa Alpha.

As Rep. Beatty notes, Delta women supported the nomination of their sorority sister Loretta Lynch, the first Black woman to serve as U.S. Attorney General. Deltas successfully petitioned Senate Majority Leader Mitch McConnell (R-KY), who blocked Loretta Lynch's nomination in 2015. Several Deltas showed up to Lynch's nomination in crimson and cream, the official colors of the sorority, to be a visible representation of support for

Sister Style. Nadia E. Brown and Danielle Casarez Lemi, Oxford University Press (2021). © Oxford University Press.
DOI: 10.1093/oso/9780197540572.003.0005

President Obama's nomination of their sister. Deltas, both inside and outside of Congress, called for Loretta Lynch to be confirmed. Americans unfamiliar with Delta Sigma Theta, and with BGLOs in general, may have been surprised by how quickly and effectively Black women mobilized in support of Loretta Lynch's nomination. However, those who were aware of Black sororities, and Delta Sigma Theta more specifically, fully expected this outpouring of political action.

All Black sororities are committed to racial uplift and to prioritizing the needs of Black women, each of the four historically Black sororities have different focuses in these areas. In this chapter, we build on the focus of Delta Sigma Theta's foundation on political activism. Delta Sigma Theta's focus is political action, and thus, this sorority is the center of our attention in this chapter. Founded at Howard University in 1913 by 22 collegiate women, Delta Sigma Theta is an organization of college-educated women who are committed to member development and public service in Black communities. Growing steadily over the century, the sisterhood of predominately Black women now has over 1,000 collegiate and alumni chapters worldwide and boasts more than 200,000 members. Delta Sigma Theta Sorority, Inc., is the largest Black women's organization in the world.

The first public action of the newly formed sorority took place on March 3, 1913, the day before Woodrow Wilson's presidential inauguration. The 1913 Woman Suffrage Procession, organized by the National American Woman Suffrage Association, was designed to call attention to women's exclusion from the democratic process. Black women participated in segregated segments of the march, although Ida B. Wells-Barnett is a notable exception as she refused to march at the end of the parade but rather integrate the racially segregated demonstration for women's suffrage. Members of Delta Sigma Theta, including Mary Church Terrell, marched in the procession[2] and were subjected to the violence of hostile protesters who manhandled and spat on them (Sydney 2020). The collegiate suffragists marched at the end of the procession in this segregated demonstration for women's voting rights.[3] The centering of racism and anti-Black sentiments within the suffragists' strategies prompts a new analysis about the role of Black women in the suffrage movement (Jones 2020). Yet, members of Delta Sigma Theta and other Black women saw the vote not just as a means of political participation but also as a way to protect themselves within a sexist, White, heteropatriarchal society (Giddings 2009). In spite of the physical and verbal harassment that members of Delta Sigma Theta endured at this suffrage march, the spirit of social action as a defining characteristic of the young sorority's identity endures to this day.

As heirs to the political action legacy put forth by their founders over 100 years ago, Deltas are highly politically active citizens who leverage their organizational ties to promote raced-gendered civic engagement. Since the sorority's founding, members have taken leadership positions in advancing civil rights both in the United States and abroad. Despite this engagement, however, BGLOs often carry a connotation of being elitist and of supporting White supremacist norms (Chambers 2017). For example, Black sororities have been critiqued for upholding problematic Eurocentric beauty standards for membership and for holding narrow gender norms and views on femininity (Whaley 2010). As an agent of political socialization, this group is an ideal subject for a study that seeks to understand how some Black women voters feel about the candidacies of other Black women. Indeed, we found that participants in our focus group made connections between beauty politics and candidate preferences. In this chapter, we center the voices of alumnae chapter members of Delta Sigma Theta Sorority, Inc., as those best positioned to assess Black women candidates.

Black Women, Black Political Institutions, and Political Socialization

Black women's high rates of political participation defy traditional political participation models. Brady, Verba, and Lehman Schlozman (1995) find that Americans need three tools to effectively engage with the political system: time, resources, and civic skills. Racism, patriarchy, and class-based oppressions have diminished Black women's abilities to effectually engage the American political structure as they often lack these tools because of structures of marginalization. As such, Black women face significant obstacles to being fully incorporated into the polity (King 1988). In spite of these structural challenges, Black women politically outperform all other demographic groups (Alex-Assensoh and Stanford 1997; Junn 1997; Farris and Holman 2014; Cole and Stewart 1996; Burns, Schlozman and Verba 2001). They are more highly engaged than other women of color, even when controlling for socioeconomic status and other traditional indicators of civic participation (Farris and Holman 2014).

Black institutions are key to Black women's political socialization. These institutions foster political mobilization, teach democratic norms, and cultivate political activity among their members (Calhoun-Brown 1996). Black women gain the skills for political participation in indigenous Black institutions such as the Black church, Black businesses, and HBCUs, as well as within sororities. These organizations aid Black women in building and developing their networks by providing access to political elites (Scott et al. n.d.). As central figures in Black organizational life (Simpson 1998), Black women have been the lifeblood of social movements. For instance, Black women's involvement in the Black Lives Matter movement (Garza 2014; Lindsey 2015), environmental justice organizing (Simpson 2014), the civil rights movement (Robnett 2000), reproductive justice organizing (Price 2010), and labor activism (Arneson 2006) demonstrates that they are highly active in issues that impact Black communities. Black women have played an integral role in race-based movements, although their participation may be obscured (Robnett 2000) because they did not have access to formal leadership roles (Dawson 2001).

Because individuals' role in an organization is a key stepping stone for their political participation, we focus our attention on Black women's participation within civic organizations. Indeed, Black women scholars have theorized the role of Black women's organizations as fostering political activism (Giddings 1984; Higginbotham 1993; Hunter 1998; Springer 2005, Smooth 2018). These institutions provide a place for Black women to develop civic skills, acquire political knowledge, develop social capital, and tap into resources that are necessary for political participation—and Black women over-participate in these organizations. In developing civic-minded organizations, Black women have created a community for their political and personal survival (Collins 2000).

Social movements, too, have been an organizational tool to connect Black women to electoral politics. Focusing on the Student Nonviolent Coordinating Committee and the National Association for the Advancement of Colored People, Payne (1990) finds that Black women had an outsized role in civil rights movement activities in the Mississippi Delta in the 1950s–60s. Black women's participation in the civil rights movement flies in the face of assertations made by political scientists that "women were less active in politics than men" (Matthews and Prothro 1966, 65). Women's reasons for their outsized participation in the civil rights movement in Mississippi did not yield a reliable pattern. Instead, participants shared that their religious beliefs or preexisting social networks led them to join the movement. Women were also trusted community leaders in this movement that had familial overtones and religious roots (Payne 1990). Similar findings emerged in social movements in northern cities like Chicago (McCourt 1977; Drake and Cayton 1970).

While these social movements and Black institutions have served as supportive and insular spaces, shielding their members from White supremacy and racism, many of them remain sites of patriarchal control, and sexism within these spaces curtails the advancement of Black women (Giddings 1984; Simien and Clawson 2004). Black women's political socialization may be most effective in spaces where these women are shielded from Black heteropatriarchy. Take for example, the Combahee River Collective's (CRC) political mobilization in the northeast United States, particularly Boston, which sought to bring political attention to the murders of Black women that garnered little police investigation and news coverage in the 1970s (Harris 2009). The CRC created a supportive space to theorize Black women's unique social location, held consciousness raising circles, and provided participants with civic skills. Holding their meetings in an inclusive space that prioritized Black women's agency from a position of community empowerment, the CRC pushed back against racism, sexism, heteronormativity, neoliberal politics, and class-based oppression.[4] As an anti-racist and anti-sexist organization, the CRC made room for political work that fought against the interlocking systematic oppression of Black women.

For Black women who resist racism and sexism, BGLOs may serve as vehicles for political participation. Pearl Ford Dowe (2018) documents how membership in Delta Sigma Theta provides its members with civic skills. To be sure, membership in Black sororities comes with a set of prerequisites that correlate with high rates of political participation (Simpson 1998). To become a member, one must have a college education, the financial means to join and sustain membership fees, and a network that is already affiliated with the organization. The social capital, financial resources, and personal networks that a Black woman has prior to joining a BGLO, or that she cultivates during her lifetime membership in a sorority, bode well for higher levels of political engagement. As Dowe (2018) shows, sorority membership is correlated with Black women seeking and gaining electoral office. Notable Deltas who were or are current public officials are Marcia Fudge (D-OH); Keisha Lance-Bottoms, the current mayor of Atlanta, Georgia; Yvette Clarke (D-NY); Carrie Meek (D-FL); Stephanie Tubbs-Jones (D-OH); and Lottie

Shackelford, mayor of Little Rock, Arkansas, and current vice chair of the Democratic National Committee.

Appearance Politics, Black Women, and Black Greek Letter Organizations

Members of BGLOs are politically grounded and civically engaged. The organizations were founded on the ethics of service, justice, and Black pride (Evans 2004). Yet, it is important to note that these organizations are not expressly civil rights organizations. BGLOs practice racial uplift in the form of service projects, educational scholarships, financial support for charities, and lobbying. The expressed goal of racial uplift, however, has connotations of elitism (Reich 2019). As mentioned earlier, W.E.B. Du Bois articulated racial uplift as a mission for the "talented tenth" of African Americans, who had access to education, middle-class status, and forms of self-autonomy, to lift the other nine-tenths of the Black American population (Gollancz 2019). A critique of uplift politics and the ideal of the talented tenth was perhaps most pointedly launched by Marcus Garvey, who held that African American elites were chiefly concerned with respectability and assimilation (Gatewood 1988). Though BGLOs embrace racial uplift politics, they often fail to holistically include the role of Black women in those politics. Historians Deborah Gray White (1993) and Darlene Clark Hine (1997) have adroitly documented Black women's involvement in club work and grassroot organizing as a form of institution building. "Lifting as We Climb," the motto of the National Association of Colored Women, used racial uplift tactics to propose solutions for racial progression that centered Black women and children. Generations of Black organizations—from the post–World War II liberation movements to the civil rights and Black Power movements of the 1960s–80s–would embrace racial uplift as a method for achieving racial equality (Reich 2019). It is within this context that BGLOs exist to serve Black communities.

BGLOs were founded between 1906 and 1963 to help Black people achieve success in higher education. These organizations mirrored White Greek Letter Organizations in their desire to build a supportive community of like-minded students (Hughey, Parks and Skocpol 2011). Next, BGLOs worked to assist Black students in gaining acceptance in American society. Members of BGLOs are notable civil rights leaders, educators, actors, musicians, athletes, entrepreneurs, corporate executives, and elected officials (Parks 2008). Furthermore, membership in BGLOs provides peer networks as well as professional and social support. Black fraternity and sorority members have successfully harnessed their organizational ties to influence popular culture and cultivate norms of Black social life.

Uniquely situated within Black culture, BGLOs have faced allegations of elitism and snobbery (Hernandez 2011). Because membership selection is opaque, critics maintain that these organizations have built and maintained a separate and privileged society that conforms to Western values and social norms (Hughey and Parks 2011). The founders of these organizations prioritized racial uplift as a method of challenging White supremacy (Gaines 2012). This form of self-help rejected claims that Black people were an inferior race and that they could not successfully assimilate into mainstream (White) American culture. Through racial uplift ideology, Black elites sought to challenge deeply racialized ideological classifications by presenting themselves as a "better class" of Blacks who could model racial progress by outperforming Whites' civility (Chambers 2017). The idea was that when Black people conformed to the best of Whiteness, they would be granted equality and citizenship (Gaines 2012). Critics claim that BGLOs followed in this tradition by both challenging racial bias and holding up White supremacist ideas (Chambers 2017). Indeed, E. Franklin Frazier (1979, 94) notes, "Although the original aim of the society [BGLO] was to bring together the aristocracy of talent, it has become one of the main expressions of social snobbishness on the part of the Black bourgeoisie."

However, Black elites' membership in BGLOs may be been motivated by their own experiences of forced exclusion (Graham 1999). The Black bourgeoisie's desire to set themselves apart as members of BGLOs, and to thereby receive privileged status in Black communities, was a reaction to their status as second-class citizens within larger American society (Frazier 1957). Combining aspects of traditional African culture and elements of Euro-American culture, BGLOs sought to serve Black communities (Brown, Parks and Phillips 2012). These organizations were a safe haven for Black people who challenged discriminatory laws, but they were also seen as traditional institutions because they were akin to organizations already present in White society (Chambers 2017).

While BGLOs are powerful conduits for Black women in politics, these organizations have been plagued with accusations of colorism and snobbery, and of emboldening divisive tensions in Black communities (Hernandez

2011). Sororities select members on the basis of their leadership potential, ability to fulfill and uplift the sorority's mission, and capacity to add to the sorority's social standing (Giddings 1988). In addition to having a high grade point average, applicants who seek membership in Black sororities must show a record of community service and dispel disparaging racial and gender stereotypes of Black women in popular culture (Hernandez 2011). Yet, an enduring perception of Black sororities is that these organizations enforce rigid appearance guidelines that are promoted by the official sorority regulations and members' informal practices. Members are socialized to be highly cognizant of their behavior, dress, and speech so that they do not act in ways that negatively reflect on the group.

Stereotypical depictions of Black women foster Black women's oppression (Collins 1991). Indeed, controlling tropes of the Mammy, the matriarch, welfare recipients, and hot mamas have normalized and naturalized racism, sexism, and poverty in America's view of Black women. These stereotypes, which are rooted in enslavement, serve as a continued justification for abuse and discrimination toward Black women (Hunter 2005). These stereotypical images of Black women stand in direct contrast to the cult of White womanhood. Black women were dehumanized and depicted as individuals who were not pristine, fragile, dependent, or passive—all traits that defined White womanhood. This defeminization left Black women without a clear gender identity (Davis 1981). These distorted views of Black womanhood reinforce Black women's marginality (Harris Perry 2011), that could be readily seen in their appearance and behavior. Sororities' use of appearance enforcement, similar to their racial uplift techniques, is a strategic response to confronting the social inequalities that Black women face in American society. It is meant to challenge controlling images of Black women by compelling sorority sisters to adhere to middle-class, White standards of dress, speech, and conduct.

While appearance enforcement serves as both a symbolic and a literal act of cultural and ideological defiance, intended to control the imagery of Black women in popular culture (St. Jean and Feagin 1997), it in fact adds another system of control for Black women. Appearance enforcement reinforces structural forms of gendered racism (Hernandez 2011). If sorority members do not adhere to group standards of speech and appearance, they are often policed by members of the sorority to correct these behaviors. Stereotypes of Black women within broader White society therefore often go unchecked.

Sorority members are aware that one woman's transgression can be seen as behavior typical of all Black women. Thus, policing Black women's bodies and behavior mirrors White supremacist tactics. Instead of challenging racist and sexist structures, they reinforce the White community's preoccupations, prejudices, and desires about Black women (Chambers 2017).

Lastly, racial, class-based, and gendered performances are inextricably linked to the evolution of respectability politics for BGLO sorority members. Consider the 2014 police killings of Michael Brown (Ferguson, Missouri), Tamir Rice and Tanisha Anderson (Cleveland, Ohio), and Eric Garner (Staten Island, New York) that sparked nationwide protests and Black Lives Matter demonstrations. National leadership of both Delta Sigma Theta and Alpha Kappa Alpha originally barred members from protesting while wearing sorority paraphernalia. Delta's national president, Paulette C. Walker, informed members, "You are solely responsible for yourself and your activities" (Grigsby Bates 2014). Deltas were permitted to wear their colors but not their letters. Disappointed in the statement, many members of the sorority pointed to the organization's long history of engaging in civil rights activities to underscore the hypocritical stance of the current sorority's leadership (Coker 2014).

By contrast, Black fraternities such Alpha Phi Alpha Fraternity, Inc., encouraged members to display their colors and wear their letters while participating in protests. Alpha Phi Alpha reminded its members that fraternity brothers Reverend Martin Luther King, Jr., and Supreme Court Justice Thurgood Marshall led and/or joined in protests (Grigsby Bates 2014). These differing reactions from BGLO fraternities and sororities evinced a continued gendered stance toward respectability politics that restricts Black women (Crosley Coker 2014). Delta Sigma Theta later reversed its opinion and allowed members to participate in Black Lives Matter activities while wearing their letters.

In what follows, we detail how alumnae members of Delta Sigma Theta Sorority, Inc., perceive Black women candidates for political office. Given the sociohistorical and cultural significance of Black women's political activism, and Black women's relationship with the politics of appearance, it is instructive for us to examine how members of a Black sorority assess Black women political elites. Because these members are a prototype of highly politically engaged Black voters, we turn to them to learn how Black women candidates' appearance may influence vote choice.

Data and Methods

In December 2019, we held a focus group with eight members of an alumnae chapter of Delta Sigma Theta Sorority, Inc. The chapter and the sorority were not official sponsors of this research. All opinions expressed in the focus group were the members' own opinions. The sorority and chapter did not sanction this study and are not liable for the comments of the members. The focus group participants spoke as individual women and not as representatives of Delta Sigma Theta Sorority, Inc. or of their alumnae chapter. In the following discussion, we identify the women with pseudonyms to provide them with anonymity.

The focus group participants ranged in age from 24 to 74 years old. All of the women were college educated, several held advanced degrees, and all either worked in or currently work in professional settings ranging from social workers to educators to healthcare workers. The participants' length of membership in the sorority also varied. A majority of the women joined the sorority through their local alumnae chapter in the mid-2010s, while others joined the sisterhood via collegiate chapters in the 1970s and '80s. While the women in our focus groups were all Deltas, they did not share similar family contexts. For instance, three of the women were grandmothers and two of the younger women were single. One woman was a mother to young children and another had been divorced for over 30 years. The women in the group also differed in their political views. For example, several shared that they were reluctant Democrats and would register as Independents if possible, while two others were staunch Democrats and had worked as partisans in their local communities. The diversity in the women's lived experiences, ages, family life, and professional roles made for a stimulating and robust conversation.

We held the focus group at a local library from 10:30 a.m. to 12:00 p.m. on a Saturday in November 2019. Using one of the library's large study rooms, we convened Deltas from a medium-sized Midwestern city to discuss their views on Black women candidates for political office. We contacted members of this alumnae chapter in advance through targeted emails and the chapter's listsserve. We advertised the focus group through the chapter's Social Action Committee, the list of newly initiated members, alumnae members of the sorority who are affiliated with the local university, and the Delta D.E.A.R.S. social group.[5]

We relied on this alumnae chapter of Delta Sigma Theta Sorority, Inc., for several reasons. First, Nadia is a member of the sorority, and we leveraged her organizational ties to recruit members for this study. Next, recruiting diverse, non-collegiate, Black women to participate in our study proved difficult. We reached out to the sorority because they fit our desired demographic profile: politically active Black women. Lastly, members of this alumnae chapter had previously expressed interest in supporting Nadia's scholarship. As individual members with strong political views, several of the Deltas expressed to Nadia that they would be open to sharing their experiences and expertise with her. When Nadia and Danielle began having difficulty recruiting Black women to participate in this study, we regrouped and reframed our data collection efforts to center on members of Delta Sigma Theta Sorority, Inc. With this new direction, we gladly focused on how to best draw on Delta while also recognizing that the participants were speaking on their own behalf and not for the sorority.

The respondents in our focus group clearly articulated their preferences for Black women candidates. The Deltas opined that appearance matters for Black women elected officials and candidates. Moreover, the focus group participants connected their identities and experiences as Black women to challenges that are faced by other Black women in political environments. We identified six key themes that were paramount during the discussion: positive assessments of Black women candidates; what non-Black women may think of Black women candidates; generational differences in participants' opinions; what a Black woman office seeker should look like; and connections to participants' own appearances.

We had the focus group transcribed to ensure accuracy of what was said during our session. We took notes during the focus group to capture the nonverbal communication and the larger themes expressed during the session. Nadia facilitated the focus group while Danielle took notes. The authors debriefed immediately after the focus group to ensure that we agreed on interpretations of what was said and physically communicated by participants.

We used an open-coding technique in which we closely examined the data and compared for similarities and dissimilarities. We then marked the text with appropriate labels for further analysis. From there, we grouped the raw data into conceptual categories to build a descriptive and multidimensional framework for analyzing the data. This process ensures the validity of the work, as it is derived directly from the raw data, the transcripts.

The following analysis is representative of participant statements from the focus group discussion. We present the data as organized around conceptual themes to best showcase how highly politically engaged Black women view Black women candidates. The politics of appearance for Black women candidates quickly became a hot topic of conversation as members of the focus group immediately drew comparisons between how a candidate looks and whether or not she is electable.

The Politics of Appearance and Assessments of Black Women Candidates

The atmosphere in our focus group was friendly, and the participants were visibly excited to see one another. As members of the same chapter, they were acquainted with one another but not overly familiar. Because of the chapter's large size, many of the Deltas in our focus group may not have previously had an opportunity to informally engage with the women in our session in a one-on-one manner. Others were line sisters, or members of the organization who were initiated into Delta Sigma Theta together via the same chapter. There was one woman who was a financial member but was inactive in the sorority programming because she was unable to attend sorority-sponsored events due to a lack of child care. The bonds of sisterhood were present during the focus group as the women hugged and warmly greeted one another. The focus group participants often laughed together and warmly smiled at one another. The facilitator, Nadia, interrupted their natural, sisterly banter to ask participants about their perceptions of Black women candidates.

Positive Assessments of Black Women Candidates

When asked to describe Black women political candidates, the women shared these nouns and adjectives: smart, strong, outspoken, confident, intelligent, prepared, fearless, hardworking, trailblazer, underdog, and multifaceted. The participants also described Black women candidates as being "equal to or better," "experienced—I think that any woman politician in these days has guts," and "alert, like always ready to respond." All agreed that Black women politicians must be multidimensional, a characteristic that Naomi, a Baby Boomer and 65-year-old retiree, added to the list. Chloe, a soft-spoken

Millennial woman in her late thirties, added that a Black woman politician "brings a different angle to the table. She brings a different insight." The women nodded in agreement with Chloe's assessment.

Nadia then asked the Deltas to describe how this Black woman politician looks in their mind's eye. Camila, a woman in her late seventies and member of the Silent Generation, quipped, "Mean!" The entire room erupted with laughter. Chloe quickly followed up to add, "She looks poised." The sorority sisters were likeminded in their assessments of Black women candidates, whom they uniformly described in positive terms. Even Camila, who light-heartedly noted that such candidates look mean, would later explain that Black women have to display a tough exterior because of racism and sexism and because people believe that Black women are incapable of being effective politicians. Therefore, Black women candidates are not necessarily mean, but they have to be "about their business," which often comes across as "being mean."

What Others Think of Black Women Candidates

Camila's comments shifted the conversation. The room became more serious as the Silent Generation retired business executive moved the discussion to non-Black women's assessments of Black women candidates. Naomi spoke first, and her once jovial demeanor changed to become more solemn. She stated, "If it's not one thing, if it's not qualifications then it's attitude. If it's not attitude, then it's down to the way they look." The other participants noticeably approved of Naomi's assessment. They nodded their heads and murmured "ah-huhs" and "yes" as she spoke. Esther, another retiree in her early seventies and a member of the Silent Generation, cosigned these sentiments to add, "And they question their ability and qualifications." Naomi qualified her statements to enhance Esther's point, explaining, "I mean, it just depends on where it's coming from, male or female. Women may question the way somebody talks or presents themselves. Men just be plain old sexist, if nothing else. So, it really depends on who it's coming from." To that end, Camila pointed to an interplay of sexism and a belief that Black women have bad attitudes. She reminded the women in the room, "[Attitudes are] not what [Black women] look like."

In response, Jayda quietly said, "I'm a little opposite though. I feel like people feel inferior to us." Jayda was the youngest participant in our focus group. At 24, she was a recent college graduate, a Millennial, and was newly engaged to be married. Jayda seemed more reserved than the other members of the focus group, as she initially only spoke when the Deltas directly spoke to her, asking about her wedding planning before the start of the focus group. Now, Jayda was unswervingly challenging the narrative of Black women candidates that the senior members of focus group put forth. Jayda continued, "I think we scare people. So, I think that a lot of [Black women candidates] may be overqualified or just as qualified and so then the expression of inferiority comes off as questioning us." The two other Millennial women in the focus group, Chloe and Talia, leaned forward during Jayda's articulation of why some may question Black women's qualifications for elected positions. They seemed to physically acknowledge Jayda's assessment.

Jayda's comments differed from Naomi, Esther, and Camila's assessment of others' views of Black women candidates. The older women in the group believed that non-Black women may not hold Black women office seekers in high esteem. Whereas Jayda presented a deeper, perhaps psychological, rationale for why some of these women may disapprove of Black women candidates, all three of the older women insinuated that non-Black women think less of Black women candidates, whether because of sexism, racism, or other prejudices. They implied that stereotypes may lead others to think that Black women are not capable of holding office. It is notable that although focus group participants listed only positive traits of Black women candidates, they all believed that others hold negative views of this group of political elites.

Black Women Candidates and Appearance

The conversation naturally progressed to a discussion of how Black women candidates look. Jayda continued the dialogue by presenting her "aunt" as an example of why she believes that others have a negative perception of Black women candidates. Jayda's "aunt" is a close family friend who has been a part of her life since she was a girl. Because of this close relationship, Jayda had a bird's-eye view of the challenges that her aunt faced as a candidate for a local office. Jayda shared,

I have an aunt, she's not a biological aunt, but she ran for office [in an affluent suburb]. And what I know her appearance to be normally and when she started to run her campaign, she totally switched her appearance. So, she wears like big curly wigs and she's very eccentric in her dress. And as soon as she decided to run, she cut her hair and permed it. And she started wearing more reserved suit separates and what not. And I was like, "I understand, but I wish it would have been just you. And just come out as you. Regardless of what the perception would have been."

One woman interrupted Jayda to remind her that the aunt was running for office in this affluent suburb as a Black woman. Another, Clara, chimed in to add, "I see it and I know it. I understand it." Clara is a retired school teacher in her early seventies and currently works as a substitute teacher in the city's public school system. She continued, "What I would hope would happen is, let us get together and get her elected. And she can go back to being the way she always was to you and your family." Clara directed her comments directly to Jayda, who attempted to answer, but Chloe interjected by asking, "But, why do we even need to have that mindset?" Chloe pushed back against Clara's more conservative view that Jayda's aunt should have presented herself in a more demure manner in order to get elected. However, Chloe and Jayda's contention was the minority opinion in the group. Esther retorted, "Well, I think the question is to know, what's the goal? What is the goal of any politician? And it's to present yourself so you can get elected." Naomi added, "That's right."

There was discernable disagreement from some of the other women with how Chloe and Jayda felt about Black women politicians' presentation. The discord among the participants was palpable as the room experienced the first lull in conversation. Then, Jayda spoke, first softly and then more forcefully: "I guess, it bothered me because I don't think that it should matter. I know that regardless of what she looks like, her thoughts and ideas are the same. So, it bothered me to switch up on the look rather than polishing the articulation of her ideals. Her first go-to was to switch up her look." In a stern retort, Clara said, "No, her first goal was to win." Chloe leapt to Jayda's defense and tried to add a similar perspective, in a different voice, as to why it is problematic that Black women have to alter their appearance to win elections:

Just being from here or at least growing up here, it just always seemed like there is a very narrowly defined standard for what is acceptable for Black women professionally. And I believe it goes over to the political side. And

if you don't fit within that narrow image, then, somehow, you are less qualified or there's some other quality about you that disqualifies you for being
competent for that position. So, that's really frustrating to me that there's
not enough diversity of mindset as to what a Black woman looks like.

Speaking as though she did not hear Chloe's comment, Naomi quickly
followed up: "What I would look for in Black women candidates is the same
thing I look for in everybody. And that's excellence. . . . You get a chance to
express your individuality once you establish that you are good. Or excellent. So, if you want [my vote], you know, I want to hear and see competence.
What you can bring to the table. In my generation we used to say 'no half
stepping.'"

As the comments here show, the generational differences, particularly
between older participants and Millennials, were unmistakable during this
conversation. The Deltas went on to address these differences head-on, in
a sisterly manner. The focus group participants did not shy away from
contestation.

Generational Differences

The differences in the values, beliefs, and opinions of generational cohorts
were reflected in the focus group participants' discussion of Black women
candidates' appearances. Spurred by Jayda's discussion of her aunt's failed
campaign, Esther led the group to dive into these issues head-on, observing,

Maybe it's generational, too. I grew up in a generation where we still had
that whole thing. "Yeah, you do have to do that." And "You have to be the
best." Now, once you're the best, once you get elected, maybe you can be
more radical or different, but the reality is for Black folks in America, we
are still in that position where we don't get the breaks. So, I think that in our
generation, we were taught that, we live that.

Nadia asked if Esther thought that things are changing now. To that, Esther
responded, "Just superficially."

Naomi tackled the issue directly, addressing her remarks to the younger
women in the room. As a mother of three Millennials, she prefaced her

comments by noting that she is aware of young people's desire to see political change:

> I think our younger folks would want it to be that way . . . and so, you know, if they've been friends or want to run for office, they would support their friend. And they wouldn't expect them to change. I think that some of us in our generation are cynical about the kids [younger generation]. But I think it's made us cynical as to whether or not people closer to our age would change and accept [change]. Our younger folks running and being who and what they are from the very beginning. That's something to support.

The mood seemed less cautious after Naomi's remarks, as the women appeared to agree with her sentiments. The hopeful nature of Naomi's comments eased some tensions. To keep the conversation upbeat and on topic, Nadia asked the younger women in the room if Naomi's interpretation was accurate. Do younger generations accept people for who they are or what they look like? Are younger voters more tuned into the policies or qualifications of a candidate and not the outward appearance of the office seeker?

Jayda was the first to respond. She shared a tentative yes, but then answered no. She rephrased her earlier comment in an attempt to clarify her words by situating how she thinks about politics:

> I'll just speak form my personal experiences. I'm open to hear and agree to disagree. So, I'm not like, "Yeah, no," but I'm open to learn and hear other experiences. So, then I can, whenever there is a disagreement, understand where somebody else is coming from. And back to the whole, the idea that you need permission to be you, I guess is the goal to win? Regardless if it's winnable or not, I'm going to stand on what I believe. So, if it's who you are and who you always are, it gives the permission for others to do the same. Rather than "I'm going to assimilate to what is expected" and everyone else is just going to follow suit. So, I think it's more than just winning for Black women candidates.

The women in the focus group attentively listened to Jayda. Her polite and persuasive tone seemed to be successful in challenging some of the older women's beliefs around the electability of Black women who do not adhere to conservative styling. Jayda persisted in questioning the perceived goal of winning election at any expense. She continued,

> I think on the surface it is that you want to win, you want to be elected. But I think it's also in so many instances, you know, you're not doing it just for you. You are opening a door that you want other people to have to come here be able to come in. So, you want to win, but you also want to open that door. So, it's like that next step beyond just winning in that case.

At this point, Talia addressed the group in direct response to Jayda's questioning whether winning is enough. A Millennial in her mid-thirties, Talia is a public health administrator for the state and is originally from a city with a Black woman mayor. Talia chimed in to support Jayda's viewpoint by offering a similar take. She said, "And if I don't win, the next Black woman behind me can win, right? So, I think that it's a heavier load for Black candidates. Especially, a Black female candidate in a political race. I see it in my city. My mayor went through a lot." Both Jayda and Chloe nodded in agreement while Talia spoke. The three younger members of the focus group suggested that Black women who run for political office without conforming to traditional models of how one should look are opening doors for other women to express themselves freely.

There was a clear generational split between the members of the focus group on this issue, which was ultimately left unresolved. The women amicably disagreed, and neither group seemed to persuade the other to change their mind. The apparent generational split provided an opportunity for each cohort of women to share how they think about Black women candidates as filtered through their own lens.

What Should Black Women Office Seekers Look Like? Connections to Participants' Experiences

The sorority sisters moved the conversation forward to discuss how their ideal candidate would look. This discussion also revealed other generational splits and the politics of their own physical appearance. Connecting respectability politics to generational differences, each group of women shared that they challenged or are currently challenging the ideal appearance of Black women.

Camila led the conversation by providing an example of her experiences in college in the mid-1960s. She stated,

> I remember when people started wearing Afros. You, I'm sure you remember, it was crazy because people were not used to natural hair. Hey, I mean, I can go so far to say that Black campus grapevine works in different ways. I remember when Howard [University's] first Miss Howard wore her hair naturally. And they made a big thing of it, you know. Bringing the new Miss Howard out and she had an Afro. Lord have mercy!

At the time, Camila was a student at Morgan State University. She vividly shared other examples of how students on historically Black campuses were challenging the norms of respectability. Nadia asked if natural hair was seen as respectable now, and Camila, who currently wears her hair in a low-cut natural, responded, "I don't think that there is a 'respectable' look. My only provision is, is it clean and neat? Then you can wear it any way you want."

Camila directed many of her comments directly to Jayda. Reliving her college days through the lens of hair politics, Camila seemed to want to connect with her young sorority sister who recently graduated from college and also wears her hair in an unprocessed state. Jayda appeared to appreciate Camila's attempt to draw her into a discussion where the two could be on the same side of an issue. In response, Jayda added,

> I think that goes too, because people look at my hair and go, 'Is it clean?' Other people don't think my hair's clean and neat. So, it goes even in the natural community. I want to go as trivial as edges. Like, I don't put gel on my edges and other naturalistas will lay their edges [down]. I'm just, the hair doesn't need to do that. You're natural. [But] I understand the whole relaxed look of a politician and their hair.

Esther quickly affirmed Jayda's position of preferring relaxed hair on Black women political elites. Using the former First Lady as an example, Esther noted, "When, after Michelle [Obama] came of out of office, didn't she receive backlash when she went natural? So, it's all the hype around natural hair. But, looking around, most of us are natural in here today. It's still, you know, still not looked upon as the best look for us by the majority." Indeed, Esther was correct, of the eight women in the focus group, seven had natural hair. Although the supermajority of the participants wore their hair in an unprocessed state, some of the older women expressed misgivings about Black women candidates having natural hair.

While Jayda was retelling an experience with older family members who encouraged her to straighten her hair, and co-workers who express curiosity over her Afro puffs, Talia seemed to have an "aha" moment. Her face lit up, and she interrupted Jayda in mid-sentence to share a reflection. Talia mused,

> It also makes me think then, how a Black female candidate must present herself. She has to stick with it because it makes me think about a time where I changed my hair. I had braids. And how an executive-level staff member walked right past me and didn't recognize me. So then, it makes me think, in that case, whatever she [the Black woman office seeker] starts out with and how she presents herself, she should stick with it. Because they [voters] won't know who she is.

Jayda immediately made a connection to Talia's example and how, for Black women candidates, changing their hairstyle might be a political liability. Again, using herself as an example, Jayda was able to connect her experiences to a potential problem that Black women candidates might face if they change their look:

> But, if she does change it, her look comes into play. It becomes the focus. Because I switch my hair—braids, then I'll straighten it, I do it all. Every time I come into work, they [White co-workers] want to ask questions about my hair. I'm at work, what about the meeting at hand? We spent 15 minutes at the start of the meeting talking about my hair. Rather than what the purpose of the meeting was about. I see that being the switch-up, in Black woman's campaign or whatever she's doing with the public. Just like even conversations like "Oh, Michelle Obama's wearing this now and she's wearing that now." I think that our hair is a focus. Anytime we do something. And we have the right to switch up our look, but it becomes the focus rather than what we're saying.

The women in the focus group nodded in agreement with Jayda's assessment that Black women's hairstyling choices are often the topic of conversation, and that at times, this distracts from what the Black woman is trying to do or say. The women acknowledged that this had happened to several of them in the past and extrapolated that this would be a problem for Black women political elites.

Esther reminded the group that this is a distinct problem that women face: "So, is it just, you know, making frivolous assumptions and evaluations of women in general? I can't tell you what Representative Jim Jordan's (R-IN) hair looks like. So why is it that women are subjected to that kind of scrutiny across the board?" Anna, a middle-aged woman who had largely been silent during much of the discussion, agreed with Esther's assertation: "Yes, I remember when Hillary [Clinton] was given slack too with the change of her hair. And I remember when she started off with the headband and then she had to take those off because she looked too young or whatever. Girl. Yeah, so I think so. I wonder if it's just a female thing. Hair?" This part of the discussion ended with renewed attention to the issues women candidates face and a reduced focus on the generational differences among the participants.

Focus Group Participants' Hair

The discussion ended with the Deltas discussing their own hair and their relationship to respectability politics. The women were all well-versed in the cultural norms of Black women's appearance. This shared acknowledgement transcended the generational divide, with the majority of participants sharing a personal example of how their natural hair has been received.

Camila articulated that Black women's relationship to natural hair is cultural: "Because some people have been programmed, you know. Hair is hair, I don't care who has an issue with it. But I'm old enough to know that this isn't just hair. But, 'cause for Black girls, little girls, from the time that you are two years old, there is an issue about hair, some way, shape, form, or fashion." The women laughed and agreed with Camila. She continued, "You know, your mom tied it up at night so that she didn't have to do it first thing in the morning. I sympathize with anybody who said that 'I'm not dealing with this.' It just has to be neat and clean, you know, and have it in some semblance of order. And after that, that's the least of my worries. But that is a cultural phenomenon that we have."

Camila expressed a desire that Black people would get away from having a preoccupation with hair, and Clara furthered this assertion, noting, "Yeah we have to get away from this slavery mentality which covers well over 200 years. I've been natural since 1962—well, I've been going back and forth. This attitude hasn't really changed since 1962. We're just not in that place yet for natural hair. It is going to take a little bit longer." Anna agreed and but added a note of optimism, arguing that older Black women can serve as positive role models for younger generations of women who need to embrace their natural hair. She said, "Because at 53 years old, I see this in my family. I'm in the middle. My mother is in her nineties, and she's always saying, 'Are you going to fix your hair?' 'Cause I'm natural, but my nieces are 16 and 17 and now they are wearing their hair natural because of my natural hair. I exposed them to natural hair." Anna believes that although her elderly mother does not approve of her hair, she is changing the norms of acceptable hairstyles in her family by showing her nieces that one can have natural hair and still be professional. When asked when she thought that natural hair would be embraced fully, Anna responded, "It's gonna take folks dying out, unfortunately, until people stop worrying about it."

However, others expressed skepticism toward this view and didn't seem optimistic about this change occurring in their lifetime. Camila advanced the notion that hair preferences for Black women have been around for a long time, and that they aren't likely to change any time soon:

> ... [T]rust me, it's been an issue since 1619, when the slave ship landed in America. And yeah, what to do with your hair. White people, on the other hand, they can put their hair in a bun and no one would know the difference. Nobody will ever say a word. But the rest of us, Black women, it's an integral part to of how people assess us. An integral part of how people see us. It really depends on where you work, what you do as to whether or not you have to think about. Having an effect on the outcome of your life because it can. If you're in corporate America, depending on the company and you know, teachers dependent on where they are teaching, and what principal they have. Um, it never goes away. It never goes away. You just have to learn to say, decide whether or not you're going to let it affect you. And you just move forward because, if not, it will drive you crazy. And hair has driven us all crazy, all of our lives.

Camila aptly summed up the feeling of the room in a reaffirming nod to natural hair and observation that the majority of women in the room had unprocessed hair: "We're not the ones walking around with lace fronts [wigs]." Talia quipped, "Shots fired" in reference to those who wear wigs. The room erupted in jubilant laughter.

Discussion and Conclusion

Rather than resting on their laurels as organizations founded on principles of civic engagement and political activism, BGLOs continue to be active today. Indeed, Deltas have been building upon this tradition. The sorority's five-point programmatic thrust includes political awareness and involvement, with the express purpose of improving the political, educational, and economic needs of Black communities. The sorority's members follow initiatives set forth by the organization's national Social Action Commission. These directives seek to influence public policy, increase voter registration and education, and engage with elected representatives. Notable Deltas, present and past, who have enhanced the sorority's political actions include Mary McLeod Bethune, Myrlie Evers-Williams, Frankie M. Freeman, Patricia Roberts Harris, Dorothy Height, Alexis M. Herman, U.S. Rep. Barbara Jordan (D-TX), U.S. Rep. Carrie P. Meek (D-FL), and U.S. Rep. Stephanie Tubbs-Jones (D-OH). These notable Deltas in politics have continued to advance Black women's activism in the areas of civic engagement and through elected or appointed government positions. The individual accomplishments of these trailblazing Deltas are part and parcel of the collective political actions of this sorority. More than just participating in the historic suffrage march of 1913, Deltas have also spearheaded or have been involved in the American Council on Human Rights and Habitat for Humanity, which demonstrates their continued political involvement. Today, the sorority hosts annual programs, Delta Days at the Nations Capital and Delta Days at the United Nations, to disseminate information and to monitor political developments that impact women and children.[6] The Deltas who participated in this study embrace their sorority's mission of public service to Black communities.

The women in the focus group were exuberant in their discussion of the politics of appearance for Black women candidates. They worked through generational differences in a sisterly manner, which enabled each Delta to freely speak her mind without fear of reproach. The atmosphere remained upbeat, even during difficult parts of the conversation. While the women did not always agree on the implications of styling choices for Black women office seekers, they were uniform in their desire to see more Black women elected officials. Speaking to a group of highly politically engaged women enabled us to learn about their preferred vote choice.

As the other chapters in this book demonstrate, Black women political elites face unique challenges, suffer electoral backlash, and confront the politics of respectability when they decide to wear their natural hair. As voters, the women in this focus group acknowledged these difficulties and added a more nuanced articulation of how the citizens that overwhelmingly support Black women candidates may assess candidates' appearances as part of their vote choice. The contestation in the group over the connection between electability and appearances reveals a lack of uniform agreement among Black women voters. While this group of civically minded and devoted voters are often portrayed as a monolith in both media depictions and scholarly studies, our work advances that there are some differences in how Black women view Black women candidates. We cannot assume that Black women will vote for a candidate who shares her gender and ethno-racial background. Philpot and Hanes, Jr.'s (2007) analysis is instructive for understanding how and why Black women support Black women office seekers. This study affirms that Black women voters are the most supportive of Black women candidates. Our research examines the other considerations that signal electability to some Black women voters.

Our findings are equally instructive in challenging notions of appearance enforcement for sorority members. We show that for some younger sorority members, internalized frames of White supremacy and White feminine ideals are not the gold standard. Instead, the Deltas in our study embrace natural hair as a personal styling choice that bears little significance in an individual's political ideology. The younger women in our study, however, vehemently disavow appearance enforcement. They believe that styling choices should have no impact on electability and they urged their older sorority sisters to question why a Black woman candidate's appearance should matter in these normative ways. All the women in our study were cognizant of the controlling stereotypical images that have shaped Black women's experiences. However, the younger Deltas in our study were the ones who vocally challenged the sustained significance of appearance within Black women's electoral outcomes.

Furthermore, we do not find that the women in our study see themselves as tied to Black elitism in ways that reinforce documented criticisms of BGLOs. The Deltas who participated in our study align more closely with the literature on political participation. These are highly engaged women who are thinking about politics in nuanced and dynamic ways. In our larger conversation, the participants opined on topics ranging from policy concerns for their communities, to a history of local Black women elected officials, to their preferred candidate for the 2020 Democratic presidential nominee, to effective strategies for grassroot organizing. These Deltas demonstrated a depth of knowledge of local, state, and national politics that was informed by their own civic involvement. Indeed, many of the women were active in social justice initiatives through other organizations, such as their churches or the Links, another Black women's organization, in addition to their work with Delta Sigma Theta Sorority, Inc.

To be sure, the Deltas who opted to join our focus group may exhibit some selection bias. The women who agreed to spend a Saturday morning talking about Black women office seekers with researchers are women who display a great deal of interest in politics. We do not claim that all members of Delta Sigma Theta Sorority, Inc., hold the same level of civic engagement or a deep commitment to electing Black women candidates. However, it is reasonable to conclude that the majority of Deltas, regardless of their ability to participate in some forms of political action, have a strong level of civic-mindedness given the founding principles of the organization.

Moving forward, we build on this chapter to argue that as voters evaluate a Black woman's qualifications for office holding, they care about how she looks. In the next chapter, we use novel data to explore whether a dominant appearance exists among the pool of Black women candidates.

6

Is There a Black Woman Candidate Prototype?

> I hope that you're the one
> If not, you are the prototype
>
> —André 3000

While we often think of candidate self-presentation as a choice, the reality is that styling choices for Black women candidates are situated within a set of constraints dictated by sociopolitical norms and laws. In *The Accommodation* (1986), a history of race and racism in Dallas, Texas, journalist Jim Schutze (1986, 86–87) recounts how U.S. Congresswoman Eddie Bernice Johnson (TX-30) learned about race relations in Dallas, Texas, during a shopping trip to buy a hat. Johnson offered some insight into her styling choices: " 'My parents taught us that, even if you couldn't buy much, you should buy the best, so I went to one of the best stores downtown, A. Harris. And I was told that I could not try on hats or shoes. They had to measure my head and then go over and measure the hat" (Schutze 1986, 87). This event took place in the 1950s, when segregation was legal. In a turn of events, it would be Stanley Marcus, of the Neiman Marcus department store, who would hire Johnson, relieving her from her position as a federal nurse, to facilitate her run for state legislature (Schutze 1986, 87; Burke 2020). Upon her first election in 1973, Johnson was the first Black woman to represent Dallas in the statehouse, and she would become the first Black person and woman to represent Dallas in the state senate (Burke 2020). Today, Johnson represents Dallas in the 30th U.S. House Congressional District in Texas.

This story illustrates that manner of self-presentation is dictated not only by personal preferences but also by constraints imposed by outsiders. As previous chapters have shown, for Black women, hair is not simply hair. Indeed, Black women candidates think carefully about how to style their

Sister Style. Nadia E. Brown and Danielle Casarez Lemi, Oxford University Press (2021). © Oxford University Press.
DOI: 10.1093/oso/9780197540572.003.0006

hair and how constituents will receive their choices. In previous chapters, we showed that these choices balance personal commitments to identity and self-expression with the reality of constraints imposed on their agency by outsiders, such as the public, party leaders, and personal advisors. In this chapter, we explore the distribution of skin tone and hairstyles among Black women candidates who ran for office in 2018 in different geographic locales, at different levels of office, and with different electoral outcomes.

Is there a dominant "type" of Black woman candidate? Do Black women candidates conform to the lighter-skinned, straight-haired ideal? Black women elites are acutely aware of how others judge their appearance, and Black voters may evaluate Black women candidates differently as individuals when skin tone and hairstyle are salient markers of difference. Yet, how prevalent is colorism and Eurocentric appearance in the pool of Black women who actually seek office? Where do these women run? What do they look like? What happens to them? In this chapter, we bring together several sources of novel data and examine the headshots of 667 Black women who sought office at the local, state, and federal levels in 2018, to determine whether the pool skews lighter-skinned and Eurocentric.

There are many reasons to believe colorism and Eurocentrism is present in the pool of Black women candidates. Colorism is an intra-ethnic hierarchy that values lighter-skinned co-ethnics (Herring 2004) and communicates that people of color with phenotypical features closer to that of Europeans are more desirable (Hunter 2005). Scholars have found that life expectancy and mate selection (Hughes and Hertel 1990; Hunter 1998), socioeconomic opportunities (Hill 2000), prison sentencing (Hochschild and Weaver 2007), trait impressions (Maddox and Gray 2002), and electoral outcomes (Terkildsen 1993; Weaver 2012; Lerman et al. 2015) are all linked to colorism. Skin color, like hair texture, has remained a powerful indicator of societal attitudes and treatment of Blacks (Neal and Wilson 1989; Okazawa-Rey, Robison, and Ward 1987). After the abolition of slavery, skin color remained a form of status acquisition (Okazawa-Rey et al. 1968). Preferential treatment was awarded, both in intra- and interracial contexts, to Black people who sought to adhere to Eurocentric bodily norms and White standards of beauty (Gatewood 1988). During the Black Power and civil rights movements, the phrase "Black is Beautiful" was used to challenge these hegemonic norms around colorism (Neal and Wilson 1989). During this era, lighter skin became less uniformly desirable, whereas dark skin remained undesirable, and a medium brown skin tone was the most highly desired (Goering 1971).

Yet, the preference for lighter skin among Black women has persisted and remains largely intact today. Lighter-skinned Black women are more likely to marry Black men of higher status than their darker-skinned counterparts (Goering 1971). Black people also receive mixed messages about skin tone. For example, within some aspects of popular culture, African Americans are taught to be proud of their skin color, but many remain "color struck"—convinced that lighter skin is more beautiful and desirable—as seen in how they respond to different shades of Black skin (Neal and Wilson 1989). Because of the nation's long history of racism and colorism, skin color is a multidimensional construct that consists of cognitive, affective, and behavioral components (Cash and Brown 1989).

Despite the pervasiveness of colorism and the dominance of Eurocentric beauty standards in American society, scholarship on race and representation is noticeably lacking in discussions of skin tone and hairstyle as they pertain to Black women candidates. To date, there is just one study (Hochschild and Weaver 2007) that briefly examines the skin tones of Black elected officials and that shows that the pool of Black elected officials skews lighter-skinned. As Hochschild and Weaver (2007) note, their research was limited to those candidates who won office. We push this single study forward by expanding our inquiry to include all Black women candidates who sought office in 2018, and we analyze their skin tone characteristics, hairstyle characteristics, geographic contexts, and electoral outcomes.

Although no similar systematic analysis of Black women candidates has been undertaken to date, we expect two potential outcomes. Consistent with prior research, we expect that the pool will generally skew lighter in skin tone, with a greater proportion of candidates wearing straightened hairstyles. We also expect that candidates with more Eurocentric appearances will tend to finish their campaigns with electoral victory than those with darker skin and natural hairstyles.

Data and Method

To explore whether the pool of Black women candidates skews lighter-skinned and Eurocentric in appearance, we conducted a content analysis of visual data. While text-based content analysis is frequently deployed in the study of elite political behavior (e.g., Brown and Gershon 2016; McIlwain and Caliendo 2011), visual content analysis is comparatively rare (Joo and Steinert-Threlkeld 2018, but see Farris and Mohamed 2018). Rather than focus on how candidates present their narratives through text, we instead focus on how candidates present their *selves* through visuals by analyzing the content of their public-facing headshots.

There are a number of ways candidates may choose to present their political personas. Scholars of political communication have shown the various strategies candidates of color adopt when crafting their personal narratives (Brown and Gershon 2016) and strategically addressing racial identity and racial issues in their campaigns (Collet 2008, McIlwain and Caliendo 2011, Perry 1991). However, as our previous chapters have shown, Black women elites recognize that there are constraints on individual agency, as they experience pressure from the political establishment to "look like a White woman" and find ways to express their personal style in everyday lawmaking activities. Depending on a Black woman candidate's strategic calculation, she may decide to adopt styles in line with Eurocentric beauty standards—those with straightened hair—or she may decide to style herself with natural hairstyles. We therefore offer the caveat that the photos we analyzed are curated images that candidates have released to the public or images of styling choices that candidates have allowed the public to see, such as at events covered by reporters.

We collected multiple sources of data. First, we identified 667 Black women candidates who ran for office in 2018 using the list from the database Black Women in Politics. This figure is a cleaned count, with listings that appear multiple times in the directory removed. This count also only includes headshots of candidates for whom we could locate a color photo with a recent date. Second, we downloaded those candidates' headshots from online sources such as campaign webpages, news stories, and Ballotpedia. Third, to code for skin color, we took two approaches. With the assistance of a graduate research assistant to automate the process, each candidate's headshot was uploaded into Betaface, a web application that utilizes facial recognition software that codes aspects such as a person's race, gender, skin color, and facial characteristics. Out of the 667 headshots, 3 were not readable, likely because of poor photo quality. The application uses hex values—unique identifiers for colors used to create images on webpages—to identify characteristics of the person in the photo. We used the hex values assigned to skin color to retrieve "lightness values," or interval numerical values that range from 0 (darkest) to 1 (lightest), from Color-Hex.com, a website that stores information about hex values. In addition, we coded each headshot with the Massey and Martin (2003) skin shade scale, which ranges from 1 (lightest) to 10 (darkest). Two coders—Danielle and a graduate research assistant—hand coded the headshots using the Massey and Martin (2003) scale. They agreed on about 50% of the observations (kappa=.38, prob > Z=.000, N=664) and were highly correlated with each other (r=.85, p=.000). To determine whether the lightness values correlated with the Massey and Martin (2003) coding, we reverse-coded each rater's Massey and Martin (2003) coding, averaged the two, then divided the averaged scores by 10. The average Massey and Martin (2003) rating is fairly highly correlated with the Color-Hex lightness values (r=.59, p=.000), suggesting that these two measures somewhat overlap in measuring skin tone. Fourth, two undergraduate and graduate research assistants coded the candidates' hairstyles using a coding scheme Nadia and Danielle developed to identify each candidate's hairstyle. The hairstyle coding proved to be one of the most difficult aspects of this data collection process. Initially, we constructed a set of directions with examples of hairstyles, including braids, locs, twists, Afros, wigs, accessories, etc. Upon receiving the coding from our research assistants, we realized our directions were not as exhaustive as we had initially thought, as one of our assistants flagged numerous headshots that they were unsure how to code. In these cases, we reviewed the flagged headshots and coded them ourselves, adhering as closely as possible to the directions the research assistants had followed. In the midst of merging the two datasets from the research assistants, we found that nine headshots had not merged between the two datasets, and we coded those. Where observations were missing values, we reviewed those headshots and coded them. Upon discovering these coding and merging challenges, we opted to focus our analysis on hairstyles that fell into five major categories (1) straight or not, (2) curly (Afro, short natural, very short, curly wigs, etc.)[1] or not, (3) braids or not, (4) locs or not, and (5) other, for hairstyles that did not fall into the other four categories.

After cleaning the data and collapsing the coding into these categories, we tested for inter-rater agreement. Overall, there was high agreement between the two coders (see Table 6.1). This agreement suggests that despite the coding challenges we encountered, our directions were sufficiently clear and consistently applied to identify hairstyles that fell into these categories.

Table 6.1 Inter-rater Agreement for Hairstyle Coding

Category	Agreement	Kappa
Straight	90.55%	.80 (Prob > Z =.000)
Curly	95.65%	.87 (Prob > Z =.000)
Braids	98.35%	.69 (Prob > Z =.000)
Locs	97.64%	.76 (Prob > Z =.000)
Other	89.81%	.41 (Prob > Z =.000)

Finally, a research assistant collected contextual information (when available) for each of the 2018 candidates in the study. Here, we report the level of office that was sought (local, state, congressional), the electoral outcome (won, lost, withdrew or was withdrawn), and the region (West, Midwest, South, Northeast). Table 6.2 reports the descriptive statistics for the context of this set of candidates. Most of the candidates included in this table sought local office, lost their elections, and ran in the South. Two candidates, Margo Davidson (Pennsylvania) and Ryana Parks-Shaw (Missouri), were coded as special cases, as they ran for multiple levels of office. Thus, we do not include these elections in our outcome or level-of-office tabulations. We also do not include runs for party positions. Appointments are included in this dataset. This multifaceted dataset allows us to explore each of our key research questions: What are the dominant appearance characteristics of Black women candidates? Where do they run? And who wins and who loses?

There are both advantages and disadvantages to using this data. To our knowledge, there is no other dataset on Black women candidates as comprehensive as this one. While scholars frequently labor to collect lists of candidates and legislators that identify the race of a candidate or legislator (e.g., Fraga et al. 2020; Klarner 2018), this list is exclusively about Black women, and it pairs visual information with contextual data. Rather than treat Black candidates as a monolith by quickly glancing at a photo and marking a candidate's race, we explicitly draw on information that tells us the extent to which a candidate may be "racialized" by the public or experience Blackness as a candidate. In doing so, we assert that the experiences of Black women are varied, and our data acknowledges that Black women with darker skin and natural hairstyles may have different electoral experiences than Black women with lighter skin and straight hairstyles.

Table 6.2 Candidate Contexts

Level of Office	
Local	48.42% (N=322)
State	40.75 (N=271)
Congress	10.83 (N=72)
Electoral Outcome	
Won	46.77 (N=311)
Lost	49.92 (N=332)
Withdrew	3.31 (N=22)
Region	
West	12.74 (N=85)
Midwest	20.09 (N=134)
South	59.07 (N=394)
Northeast	8.10 (N=54)

Because datasets that track candidate race and ethnicity are limited in availability, our data is restricted to 2018. Relying on this snapshot of data has a few implications for its composition and our conclusions. Because President Trump's 2016 election may have inspired more Democratic candidates' campaigns for office (Lawless and Fox 2018), and because of the influence of Stacey Abrams's 2018 historical run for Governor of Georgia, our dataset may have a more diverse sample of Black women who ran for office. The climate in 2018 may have facilitated more Black women running than prior to 2018. This context is important for the bounds of our data. Furthermore, 2018 may have offered more opportunities for lighter-skinned Black women already in office (e.g., Hochschild and Weaver 2007) to advance their political careers faster, and the election cycle may have unearthed more opportunities for Black women with darker skin and natural hairstyles to enter the political arena. This snapshot of data does not include Black women who never entered the candidate pool, precluding us from exploring the extent to which skin tone and hairstyle serve as barriers to candidate entry (e.g., Silva and Skulley 2019; Fraga and Hassell 2020).

We recognize that measuring skin tone is fraught with a host of normative and methodological issues. By using two measures of skin tone, we hope to circumvent these issues. The Massey and Martin (2003) skin shade scale is one of the most common scales used to measure skin tone. The scale consists of pictures of hands that range from very light to very dark, and individuals are typically asked to place themselves along the scale, or interviewers are instructed to place others on the scale. One of the drawbacks to using this scale, however, is that our perceptions of others' appearances depends on other known information about an individual (e.g., Saperstein 2012), or even our own experiences (e.g., Campbell et al. 2020). Skin tone, in other words, is in the eye of the beholder.

At the same time, we know that artificial intelligence software is riddled with racism (Noble 2018). For this reason, rather than use the Betaface data that assigns race or gender to a photo, we instead used the data on the actual color that is used to print an image on a webpage. Whereas coding skin tone with the Massey and Martin (2003) scale is subject to an individual's biases, the color used to print an image merely reflects the quality of the photo. Still, we recognize that a software's ability to recognize a range of colors hinges on the quality of the training data. For these reasons, we use both measures of skin tone and skin color to classify candidates' headshots.

Finally, we do not make causal claims about this data. Skin tone is one attribute that we cannot randomly assign (Sen and Wasow 2016), as skin color and hair texture are biological. Yet, one's early-life social and economic resources—which constrain or facilitate running for office later on—are cor-related with skin tone (Hunter 2005). Hairstyles are chosen within socially constructed parameters. Our goal with this research is to explore the charac-teristics of Black women candidates in the pool of such candidates in a single election cycle.

Findings

We report several sets of descriptive statistics by skin tone, by hairstyle, and by both skin tone and hairstyle. We report these statistics by level of office pursued, electoral outcome, and region.

Skin Tone

Table 6.3 reports the average and median skin tone values for all candidates in our dataset, excepting the three candidates we were unable to code. In the left column are the mean, median, standard deviation, and minimum and maximum values for the averaged intercoder Massey and Martin (2003) scores (not reverse-coded), and in the right column are these statistics for the Color-Hex lightness values. Higher Massey and Martin (2003) scores indicate darker skin tones on a scale of 1 to 10, and lightness values closer to 1 indicate lighter skin tones.

As Table 6.3 shows, the candidates in our dataset skew relatively light, supporting the hypothesis that colorism pervades representational politics. The average skin tone score on the Massey and Martin (2003) scale is 4.29 and the median is 4, indicating that most Black women who ran for office in 2018 fell on the lighter end of the scale. The darkest Massey and Martin (2003) value in our dataset is 8.5 out of 10. The lightness values also show that the candidates skewed relatively light, as the mean and the median scores are .57. Importantly, the standard deviation for the Massey and Martin (2003) coding is 1.34, and for the lightness values it is .11. This suggests that the pool skews relatively light, and on average, there is little deviation from this lightness within the pool. In short, the pool of Black women candidates is relatively light in skin tone.

In Table 6.4, we show the mean and median skin tone scores by level of office pursued, electoral outcome, and region. Again, skin tone generally skews lighter across the board for Black women candidates. Notably, however, there are no substantive skin tone–related differences between levels of office, electoral outcomes, or regions. Chi-squared tests reveal no statistically significant relationship between skin tone and any of these variables.

Table 6.3 Mean and Median Skin Tones for 2018 Black Women Candidates

	Massey and Martin (2003) (N=664)	Color-Hex Lightness Value (N=664)
Mean	4.29	.57
Median	4	.57
Std. Dev.	1.34	.11
Min. and Max.	1, 8.5	.14, .85

Table 6.4 Skin Tone by Level of Office, Electoral Outcome, and Region

	Massey and Martin (2003)	Color-Hex Lightness Values
Level of Office		
Local (N=319)	Mean: 4.26, Median: 4	Mean: .57, Median: .58
State (N=271)	Mean: 4.33, Median: 4.5	Mean: .56, Median: .56
Congress (N=72)	Mean: 4.26, Median: 4	Mean: .57, Median: .58
Electoral Outcome		
Won (N=308)	Mean: 4.23, Median: 4	Mean: .57, Median: .58
Lost (N=332)	Mean: 4.35, Median: 4.5	Mean: .56, Median: .57
Withdrew (N=22)	Mean: 4.16, Median: 3.75	Mean: .59, Median: 59
Region		
West (N=85)	Mean: 4.09, Median: 4	Mean: .59, Median: .6
Midwest (N=134)	Mean: 4.20, Median: 4	Mean: .57, Median: .58
South (N=391)	Mean: 4.33, Median: 4.5	Mean: .56, Median: .57
Northeast (N=54)	Mean: 4.47, Median: 4.5	Mean: .55, Median: .56

Hairstyles

To analyze the descriptive characteristics of the hairstyle data, we created new variables that combined the coding from the research assistants. Where the assistants disagreed, Danielle reviewed the headshots and resolved the differences. Based on our coding, about 66% (N = 443) of the women who sought office wore straightened hairstyles. About one-fifth (22.19%, N = 148) of the sample wore curly styles. Only about 2% (16) of the sample wore braids, and just over 5% (N = 36) wore locs. Twenty-four (3.60%) candidates wore other styles, such as twists, head coverings, or hijabs. Table 6.5 reports the distribution of hairstyle values for each hairstyle by level of office sought, electoral outcome, and region. The columns depict the distribution of hairstyles across each category (e.g., the percentage of straightened hairstyles at each level of office). Most candidates in our dataset sought local or state office, and as a result, few hairstyles at the federal level were represented. The data for hairstyle at level of office sought shows that straight and curly hairstyles are similarly common at both local and state levels. While the numbers are small, in this dataset, braids and locs are primarily seen at the local level of office. This suggests that candidates at the local level choose to present themselves with hairstyles that go against the dominant straightened style commonly found throughout the pool. This also suggests that candidates for local

Table 6.5 Distribution of Hairstyles

	Straight	Curly	Braids	Locs	Other
Level of Office*					
Local	46.61 (N=206)	48.30 (N=71)	75.0 (N=12)	63.89 (N=23)	41.67 (N=10)
State	41.86 (N=185)	42.86 (N=63)	25.0 (N=4)	30.56 (N=11)	33.33 (N=8)
Congress	11.54 (N=51)	8.84 (N=13)	0	5.56 (N=2)	25.0 (N=6)
Total	100.0 (N=442)	100.0 (N=147)	100.0 (N=16)	100.0 (N=36)	100.0 (N=24)
Electoral Outcome					
Won	48.64 (N=215)	44.90 (N=66)	25.0 (N=4)	38.89 (N=14)	50.0 (N=12)
Lost	48.42 (N=214)	50.34 (N=74)	75.0 (N=12)	55.56 (N=20)	50.0 (N=12)
Withdrew	2.94 (N=13)	4.76 (N=7)	0	5.56 (N=2)	0
Total	100.0 (N=442)	100.0 (N=147)	100.0 (N=16)	100.0 (N=36)	100.0 (N=24)
Region*					
West	11.06 (N=49)	15.54 (N=23)	37.50 (N=6)	16.67 (N=6)	4.17 (N=1)
Midwest	19.86 (N=88)	20.27 (N=30)	12.50 (N=2)	27.78 (N=10)	16.67 (N=4)
South	60.72 (N=269)	58.11 (N=86)	37.50 (N=6)	50.0 (N=18)	62.50 (N=15)
Northeast	8.35 (N=37)	6.08 (N=9)	12.50 (N=2)	5.56 (N=2)	16.67 (N=4)
Total	100.0 (N=443)	100.0 (N=148)	100.0 (N=16)	100.0 (N=36)	100.0 (N=24)

*$p > .10$

office may grapple with fewer constraints on their styling choices on the path to office than they would at higher levels of office where party networks, and perhaps increased media coverage, become more relevant. In addition, there is a marginally statistically significant relationship between hairstyle and level of office sought ($\chi^2(8)=15$, Pr=.06).

Turning to electoral outcomes, there is no statistically significant relationship between hairstyle and outcomes. While the distribution of winners and losers is close for those who wore straightened styles, there is about a 5 percentage point gap between the winning and losing rates of those with curly hair. This suggests that candidates who have curly hairstyles may suffer a slight penalty. Again, while the numbers are small for those who wore braids or locs, 75% of candidates who wore braids lost, and about 56% of candidates who wore locs lost. This suggests that candidates who wear braids or locs may be disproportionately more likely to lose their elections, though it should be noted that these groups make up just 2% and about 5% of the hairstyle pool, respectively.

Recall that in our conversations with Black women elites (Chapter 3), we learned that some Black women candidates may not face pushback from voters in locales with a rich histories related to Black women hair entrepreneurs (e.g., St. Louis, Missouri), but that for some elites, regional culture, such as Southern culture, may constrain the range of styling possibilities available to Black women candidates. Thus, it is possible that the acceptability of a given hairstyle may vary by region. Turning to the regional distribution of hairstyles, we found a marginally statistically significant relationship between region and hairstyle ($\chi^2(12)=18.74$, Pr=.095). Straightened hair is overwhelmingly common in the South (60.72%), and curly hair is overwhelmingly common in the South as well (58.11%). Braids are equally common in the West and the South (37.50%), while locs are most common the South (50%). All other styles are most common in the South (62.50%). Taken together, these patterns suggest that Black women who pursue office in the South may have a greater range of hairstyle choices to select from when creating their political self-presentations.

Skin Tone and Hairstyle

The politics of appearance is not solely about either skin tone or hairstyle. As we have discussed and shown in previous chapters, there is an ideal type to which Black women are expected to conform in order climb the social, economic, or political ladder in White America: an appearance that is aligned with Eurocentric beauty standards to the greatest extent possible. In Table 6.6, we therefore report descriptive statistics both by hairstyle and

Table 6.6   Hairstyle and Skin Tone by Median

	Massey and Martin (2003)*		Color-Hex Lightness Value	
	Below	At or Above	Below	At or Above
Hairstyle				
Straight	70.0% (N=161)	64.53% (N=282)	63.28% (N=212)	69.58% (N=231)
Curly	23.48 (N=54)	21.51 (N=94)	22.99 (N=77)	21.39 (N=71)
Braids	1.30 (N=3)	2.97 (N=13)	2.39 (N=8)	2.41 (N=8)
Locs	3.04 (N=7)	6.64 (N=29)	7.46 (N=25)	3.31 (N=11)
Other	2.17 (N=5)	4.35 (N=19)	3.88 (N=13)	3.31 (N=11)
Total	100.0 (N=230)	100.0 (N=437)	100.0 (N=335)	100.0 (N=332)

*p < .10

by whether a candidate's skin tone was at or above or below the median skin tone value.

In the left column, we report hairstyles by the Massey and Martin (2003) coding, and in the right column we report hairstyles by the Color-Hex lightness values coding. There is a marginally statistically significant relationship between hairstyles and the Massey and Martin (2003) median values ($\chi^2(4)=8.28$, Pr=.08). Candidates who fell below the median, or who were lighter-skinned, overwhelmingly had straight hair (70%). By contrast, candidates who were at or above the median, or who were darker-skinned, had more varied hairstyles, as only about 65% wore straightened hair, with 2.97% wearing braids and 6.64% wearing locs 6.64%. While the relationship between hairstyles and lightness values is not statistically significant, there is a trend of similarity: candidates who have higher lightness values, or who are lighter-skinned, tend to wear straightened hairstyles (69.58%). Looking at the locs styles, candidates who wear locs (7.46%), also tend to be darker-skinned. This suggests that choices of hairstyles and skin tones tend to co-occur, with candidates who have lighter or darker skin tending to select specific hairstyles. Due to the small sample sizes, we do not disaggregate by hairstyle, median skin tone, and level of office, electoral outcome, and region.

Discussion and Conclusion

In this chapter, we have presented exploratory findings on the appearances of Black women who ran for office in 2018. Within this set of candidates, most wore straightened hairstyles and the average candidate skewed lighter-skinned. To be sure, this analysis is of Black women candidates compared with other Black women candidates—not with the general population. These findings should therefore not be generalized to other contexts, such as the relationship between skin tone, hairstyle, and employment outcomes, for instance. These findings are consistent with previous findings on colorism and elected office, and in many ways, they are not surprising. As we discussed earlier in this chapter, this dataset consists of individuals who were already on the campaign trail. While these findings are limited to candidates who had sufficient resources to declare their candidacy, they offer insight into what potential candidates may experience, and these patterns are consistent with what the Black women candidates and elected officials told us in previous chapters. That our dataset skews lighter-skinned is a reflection of the general advantages afforded to lighter-skinned Black people in the United States. These candidates may have declared their campaigns while already having a robust set of credentials and resources to aid them in running for office.

This dataset, to our knowledge, is the first of its kind in political science. Taking into account the small sample size, the tabulations reported here offer several implications for candidates hoping to enter the political arena. Colorism and hair discrimination may contribute to a pipeline blockage at lower-level offices (e.g., Mariani 2008). If Black women who wear locs tend to start their political careers in local offices and also tend to lose, this suggests that Black women who wear locs may face a constrained pathway to office. Such candidates may find themselves needing to make choices that candidates who wear straightened hairstyles from the start do not need to make. While further research is needed to assess causality, these patterns suggest that candidates who wear straightened hair at the onset of their careers may enjoy more opportunities to run in the future due to success at the local level. For

Black women who wear locs, the doors to political office may close prematurely, and the ideal type of Black woman representative may remain one who is lighter-skinned with straightened hair. Further research is needed to disentangle the effects of district composition; however, these findings tentatively suggest that Black women who run in the South may have, or may perceive, a greater opportunity to wear a range of hairstyles than that enjoyed or perceived by Black women in other parts of the country.

7

Voter Responses to Black Women Candidates

They don't think I'm viable, because I'm a Black woman with natural hair and no husband.
—Stacey Abrams, candidate for governor of Georgia, 2018

Stacey Abrams secured a place in the history books by becoming the first Black woman to win a major party's nomination for governor in Georgia when she won the state Democratic primary on May 22, 2018. As the former minority leader of the Georgia statehouse, and a small business owner, novelist, and Spelman College and Yale Law School graduate, Abrams was arguably the most qualified candidate in the race. Yet, during an interview with *The Breakfast Club*, a syndicated hip-hop/urban radio show based in New York City, Abrams told the hosts, "They [doubters] don't think I'm viable, because I'm a Black woman with natural hair and no husband. That is a sentiment that is held by some. But what I will say, is that I am the most qualified candidate—Democrat or Republican—running" (Breakfast Club Power 105.1 FM 2018, 2:49). Here, Abrams directly responds to critics who view her looks and marital status as impeding her ability to serve as governor of Georgia. Stacey Abrams's looks were also the center of an attack ad, put out by a political action committee that ran in the Atlanta metro area, in which the focal point was Abrams's decision to wear her natural, unprocessed hair. On social media, Stacey Abrams—who has ebony skin, is heavy-set, and wears a natural twist out hairstyle—has been contrasted with Keisha Lance Bottoms, the current mayor of Atlanta, who has honey-brown skin, is slender, and has straight hair that is coiffed in a close-cropped style. In Abrams's historic candidacy, and as the political careers of these two women progress, their appearances as Black women will continue to be salient to voters and political commentators alike.

Sister Style. Nadia E. Brown and Danielle Casarez Lemi, Oxford University Press (2021). © Oxford University Press.
DOI: 10.1093/oso/9780197540572.003.0007

What is the effect of variation in skin tone and hairstyle on evaluations of Black women candidates? The first thing people notice when they see political candidates is the candidate's appearance. Scholars working on candidate evaluation have noted that simply looking better is a bonus for candidates (e.g., Banducci, et al. 2008; Ahler, et al. 2017), while those working on race and candidate evaluation note that skin color is consequential for Black candidates (Terkildsen 1993; Weaver 2012; Lerman et al. 2015). At the same time, decades of research has tested whether gender stereotypes undermine the candidacies of women (e.g., Dolan and Kropf 2004; Kahn 1994; Sanbonmatsu 2002; Bejarano 2013). To date, however, no study in this literature speaks to how *Black voters* evaluate *Black women candidates* who vary in phenotype. In this chapter, we present findings from two survey experiments on Black voters. As many Black candidates run in majority-minority districts (Swain 1993; Grose 2011), our focus on Black voters approximates realistic scenarios. In Experiment 1, we focus on Black voters' evaluations of a single candidate as we vary her skin tone and hairstyle. In Experiment 2, we focus on Black Democratic voters' evaluations of two Black women candidates to determine whether appearances have the potential to split Black Democrats' votes. This experiment approximates real-world scenarios like the 2019 mayoral election in Chicago between Lori Lightfoot and Toni Preckwinkle.

Theory and Hypotheses

We employ a social-psychological approach—social identity theory—to gain insight into how voters respond to Black women candidates who vary in phenotype. Social identity theory holds that when individuals view themselves as belonging to a social group, whether it be defined by race, gender, class, or some other identifier, they seek to enhance their group status as an effort to preserve self-esteem (Tajfel 1974, 77–82). In situations where a social identity becomes salient—as when a person of color is in a room of White people, or a woman is in a room of men, etc.—people make comparisons between their group and other groups and recognize differences in group status (Tajfel 1974, 77–82). As a result, people may decide to reassign as positive what is typically viewed as negative about their group (Tajfel 1974, 77–82).

One example of a reinterpretation of what was once negative as something positive is the creation of the concept "Black is Beautiful" (Tajfel 1974, 83; Tajfel and Turner 1986, 20). In this vein, Black hairstyles are a cultural aesthetic that seeks to valorize Blackness. For example, consider Marcus Garvey's instructive state-ment, "Do not remove the kinks from your hair—remove them from your brain" (Byrd and Tharps 2001, 38). During the civil rights and Black Power movements of the 1960s and 1970s, both the Afro and locs styles redefined Blackness as a de-sirable attribute. The symbolic and political meanings of some natural hairstyles signal a shift during that period away from the stigma of curly, kinky hair and toward embracing these natural, emblematical hairstyles as demonstrating pride and pro-Blackness. The Afro symbolized Black pride, as Black Panthers and Angela Davis wore this style. Locs also symbolized racial pride, Black conscious-ness, and perhaps religious (i.e., Rastafari) connections. Today, it is common to see these styles worn by both men and women. Often, these hairstyles are worn more as a fashion statement than a political statement. Yet, as Mercer (1994) aptly points out, these styles have origins in radical political traditions.

The past decade has witnessed the rise of the Natural Hair Movement, which rejects the application of dominant Eurocentric beauty standards to Black women's beauty. In choosing to redefine the norms of Black women's beauty, naturalistas have begun to wear their natural hair and challenge con-ventional norms of what is acceptable, attractive, appropriate, and profes-sional. Indeed, there has been a 34% decline in the market value of hair relaxers (McGill Johnson et al., 2017). Because of their connection to expressions of Black pride, many people view unstraightened or natural hairstyles as an outward manifestation of pro-Black political ideology (Mercer 2005). Given the political connotation of hairstyles for Black women, particularly natural hairstyles, Black women voters may experience the sight of a candidate with darker skin and natural hair as empowering, and may respond favorably to a candidate displaying these Afrocentric characteristics. Such a candidate's appearance may communicate to voters, "I am one of you" (Fenno 1978, 58). One study suggests that some Black voters respond favorably to darker-skinned male candidates (Lerman et al. 2015). Two studies on Black women candidates give us further reason to believe that Black voters will also re-spond favorably to Black women candidates with darker skin and natural hairstyles. Orey and Zhang (2019) found that, relative to a Black man candi-date, Black voters rate Black women with any skin tone and hairstyle as more likely to represent the interests of women, but that lighter-skinned women score lower on their perceived alignment with Black nationalism. Burge et al. (2020) found that, relative to a lighter-skinned Black woman candidate, Black voters viewed a darker-skinned Black woman candidate as more viable among Black voters. Taken together, these findings suggest that Black women with natural hairstyles may be especially favored among Black voters, relative to their lighter-skinned, straight-haired counterparts—despite their relative infrequency in the candidate pool. Previous research illustrates that Black voters have a deep sense of linked fate—a sense that what happens to the rest of the group affects the individual—that guides political behavior (Dawson 1994), and research on Black women specifically suggests that Black women feel a distinct sense of linked fate with other Black women, which shapes their support for Black women candidates (Philpot and Walton 2007). Thus, the empowering effect of seeing Back women candidates may be especially true for Black women voters.

At the same time, communities of color in the United States experience pressure to assimilate and to police members of their own group who fail to emulate Whiteness. One underlying current of the notion of assimilation is that non-Whites, immigrants and non-immigrants alike, are expected to adopt Whiteness, relinquishing all attachments to non-Anglo culture (Gordon 1961; Alba and Nee 1997; Portes and Zhou 1993, 76). The social and economic benefits of assimilating into Whiteness create opportunities for intragroup conflict. Intragroup discrimination may occur against those who are perceived as less assimilated into American Whiteness. For example, discrimination from other Latinx is salient to Afro-Latinx (Lavariega Monforti and Sanchez 2010), Asian Americans may invoke the term "FOB (fresh off the boat)" to describe new immigrant co-ethnics (Pyke and Dang 2003), and color-based discrimination is salient to darker-skinned Black women in interactions with Black and White people (Uzogara and Jackson 2016). In response to the pressure to conform to Whiteness, some communities of color, and in the context of this study, Black Americans, may adopt the politics of respectability, or the belief that if individuals adjust their behavior, they can avoid the constraints of systemic racism and prejudice (Harris 2014; Jefferson 2018).

While Black women who choose to wear their hair naturally may do so to reject imposed Eurocentric beauty standards, Black women who opt to straighten their hair are also making political statements. Black-owned companies, including those founded by Black women such as Madame C.J. Walker, Sara Washington, and Annie Turbo Malone, promote straight or wavy hair as a method of treating damaged hair, addressing scalp disease, and encouraging hair growth (Walker 2007). African American beauty culturists straightened their hair to illustrate how to care for Black hair in a progressive and modern way. These culturists countered the negative images of Black womanhood by presenting positive and healthy images, and promoted a strong racial identity through empowering women to feel beautiful in their skin. While Black beauty culture as a consumer enterprise demarcates class dynamics within the Black community, it also epitomizes Black economic independence. This was particularly the case until White businesses began to incorporate Black hair care products—L'Oreal's purchase of Soft Sheen in 1998 being one example (Walker 2007). Straightened tresses, for some Black women, enable social mobility. Rejecting ethnic communalism in favor of assimilation is a survival strategy for some who try to gain acceptance in White mainstream society (hooks 1995). Thus, a Black woman who chooses to straighten her hair may ultimately choose to assimilate into Eurocentric beauty standards to advance socioeconomically. As our previous chapters show, a Black woman politician who presents herself as more Afrocentric may encounter co-racial resistance, as Black voters may hold a negative of view of her unwillingness to assimilate into White standards of beauty and behavior to rise socioeconomically.

This discussion leads us to three hypotheses about what we expect to see if we manipulate a candidate's phenotype to be darker-skinned with natural hair. The *closeness hypothesis* focuses on the candidate's perceived closeness to Blackness. It is plausible that a Black woman candidate's darker skin and naturally curly or braided hair communicates her solidarity and identity with the group, and that in turn, her appearance helps cultivate support from that group. Thus, we hypothesize that relative to a lighter-skinned candidate with straight hair, a more Afrocentric-appearing candidate will be more closely associated with Black people and with serving Black interests. We also identify what we call the *empowerment hypothesis*, which posits that Black voters may be more likely to vote for a candidate with a phenotype that is more Afrocentric, and that they may view that candidate more favorably than a lighter-skinned, straight-haired candidate.[1] At the same time, we also consider what we call the *internal discrimination hypothesis*, which suggests the opposite of the empowerment hypothesis. If we find that a candidate's more Afrocentric appearance results in a decreased likelihood of Black voters voting for and describing the candidate with favorable traits, then this hypothesis will be supported.

Two Experiments

To explore how Black voters respond to Black women candidates who vary in phenotype, we conducted two online experiments with nationwide samples (see the Appendix for more detail). We decided to conduct these experiments for two reasons. First, we are interested in whether changing an individual's phenotype causes changes in how others evaluate them. Experiments help us determine this by maximizing our control over the study. While focusing on real-world elections of Black women might be useful, the real world is simply too noisy for us to isolate a clean estimate of the effect of phenotype on evaluations of the candidate, and the real world only allows us to measure vote returns, not subjective evaluations of the candidate. Second, we needed to maximize our sampling reach to go nationwide. If we were to just conduct our experiment on Black voters in one locale, our conclusions might be limited to Black voters in that locale.

In our two experiments, Black respondents logged onto our surveys and answered a series of questions before seeing webpages describing Black women candidates. Adobe Photoshop was used to manipulate the skin tone and hairstyle of our candidates. In the first experiment, people read the webpage of a single candidate. Our goal here was to determine whether phenotype mattered at all. In the second experiment, we introduced a light-skinned, straight-haired opponent and varied the phenotype of one of the candidates. Our thinking here was that appearances are relative—what is considered light or dark, and straight or curly, all depends on the presence of a comparison candidate. Below, we report our findings for men and women respondents separately, since we believe that these groups may respond differently to Black women candidates.

Experiment 1

We conducted an online survey experiment on 1,292 respondents who identified as belonging to a non-White category. The survey was conducted on May 17, 2017, on Amazon Mechanical Turk (MTurk), and respondents were paid $1.00 for their participation. We focus our findings on the 516 Black respondents. Our sample includes about 51% women, 52% Democrats, 12% Republicans, and 33% Independents (see the Appendix for more descriptive statistics from Experiment 1). The merit of using MTurk for experimental research is a subject of ongoing debate (e.g., Clifford, Jewell, and Wagonner 2015; Berinsky, Huber, and Lenz 2012; Logan, et al. 2017; Huff and Tingley 2015; Thomas and Clifford 2017). We recognize the strengths and weaknesses of using MTurk for research. On the one hand, the sample we collected from MTurk skews relatively young: the average age of Black women in our sample is about 35 (34.6), while the average age for Black men is about 31 (30.7), and it is possible that MTurk is unlikely to include older generations of Black respondents. Given generational differences in the decision of Black women to straighten their hair or wear it naturally, one of the drawbacks of using MTurk is that we may be less likely to receive responses from Black women who would punish a Black woman candidate for wearing her hair naturally. On the other hand, considering the current wave of candidates for office and the large young population of potential voters of color more generally, the younger respondents on MTurk offer a glimpse into the future of American politics. However, future studies should aim for more nationally representative samples.

We used Adobe Photoshop Creative Cloud to create six conditions in which we altered the hairstyle (braids, straight hair, or naturally curly hair) and skin tone (lighter or darker) of a Black woman. We used templates from Black women politicians' websites to create a fictional webpage and named our candidate Brenda Johnson. We programmed our survey using Qualtrics. After providing informed consent and answering demographic questions, respondents answered questions about identity, as well as other questions used both in larger surveys, such as the American National Election Study and the 2008 National Asian American Survey (Ramakrishnan, et al. 2012), and in previous candidate evaluation and political behavior research (Lerman, McCabe and Sadin 2015; Adida, Davenport and McClendon 2016; Newman, et al. n.d.). These included questions, used in other research on women candidates (Merolla, Sellers, and Lemi 2017), that measure candidate gender stereotypes (Dolan 2014b), and questions that reflect past theories of evaluations of Black women candidates (Philpot and Walton, Jr. 2007, 60) that use the concept of "linked fate" (Dawson 1994). Participants were randomly assigned to one of six experimental conditions using the Qualtrics randomizer. After exposure, respondents answered questions commonly asked in research on candidate evaluation (Weaver 2012; Terkildsen 1993; Sigelman, et al. 1995; Lerman, McCabe, and Sadin 2015; Alexander and Andersen 1993; McConnaughy et al. 2010). We also included dependent measures that asked respondents which groups within the legislature the official is likely to work with, and which organizations she is likely to work with and donate to, as past work on minority elites suggests phenotype may condition legislators' perceptions of political relationships (e.g., Brown 2014; Lemi 2018). The order in which our dependent variable questions were asked was randomized.

Table 7.1 Treatment Conditions
for Experiment 1

Condition	Skin tone	Hairstyle
Light Straight	Light	Straight
Dark Straight	Dark	Straight
Light Curly	Light	Curly
Dark Curly	Dark	Curly
Light Braids	Light	Braids
Dark Braids	Dark	Braids

Our six conditions are as follows: light skin and straightened hair (Light Straight), dark skin and straightened hair (Dark Straight), light skin and naturally curly hair (Light Curly), dark skin and naturally curly hair (Dark Curly), light skin and braided hair (Light Braids), and dark skin and braided hair (Dark Braids) (see Table 7.1). We are interested in the difference between Light Straight and all other conditions.

Findings

Recall that in our **closeness hypothesis**, we suspected that a more Afrocentric-appearing Black woman candidate would be more closely associated with Blackness, relative to a lighter-skinned, straight-haired candidate.[2] To measure a candidate's "closeness to Blackness" we asked respondents a number of questions about the candidate's perceived ideology, her issue qualifications, and who she was likely to serve and work with. We expected that respondents would view a more Afrocentric-appearing candidate as more liberal, more likely to focus on race relations, and more likely to serve Black Americans and work with organizations that serve Black people.

Ideology

In Figure 7.1, we report the difference between Light Straight and all other conditions. Estimates that cross the dotted line indicate that our treatments caused a difference in ratings, while estimates that do not cross the dotted line suggest our treatments did not cause differences. Positive estimates

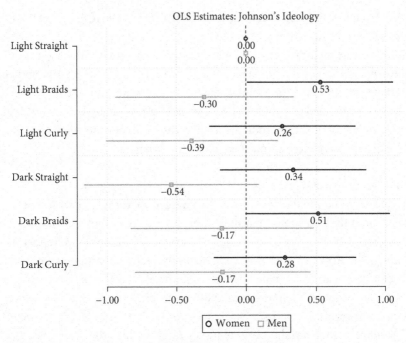

Figure 7.1 OLS estimates of Johnson's Ideology Ratings
Note: Bars are 95% confidence intervals.

mean respondents thought our candidate was more conservative; negative estimates mean respondents thought our candidate was more liberal. As the figure shows, relative to Light Straight, we cannot say with much confidence that our treatments caused shifts in ideology ratings; many of these estimates cross the dotted line at zero, indicating null effects. However, women tend to view Johnson as more conservative than Light Straight in all other conditions, especially in the Braids conditions (Light Braids: .53, p = .047; Dark Braids: .51, p = .052). By contrast, men consistently rate Johnson as more liberal than Light Straight in all other conditions. So far, this suggests that phenotype does not cause obvious shifts in ideology ratings, and we can reject our first hypothesis about the candidate's perceived closeness to Blackness—it does not apply to ideology.

Issue Qualifications

We now turn to which issues respondents believe Johnson is most qualified on (Weaver 2012), among immigration, economy, health care, education, safety, environment, women's issues, and race relations. Due to our small sample size, we are unable to accurately analyze these effects for women respondents, as issues such as immigration and health care received as few as three selections. However, our analysis suggests that, relative to the environment (an issue not explicitly about race or gender [e.g., Merolla et al. 2017]), phenotype makes no statistically significant difference in the issues respondents believe Johnson is qualified on. Thus, we can conclude that phenotype does not lead respondents to view the candidate as closer to Blackness, to the extent that issue qualifications communicate one's group closeness.

Advocacy for Group Interests

We asked respondents how much they agreed or disagreed with a statement about the candidate attending to the interests of different groups in the state, where 1=Strongly disagree and 7=Strongly agree. Here, we report the findings for African American residents in the state. We find no significant effect of our treatments on perceptions of Johnson serving African American residents, although men are marginally more likely to say Johnson serves African Americans when she is darker-skinned with braids (.55, p=.085). This suggests that variation in phenotype does *not* lead to perceptions that Johnson "serves African Americans."

Relationships in the Legislature

We now consider who respondents thought Johnson was likely to work with in the legislature. Here, we are interested in whether respondents said Johnson works with the Black Caucus. In Figure 7.2, we find no statistically significant effect for women. Black men are statistically significantly more likely to say Johnson works with the Black Caucus in the Dark Straight, Dark Curly, Light Braids, and the Dark Braids conditions than in the Light Straight condition. We find no evidence that variation in phenotype leads to different perceptions of Johnson working with the Democrats. Thus, to the extent that Johnson is viewed as closer to Blackness when she is shown with darker skin and non-straight hair, it is through the perception that she advocates for Black people in the legislature in an organized group that explicitly advocates for Black interests.

Organizations Johnson Works With

Here, we report whether respondents were more likely to list the National Association for the Advancement of Colored People (NAACP) as an organization Johnson works with or donates to. Again, we suspected that by

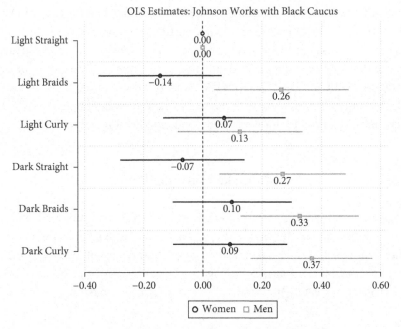

Figure 7.2 OLS Estimates of Johnson Working with Black Caucus
Note: Bars are 95% confidence intervals.

manipulating Johnson's phenotype to bring her closer to Blackness, people might be more likely to associate her with the NAACP. Responses were coded so that 1=Definitely works with this group and 4=Definitely does not work with this group. Positive estimates would suggest Johnson does not work with the group, while negative estimates suggest she does. Relative to Light Straight, men tend to be more likely to select the NAACP as a group Johnson works with or donates to in all conditions except Light Braids. Relative to Light Straight, women are statistically significantly more likely to list the NAACP as a group Johnson works with in the Dark Braids condition (−.31, p=.022), and significantly more likely to say she donates to the NAACP in the Dark Curly condition (−.36, p=.028).

Summary
So far, we find that more-Afrocentric phenotypes lead Black respondents to perceive a candidate to be closer to Blackness, at least to the extent that she works with organizations that serve Black interests. We find that phenotype does *not* matter for perceptions of ideology or issue qualifications. However,

relative to her presentation as Light Straight, Black men tend to view Johnson as more liberal in all other conditions. Furthermore, Black men tend to be more likely to say Johnson works with the Black Caucus in the legislature as she deviates from Light Straight. And Black men tend to say Johnson associates with the NAACP. Thus, Black men are the voters likely to view Black women candidates with darker skin and non-straight hair as closer to Blackness. The findings for women respondents are more mixed.

Candidate Favorability

We now turn to our empowerment and internal discrimination hypotheses. Recall that we expected Black men and women to react to our candidate in one of two ways—favorably or negatively. After randomly exposing respondents to one of the six webpages, we measured three variables: likelihood of voting, feeling thermometer ratings, and trait evaluations.

Likelihood of Voting

We find few significant effects. In Figure 7.3, we report the average treatment effects relative to the Light Straight baseline. As the figure shows, there is no statistically significant difference between Light Straight and any other condition among both women and men. However, the estimates tend to be positive. With the exception of Light Braids, women tend to say they would be more likely to vote for Johnson in the more Afrocentric conditions, and a similar trend occurs among men. Overall, there appears to be tentative support for the empowerment hypothesis among both men and women on the likelihood of voting for Johnson.

Feeling Thermometer

We find no statistically significant effect of our treatments on feeling thermometer ratings either. However, relative to Light Straight, both men and women tend to feel warmer toward Johnson in the Dark Straight, Light Curly, and Dark Curly conditions, and cooler toward Johnson in the Light Braids condition. Men and women diverge in the Dark Braids condition, with men feeling warmer toward Johnson and women feeling cooler. Again, this suggests tentative support for both the empowerment hypothesis and the internal discrimination hypothesis—empowerment for men and internal discrimination for women.

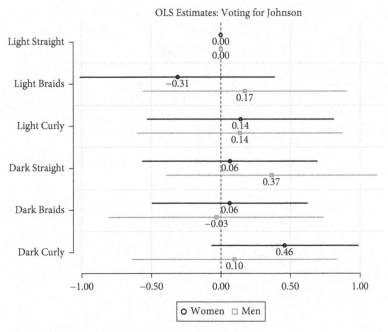

Figure 7.3 OLS Estimates of Voting for Johnson
Note: Bars are 95% confidence intervals

Trait Evaluations

We now turn to trait evaluations. Again, most of our effects are not statistically significant, but they reveal interesting differences among women and men. In Figure 7.4, we report perceptions of Johnson as experienced, where higher values indicate that respondents view her as more experienced. Black women tend to rate Johnson as more experienced in the darker-skin/non-straight hair conditions, relative to Light Straight. By contrast, Black men consistently rate Johnson as less experienced. This suggests tentative support for both hypotheses again: Johnson's phenotype appears to have a positive effect on experience ratings among women, and a negative effect among men. So far, distance from a Eurocentric appearance leads women to rate our candidate more favorably on experience, supporting the empowerment hypothesis.

We find some evidence that Black women also view Johnson as more hardworking in conditions other than Light Straight, supporting the empowerment hypothesis. Women tend to say that "hardworking" describes Johnson well in the Light Curly condition (.34, p=.061). Turning to trustworthiness,

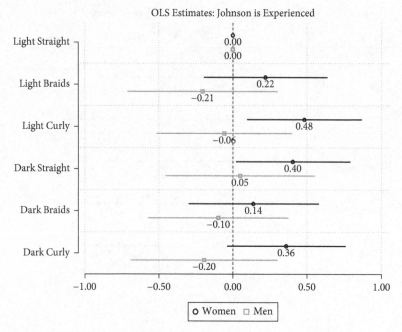

Figure 7.4 OLS Estimates of Johnson as Experienced
Note: Bars are 95% confidence intervals

we find no statistically significant treatment effects. Women and men also diverge on perceptions of Johnson as intelligent. Relative to Light Straight, women tend to give Johnson higher intelligence ratings in all conditions except the braids conditions, while men tend to give her lower ratings across all conditions.

Turning to perceptions of Johnson as qualified, women give Johnson a statistically significantly higher qualified rating in the Light Curly condition (.39, p=.030), while men give Johnson a higher qualified rating in Dark Straight (.41, p=.080). Women and men also diverge on their assessments of Johnson as warm. As Figure 7.5 shows, men assign more positive warmth ratings to Johnson in the Dark Straight (.56, p=.015) and Light Curly (.57, p=.013) conditions. By contrast, women tend to give Johnson negative warmth ratings relative to Light Straight. The men are consistent with the empowerment hypothesis, the women with the internal discrimination hypothesis.

We find no statistically significant differences in ratings of Johnson as compassionate. However, women tend to assign Johnson lower compassion

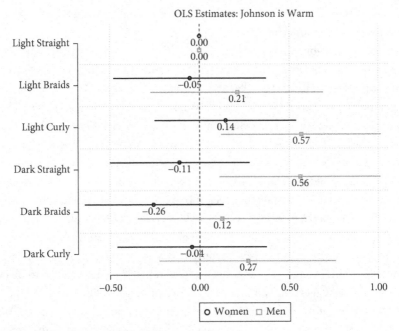

Figure 7.5 OLS Estimates of Johnson as Warm
Note: Bars indicate 95% confidence intervals

ratings in the Dark Straight, Light Braids, and Dark Braids conditions, relative to Light Straight. By contrast, men assign Johnson higher compassion ratings than Light Straight in every other condition except for Dark Braids. Similarly, we find no statistically significant effect on Johnson's ratings as being able to compromise. Both men and women tend to give Johnson a lower rating on this trait in the Dark Braids condition, relative to Light Straight.

We now turn to traits that are often uniquely applied to Black women. We find no statistically significant effect of our treatments on resilience ratings. We also find that women in the Light Braids condition tend to say Johnson is uncontrolled, relative to Light Straight (.45, p=.065), with no statistically significant effects for men. Turning to the last trait, self-reliance, we find that women view Johnson as more self-reliant than Light Straight in the Dark Straight (.40, p=.039), Light Curly (.48, p=.015), and Dark Curly (.36, p=.076) conditions. By contrast, men generally give Johnson lower self-reliance ratings in all conditions except the Dark Straight condition. Thus far, we find tentative support for both hypotheses regarding voting, feeling thermometer ratings, and trait evaluations.

The findings for Experiment 1 are puzzling. Contrary to what theory and past research would suggest, Black women tend to view Johnson less favorably on personable traits—warmth, compassion, ability to compromise, etc.—but more favorably on traits associated with a competent leader—experienced, hardworking, self-reliant, and intelligent. Why? We hypothesize that, for Black women, exposure to a more Afrocentric phenotype may activate a gender-race linked fate for action, but not necessarily a personal affinity for a candidate (Dawson 1994; Philpot and Walton, Jr. 2007). Voting is an action, and it is plausible that even if Black women tend to view the candidate as less likeable, for example, they will not necessarily withhold their vote or doubt her leadership qualities, absent all other information about the candidate. Furthermore, given Black women's tendency to label Johnson as "uncontrolled" in the Light Braids condition—a stereotype often applied to Black women—we suggest that an internal politics of respectability (e.g., Jefferson 2018) may be at play and may operate differently among Black women. We note that the term "uncontrolled" may have multiple interpretations, referring to someone who is not easily controlled by others or to someone who is uncontrollable. We left the meaning of this trait in the experiments open to the respondents' interpretation.

In line with findings from our focus groups, Black women may have specific impressions of a Black woman candidate who wears a natural hairstyle, but when it comes to voting and rating her qualifications for the job, support is still possible. Thus, there is a specific dynamic among Black women: Black women voters may infer that a more Afrocentric candidate is a more qualified leader who will advocate for their interests and thus may vote for her, but they may also believe that the candidate will have a harder time as a leader given her Afrocentric phenotype. It is possible that Black women's responses to the candidate are a form of the appearance enforcement that also occurs in Black Greek Letter Organizations (see Chapter 5).

These findings differ from previous studies in specific and meaningful ways. Terkildsen's (1993) study on White evaluations of lighter and darker Black men candidates illustrated the complex relationship between level of prejudice toward Black people (1051) and the tendency to "self-monitor" (1037), where the most prejudiced Whites, without a filter for political correctness, expressed more support for a lighter-skinned candidate, while those with a filter inflated their support for a darker-skinned candidate

(1046). While we do not include measures of prejudice or self-monitoring in Experiment 1, we suggest that for Black respondents, racial prejudice and self-monitoring may not apply to evaluations of Black women candidates, as there is a descriptive representative element, or the presence of a Black candidate representing Black voters, to evaluations of Black women candidates (i.e., Mansbridge 1999). Future research may explore such a dynamic.

Our findings contrast with Lerman et al. (2015), who found that Black conservative Democrats were more likely to prefer a darker-skinned Black man candidate over a lighter-skinned one (64), arguing that Black Democratic conservatives use skin tone to infer Black candidates' issue stances as conservative (66, 74). Our sample characteristics and small sample size in Experiment 1 do not permit us to speak to the behavior of Black Democratic conservatives—the majority of Black women in our sample are Democratic (64.89%) and somewhat liberal (mean=3.66, 1=very conservative to 5=very liberal). This ideological pattern is similar among Black men (mean ideology=3.40), though fewer Black men are Democrats (39.68%). It is possible that Black women in this sample were "projecting" their ideology onto the candidate (Lerman and Sadin 2016, 150, 153–54), but our sample is not large enough to thoroughly test this explanation. Still, this research suggests that Black women's support for Black women candidates may be conditional on phenotype.

Our findings also differ from Weaver (2012), who hypothesized that White women would not discriminate against darker-skinned Black men candidates (170), and found that support for the Black candidate was highest when he was darker-skinned (179, 182). Weaver (2012) suggested that "race and color are operating as a signal for female and liberal voters about . . . a compassionate/non-compassionate dimension" (185). Black respondents may use skin tone and hairstyle in this way as well, but we suggest that there is a tension in how skin tone and hairstyle are used among Black women respondents. Perhaps dark skin and natural hair are used to infer the candidate's ability get the job done, thus support from voters, as well as the candidate as a person, thus poor trait evaluations of the candidate by the voter when voting. We do not preclude the possibility that changing the candidate's phenotype changed other variables relevant to our outcomes, such as perceptions of the candidate's socioeconomic class.

Our findings illustrate that hairstyle and skin tone may matter to Black voters in their evaluations of Black women candidates. However, appearances are relative. As a result, our findings differ from Orey and Zhang (2019), who compared Black women candidates who varied in skin tone and hairstyle to a Black man candidate who served as the control condition. Our findings are consistent with Burge et al. (2020).

How is a Black woman candidate with a more Afrocentric appearance evaluated when she runs against a Black woman with a more Eurocentric appearance? How do Democrats, the voters most likely to be faced with a choice between two Black women, respond to such differences? To answer these questions, we turn to Experiment 2.

Experiment 2

Our second experiment was designed much like the first. We targeted 2,400 Black and White Democratic survey respondents from Lucid, a market research firm. We report findings for Black respondents here. The experiment was conducted from December 17, 2018, to January 2, 2019. Our sample is a nationwide sample of about 46% women with a mean age of about 42 years, who on average have some college or an associate's degree and on average have household incomes between $40,000 and $49,999 (see Appendix for a table of descriptive statistics). This study included six conditions in which a candidate named Brenda Johnson, who was presented with a variety of skin tones and hairstyles, ran against Tiffany McKinsey, a light-skinned Black woman with straight hair. The goal of this design was to make phenotype salient to Black voters (Weaver 2012, Study 2). The photos of the candidates were edited to vary the skin tone and hairstyle of Brenda Johnson while holding Tiffany McKinsey's constant. The six conditions featured Johnson as Light Straight, Dark Straight, Light Curly, Dark Curly, Light Locs, and Dark Locs, while McKinsey's phenotype was Light Straight. The photos in Figures 7.6–7.11 display the conditions.

The election we constructed was a special election Democratic one, as most Black women, and minority women generally, in office are Democrats (Center for American Women and Politics 2017; see Merolla, Sellers, and Lemi [2017] for an analysis that separates gender from party). As in Experiment 1, our survey was programmed in Qualtrics and participants were randomly assigned to an experimental condition using the randomizer. Pretreatment, respondents answered a series of questions about social and political attitudes, as well as questions about race and gender identity.

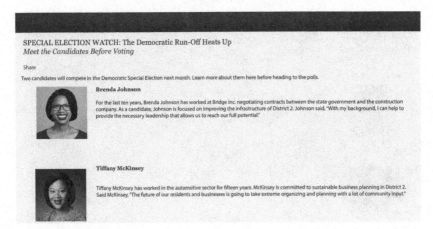

Figure 7.6 Light Straight

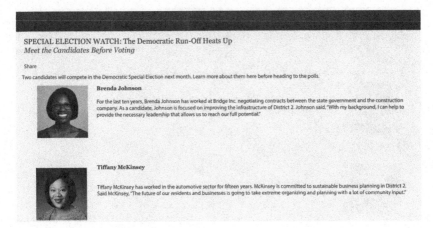

Figure 7.7 Dark Straight

Findings

As in Experiment 1, we focus our findings in this experiment on Black respondents and on results that were marginally or statistically significant. We use two models to estimate the effects of our treatments on two groups: Black women and Black men. We explore several dependent variables: who respondents think will win the election, perceptions of the candidates' closeness to various groups, trait evaluations, the respondents'

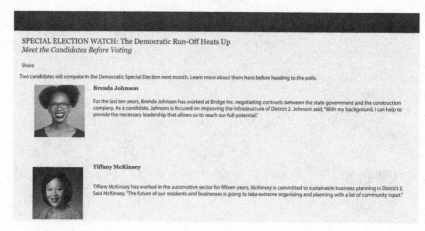

Figure 7.8 Light Curly

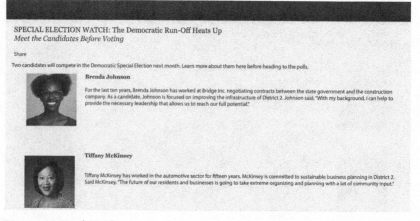

Figure 7.9 Dark Curly

commonality with the candidates, and the issues respondents believe the candidates support. In what follows, we find that our treatments had distinct effects on Black women and Black men.

Who Will Win?

After exposure to the article describing the candidates, we asked respondents, "Which candidate do you think will win this election?" We chose this question instead of "Which candidate would you vote for?" to gain

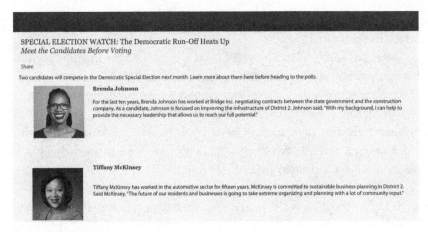

Figure 7.10 Light Locs

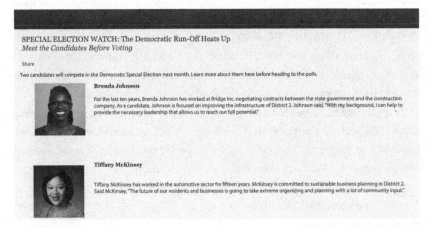

Figure 7.11 Dark Locs

a more accurate impression of respondents' perceptions of the candidates, as it may be difficult to imagine oneself voting for a candidate outside one's own district (Bauer and Carpinella 2018, 898). Overall, about 56% of Black respondents said Johnson would win, and about 44% of respondents said McKinsey would win. To determine the effects of our treatments on respondents' perceptions of who would win, we conducted a linear regression with robust standard errors, where our outcome variable is 1=Johnson is listed as the probable winner and 0=McKinsey is listed as the probable winner. This allows us to measure the likelihood of one candidate being selected relative to the other.

There are few statistically significant differences by treatment group in assessments of the probable winner. Among Black women, on average, Johnson is less likely to be selected as the probable winner, relative to McKinsey, when Johnson presents as Light Curly (−.15, p = .052). Substantively, this suggests that Johnson's light skin and curly hair pushes Black women toward McKinsey, a Black woman who is similarly lighter-skinned but with straight hair. While not statistically significant, and excepting the Dark Straight condition, each change in Johnson's phenotype from Light Straight has a negative effect on listing Johnson as the probable winner.

Among men, on average, Johnson is more likely than McKinsey to be selected as the probable winner in all treatment conditions, though these effects are not statistically significant. As with Black women, when Johnson is Dark Straight, Johnson tends to be more likely than McKinsey to be selected as the probable winner (.14, p=.052). That McKinsey tends to be less likely to be selected when Johnson is darker-skinned with straight hair suggests that when Black men are presented with two Black women candidates with straight hair, they tend to support the darker-skinned candidate.

Thus far, we have two distinct patterns. These findings suggest that when Black Democrats are presented with two Black women Democrats with straight hair, they may be more likely to support the darker-skinned woman (e.g., Burge et al. 2020). However, if one of the women is lighter-skinned with curly hair, Black women may be pushed toward her lighter-skinned, straight-haired opponent. By contrast, on average, Black men tend to view a darker-skinned candidate as a probable winner.

Group Closeness

Our core investigation explores how phenotypical markers and choice of hairstyle communicate a Black woman candidate's "degree of Blackness." To this end, we asked respondents which groups each candidate was "very close" to and gave them the option to check numerous groups in randomized order. Here, we are interested in the extent to which Black respondents view our candidates as "very close" to Black Americans and White Americans. The idea is that a more Afrocentric candidate will be viewed as close to Black Americans, while a more Eurocentric candidate will be viewed as close to White Americans. We report three sets of results: (1) Johnson's closeness to

Black and White Americans, (2) McKinsey's closeness to Black and White Americans, and (3) the relative difference in the probability of listing each candidate as close to Black and White Americans.

We find no statistically significant effect of our treatments on perceptions of Johnson's closeness to Black *or* White people. We also find no significant effect of variation in Johnson's phenotype on perceptions of McKinsey's closeness to Black Americans among Black women. When Johnson is Dark Straight (−.13, p=.057) and Dark Locs (−.21, p=.003), men are less likely to select Black Americans as one of the groups to which McKinsey is very close.

Turning to McKinsey's closeness to White people, we find that manipulating Johnson's appearance has statistically significant effects on perceptions of McKinsey. Relative to Light Straight, Black women participants viewing Johnson in the Dark Curly condition (.16, p=.008) as well as the Dark Locs condition (.12, p=.050) are more likely to list McKinsey as very close to White people. Black men see McKinsey as very close to White people when Johnson is Dark Straight (.10, p=.044) and Dark Locs (.09, p=.093).

We now turn to the relative difference in the likelihood of listing Johnson and McKinsey as very close to Black or White Americans. Here, we use ordinary least squares regression, and we create four variables where 1=Johnson was listed as very close to Black (White) people and 0=McKinsey was listed as very close to Black (White) people. This allows us to measure whether Johnson is more likely than McKinsey to be viewed as close to Black or White people. We find no statistically significant effect in the responses of Black women. Black men are more likely to say Johnson is very close to Black people than they are to say McKinsey is very close to Black people in all conditions: Dark Straight (.19, p=.003), Light Curly (.13, p=.042), Dark Curly (.12, p=.071), Light Locs (.12, p=.059), and Dark Locs (.22, p=.002).

In terms of relative closeness to White people, Black women tend to be more likely to see McKinsey as very close to White people when Johnson is Dark Locs (−.31, p=.066). There are no statistically significant differences among men's responses. Taken together, these findings suggest that when two Black women run against each other, both Black men and Black women make inferences about the candidates' closeness to Black and White people. If one candidate is darker-skinned and/or wearing natural hair, both men and women view the candidate as close to Black people. Phenotype does not appear to distance the candidate from White people in the eyes of Black voters, but the candidate's appearance pushes the candidate closer to Black people. The presence of a more Afrocentric candidate also alters perceptions of the opponent among Black men and women, but in different ways. While Black men are less likely to view a lighter-skinned, straight-haired candidate as close to Black people when she runs against a darker-skinned woman with locs, seeing the two candidates together does not push women to view the lighter-skinned candidate as close to Black people as an individual.

When it comes to relative closeness ratings, Black men consistently view the more Afrocentric candidate as close to Black people, but Black women's relative evaluations of the candidates' closeness to Black people generally do not differ.

Commonality

Previous research suggests Black women have a strong connection to Black women candidates that differs from the connection Black men might have to Black women candidates (Philpot and Walton 2007). We wanted to know how much in common Black respondents perceived they had with our candidates. Post-treatment, they were asked, "How much do you personally have in common with the candidate?" This variable is coded so that lower values mean less in common and higher values mean more in common.

We first report effects on commonality ratings with Johnson. On average, variation in Johnson's phenotype has no statistically significant effect on Black women or men's responses. Black women in the Dark Straight condition give McKinsey statistically significantly higher commonality scores (.28, p=.036). Looking at Black men's ratings of commonality with McKinsey, again, we find no statistically significant effects. Turning to relative differences with a variable where 1=Johnson's commonality score is higher than McKinsey's and 0=McKinsey's score is higher than Johnson's, we generally do not find statistically significant differences.

Trait Evaluations

When we look at trait evaluations, the evidence suggests that some phenotype conditions affected ratings given to Johnson and McKinsey, but primarily for Black women. As with Experiment 1, we asked respondents to rate how well various words and phrases described each candidate: experienced, hardworking, intelligent, warm, compassionate, resilient in tough times, able to compromise, uncontrolled, self-reliant, and professional.

We begin with the ratings of Johnson. We find no statistically significant effects on experience ratings for Johnson. Black women give Johnson marginally significantly higher hardworking ratings in the Light Locs condition (.26, p=.060). Turning to intelligence ratings, Black women view Johnson as more intelligent in the Dark Curly condition (.28, p=.059). In terms of warmth, among women, relative to Light Straight, Johnson is rated warmer in the Light Curly (.31, p=.053) and Light Locs (.27, p=.082) conditions. We find no differences in compassion ratings.

Turning to resilience, there is no significant phenotypic effect on Black men. By contrast, Black women give Johnson higher resilience ratings in the Dark Straight (.29, p=.090), Light Curly (.32, p=.047), Dark Curly (.34, p=.035), and Light Locs (.47, p=.005) conditions. When we consider ratings of Johnson as uncontrolled, relative to Light Straight, Black men rate Johnson as more uncontrolled in the Light Locs condition (.40, p=.054). These findings show that Johnson's phenotype has no effect on women's ratings of her as uncontrolled. In short, relative to Light Straight, Black women view Johnson as more resilient and intelligent, and Black men perceive Johnson as uncontrolled when she wears a natural hairstyle.

Turning to perceptions of Johnson as self-reliant, we find no significant differences among Black men or women. When we consider perceptions of Johnson as professional, Black women tend to rate Johnson as more professional in the Dark Straight condition (.25, p=.078). While we find no significant effects on Black men, relative to Light Straight, Johnson is rated as less professional in all conditions. Thus far, Black women tend to assign positive traits to Johnson when she appears Afrocentric.

Trait Evaluations of McKinsey

We now turn to trait assessments of McKinsey, where again, most of the effects are on women. We find no statistically significant effects on the experience, intelligence, compassion, resilience, self-reliance, or uncontrolled ratings. Black women rate McKinsey as more hardworking in the Dark Straight (.35, p=.014) and Light Curly conditions (.27, p=.073). Black men view McKinsey as less hardworking in the Dark Straight (−.25, p=.068) and Dark Curly (−.26, p=.075) conditions. Turning to warmth ratings, relative to Light Straight, Black women tend to rate McKinsey as warmer in the Dark Straight condition (.29, p=.074).

In terms of professionalism ratings, Black women rate McKinsey as more professional in the Dark Straight (.25, p=.068) and Light Curly conditions (.22, p=.095), relative to the Light Straight condition. By contrast, Black men view McKinsey as less professional in the Dark Straight condition (−.22, p=.095). These results suggest that when two Black women run against each other, if phenotype is made salient, both candidates may fare better with Black women.

Relative Differences in Trait Evaluations

As with previous outcomes, we are interested in the relative differences in trait evaluations between the candidates. While we have evidence that varying one candidate's phenotype affects evaluations of the candidates as individuals, what matters is if a candidate's appearance offers her a competitive advantage. Here, we report whether Johnson received a higher score than McKinsey on a given trait. Again, as with Experiment 1, the baseline experimental category is the Light Straight condition because we are interested in how voters evaluate Black women candidates who do not conform to Eurocentric beauty standards. We created several dependent variables where 1=Johnson has a higher score on the trait than McKinsey and 0=Johnson has a lower score on the trait than McKinsey. Using linear regression to estimate average treatment effects, the interpretation is the average change in probability that Johnson is assigned a higher score than McKinsey.

Women are statistically significantly more likely to give Johnson a higher hardworking score than McKinsey in the Dark Curly condition (.25, p=.037). On intelligence, Black men view Johnson as more intelligent than McKinsey in the Dark Straight condition (.21, p=.049). Women are more likely to rate Johnson as more compassionate than McKinsey in the Light Curly (.22, p=.060) and Dark Curly (.28, p=.013) conditions. Relative to Light Straight, women view Johnson as more resilient than McKinsey in the Dark Curly condition (.25, p=.023). These findings suggest that the more Afrocentric Johnson appears, the higher the ratings she receives on these traits, relative to McKinsey.

Taken together, these findings suggest that when two Black women run against each other, the appearance of one affects the trait evaluations of the other. As individual candidates, Black women tend to view both candidates in a positive light the more Afrocentric one candidate becomes. We find little evidence that Black men respond to either candidate when we vary the phenotype of one, as we find few statistically significant differences among men. This suggests general support for the empowerment hypothesis for individual candidates, particularly among Black women.

Issues

We now turn to perceptions of the issues each candidate supports. Post-treatment, respondents were asked to select the issues they believe the candidates support: (1) building affordable housing, (2) growing public transportation, (3) allowing undocumented immigrants to access state services, (4) making it easier for small businesses in the state, (5) giving tax breaks to large corporations, (6) increasing access to contraceptives in high schools without parental consent, (7) using state funds to support pre-kindergarten programs, (8) developing programs to clean up pollution in the state, (9) and providing paid family leave for state workers. These issues are a combination of raced, gendered, and seemingly race- and gender-neutral issues, and their use here follows previous research (e.g., Merolla et al. 2017).

Johnson
We begin with Johnson, where we find few differences among men and women's responses. Black women are less likely to say Johnson supports granting undocumented immigrants' access to state services in the Dark Curly (−.13, p=.098), Light Locs (−.19, p=.014), and Dark Locs (−.20, p=.015) conditions, relative to Light Straight. This suggests that Black women perceive Johnson as less liberal on immigration issues in more Afrocentric conditions, perhaps due to the perception of poor relations between Latinx immigrants and Black Americans (e.g., Hero and Preuhs 2013). Black women are also less likely to say Johnson supports corporate tax breaks in the Light Curly (−.18, p=.025), Dark Curly (−.24, p=.002), and Dark Locs (−.16, p=.055) conditions, as are Black men in the Dark Straight (−.14, p=.058) condition. Women are more likely to say Johnson supports pre-kindergarten programs in the Dark Curly condition (.15, p=.059), relative to Light Straight. While we find null effects among women on perceptions of Johnson's stance on pollution, Black men are less likely to say Johnson supports pollution programs in all conditions, relative to Light Straight. On family leave, we find no average differences among women, but relative to Light Straight, men are less likely to say Johnson supports family leave in the Dark Curly condition (−.15, p=.048). Thus far, the evidence suggests that varying Johnson's phenotype caused shifts in perceptions of her stances on some issues, primarily among Black women.

McKinsey
Assessing evaluations of McKinsey, we find that Black women tend to view her as less likely to support affordable housing when Johnson is presented in the Dark Curly (−.14, p=.063), Light Locs (−.18, p=.016), and Dark Locs (−.20, p=.012) conditions, as do Black men in the Dark Straight condition (−.14, p=.061). Black women view McKinsey as more likely to support granting undocumented immigrants' access to state programs when Johnson

is Dark Curly (.14, p=.075), but less likely to support small businesses when Johnson is Dark Locs (−.13, p=.098). When Johnson is Dark Curly, women are more likely to say McKinsey supports corporate tax breaks (.18, p=.022). On pre-kindergarten programs, relative to Light Straight, Black women view McKinsey as less likely to support such programs in *every* condition. Thus far, the findings suggest that varying Johnson's phenotype led to changes in perceptions of McKinsey's issue stances, primarily among Black women.

Relative Differences in Issue Stances

We now consider the relative differences in perceptions of the candidates' issue stances. Is Johnson more or less likely to be viewed as supportive of a particular issue relative to Johnson? We conduct several linear regressions where the outcome variable is 1=Johnson supports an issue and 0=McKinsey supports an issue. This allows us to determine if Johnson is more or less likely than McKinsey to be listed as supporting a given issue by respondents. If there is no statistically significant difference, this may be interpreted as respondents being equally likely to list a given issue as an issue that Johnson and McKinsey support.

Among women, Johnson is perceived to be more likely than McKinsey to support affordable housing (Dark Curly: .17, p=.022; Light Locs: .21, p=.007; Dark Locs: .20, p=.013), less likely to support granting undocumented immigrants access to state services (Dark Curly: −.18, p=.038), more likely to support small businesses (Light Locs: .13, p=.092; Dark Locs: .15, p=.065), less likely to support corporate tax breaks (Dark Curly: −.21, p=.016), and more likely to support state-sponsored pre-kindergarten programs in all conditions, relative to Light Straight. Among men, Johnson is perceived to be more likely than McKinsey to support affordable housing (Dark Straight: .12, p=.089), more likely to support public transit (Dark Straight: .12, = .091), less likely to support small businesses (Dark Curly: −.12, p = .096), and less likely to support clean-up programs (Dark Curly: −.14, p = .067). Again, phenotype matters for issue stances—but mostly for Black women.

Discussion of Experiment 2

These findings suggest that when two Black women run against each other, if one deviates from Light Straight in hairstyle or skin tone or both, Black voters may adjust their perceptions of both candidates individually and relative to each other. Previous research does not offer a clear explanation for these patterns, especially for men. However, that Black respondents tend to see Johnson as more liberal on some issues in the more Afrocentric phenotype conditions is consistent with the notion that minority candidates are perceived as more ideologically liberal (Sigelman et al. 1995).

Of course, by manipulating Johnson's phenotype, we may have manipulated cues about her socioeconomic status. Straightened hair may be indicative of a higher class (Lindsey 2017). To gauge this, post-treatment, we asked respondents how much debt they believed each candidate carried. This question was inspired by coverage of Stacey Abrams's debt during her campaign.[3] Across all Black respondents, we find minimal evidence that variation in Johnson's phenotype led to changes in perceptions of how much debt each candidate had. On average, Johnson receives lower debt ratings in the Dark Locs condition (–.16, p=.599), and this is not statistically significant. Black women give McKinsey in the Light Locs condition higher debt ratings than McKinsey in the Light Straight condition (.71, p=.079). These findings are the opposite of what we might expect, as one might expect a woman with straightened hair to be perceived as having less debt and to be of a higher socioeconomic level. We do not believe our conditions caused systematic changes in respondents' inferences about the candidates' socioeconomic backgrounds in a way that matters for our findings.

The findings presented here raise additional research questions. Do these patterns vary by a sense of racial and/or gender consciousness? Why does a more Afrocentric-appearing Johnson result in the consistent perception among Black women that Johnson supports state-sponsored prekindergarten programs? Why does phenotype primarily move the issue perceptions of women but not men? In the next chapter, we turn our attention to the role of linked fate in evaluations of Black women candidates.

8

Linked Fate, Black Voters, and Black Women Candidates

> Black women sharing close ties with each other, politically or emotionally, are not the enemies of Black men.
>
> —Audre Lorde

In April 2020, *Politico* ran a story about the Ohio Congressional Democratic primary race between the incumbent, Representative Joyce Beatty, and the challenger, Morgan Harper (Mutnick et al. 2020). The headline declared, "Black Caucus seeks to squash liberal insurgents" and featured a photo of Beatty standing in front of a crowd while speaking and Harper appearing to wait behind Beatty for her turn to speak. Thirty years separate the two politicians, as Beatty is a Boomer and Harper is a Millennial (Cohen and Grim 2019). While Beatty wears a short, coiffed, straightened hairstyle, Harper's hair is shoulder-length with loose curls. Relative to each other, Beatty is darker-skinned and Harper is lighter-skinned. The article asserted that the Congressional Black Caucus backed Beatty, with Beatty stating, "When you attack a hard-working member of the Congressional Black Caucus, we fight back" (Mutnick et al. 2020). While Harper represented a disruption to the status quo and was part of the progressive wing of the Democratic Party, the article noted that Beatty had followed "the old rules of Democratic Party politics" and "[had] done everything right" (Cohen and Grim 2019). Harper ultimately lost the primary election.

This electoral example illustrates the complex power dynamics of internal group differences among Black Democrats by generation, skin tone, and styling choices. This story also raises questions about the future of the Democratic Party and about Black women as the "backbone" of the party (Gillespie and Brown 2019). If it is the case that Black women Millennials tend to be naturalistas, and that this generation poses challenges to the Black

Sister Style. Nadia E. Brown and Danielle Casarez Lemi, Oxford University Press (2021). © Oxford University Press.
DOI: 10.1093/oso/9780197540572.003.0008

Democratic establishment, do differences in appearance have the potential to cause a split among Democratic voters who have strong racial and gender identities? In other words, do the appearances of Black women candidates activate group identity for Black voters?

In this chapter, we examine how linked fate may shape how Black voters respond to Black women candidates. We provide a brief review of the relevant literature on linked fate and colorism, a novel inclusion to this foundational concept in Black politics. In this chapter, we include colorism in an analysis of linked fate and its significance to vote choice, and we more fully flesh out these implications for the appeal of Black women candidates to men and women voters who report a sense of linked fate. Using experimental data, we do not find strong evidence of heterogeneity by linked fate. We end the chapter with a discussion of how Black women candidates' bodies influence vote choice.

Linked Fate, Colorism, and Black Women

Linked fate is one of the most important concepts in the study of race and political behavior in political science. The concept, theorized by Dawson (1994), was initially developed out of the political experiences of African Americans. When individuals feel that race is a determinant of their life chances, or that their race is linked to their life fate, it is rational for those individuals to make political decisions based on group racial interests (Dawson 1994, 61). A sense of racial linked fate, then, becomes a measure of group political consciousness (McClain et al. 2009). The concept has been applied to numerous other contexts in which a particular identity may be salient. For example, skin tone (Sanchez and Masuoka 2010), partisanship (Morin et al. 2020), discrimination (Masuoka 2006), candidate preferences (Schildkraut 2017), religiosity (Cassese and Holman 2016), marital status (Stout et al. 2017), and other identities, such as class (Gay et al. 2016, 128), are all associated with linked fate. Exporting a concept developed out of Black American politics to newly created "groups" like Latinx and Asian Americans may make little analytical sense (e.g. Lee 2008; McClain et al. 2009; Mora n.d.; Junn and Masuoka 2008). Sanchez and Vargas (2016), for example, recommend against using linked fate to analyze the political behaviors of non-Black Americans. Still, the concept remains the preferred tool for linking identity to politics (Lee 2008; Masuoka and Junn 2013, 105).

To date, however, scholars have yet to consider distinct forms of race-gender linked fate (Simien 2005) as it relates to preferences for particular raced-gendered candidates. Race-gender linked fate is the idea that individuals feel their life chances are tied to members of their gender group within their racial group (Simien 2005). Some evidence suggests that women of color who have a stronger sense of linked fate with other racial minorities are those more likely to support women of color candidates (Gershon et al. 2019). Previous work has found that Black women report higher levels of racial linked fate than gender linked fate (Gay and Tate 1998, 175). Indeed, Black women may have a unique sense of race-gender linked fate that encourages support for Black women candidates (Philpot and Walton 2007, 60). Yet, other work has found no statistically significant relationship between racial linked fate and evaluations of Black men candidates who vary in skin tone (Lerman et al. 2015). Whether race-gender linked fate has any bearing on Black voter evaluations of Black women candidates who vary in phenotype has yet to be studied.

Another gap in existing research is the relationship between skin tone and linked fate among Black Americans. In one study (Hochschild and Weaver 2007, 658), variation in skin tone was found to be irrelevant to reported linked fate, in large part, the authors argued, because internal colorism does not necessarily conflict with racial group unity. By contrast, Lemi and Brown (2020) found that skin tone was indeed consequential for feeling racial linked fate—among Black women. Using data from the 2016 Collaborative Multiracial Post-Election Survey, Lemi and Brown (2020) found that the darker Black Americans perceive their skin tone to be, the more likely they are to report feeling linked fate, and that this relationship was driven by Black women.

Taken together, the evidence to date suggests three potential outcomes regarding the role of linked fate in Black voter evaluations of Black women candidates who vary in skin tone and hairstyle. A first hypothesis is that there may be no statistically significant differences between Black voters who feel linked fate and those who do not. This hypothesis stems from Hochschild and Weaver's (2007) null finding on the relationship between linked fate and skin tone, as well as Lerman et al.'s (2015) null finding of an interaction between linked fate and Black voter preferences for lighter- and darker-skinned Black men candidates.

A second hypothesis is that Black voters with linked fate will rate a more Afrocentric candidate more favorably. This hypothesis builds on the hypothesis, from Experiment 1 in Chapter 7, that Black voters associate darker skin and natural hairstyles with closeness to Blackness, a salient identity that informs their political preferences. Indeed, Black voters associate darker skin and natural hairstyles with an ability to represent Black interests (Orey and Zhang 2019; Burge et al. 2020).

A third hypothesis is that there will be heterogeneity by race-gender linked fate among Black men and women. Previous research shows that race linked fate and gender linked fate interact to shape Black women's opinions on racial issues (Gay and Tate 1998; Simien 2005). Building on this finding, Simien (2005) has argued that rather than focus on race linked fate in studies of Black American political behavior, scholars should instead consider how Black women feel a sense of linked fate with other Black women and how Black men feel a sense of linked fate with other Black men. Simien (2005, 543) found that Black women were less likely than Black men to feel a sense of racial linked fate. Thus, we hypothesize that there will be heterogeneity among Black men and women by their sense of race-gender linked fate.

Findings

We return to the experiments conducted in the previous chapter and examine how Black voters may differ by linked fate in their responses to Black women candidates who vary in skin tone and hairstyle.

Experiment 1

In Experiment 1, recall that we had six experimental conditions: Light Straight, Light Braids, Light Curly, Dark Straight, Dark Braids, and Dark Curly. All respondents were asked whether they felt that what happens to their racial group affects them as an individual. We interacted an indicator variable for linked fate with treatment condition. Because of our small sample size, we do not disaggregate by gender. Using OLS with robust standard errors, we do not find a statistically significant interaction between linked fate and treatment conditions for all but two of our outcome variables from Experiment 1. Respondents with linked fate in the Dark Braids condition were more likely to list the Black Caucus as an organization with whom the candidate works (.467, p = .031). However, respondents with linked fate in the Dark Curly condition rated the candidate an average of about 2.5 points cooler on the feeling thermometer (–2.51, p = .050).

Experiment 2

In Experiment 2, recall that there were two candidates: Brenda Johnson and Tiffany McKinsey. We manipulated the appearance of Johnson to be Light Straight, Dark Straight, Light Curly, Dark Curly, Light Locs, and Dark Locs, while holding McKinsey's appearance stable with light skin and straight hair. For this analysis, we interacted indicator variables for racial linked fate and race-gender linked fate with treatment conditions. Recall that in Experiment 2, we were interested in the comparisons that voters draw between two Black women candidates running against each other—one with lighter skin and straight hair, and the other with an appearance that varied. As such, we assess whether Black voters with racial linked fate and race-gender linked fate are more likely to rate Johnson in a specific way in particular conditions than respondents without linked fate with a series of indicator variables.

Racial Linked Fate

We do not find differences by racial linked fate across all respondents. Across all respondents' perceptions of differences between the candidates—Johnson's likelihood of winning, Johnson's closeness to Black and White people relative to McKinsey's closeness, Johnson's commonality with respondents relative to McKinsey's, trait assessments of Johnson relative to McKinsey, and the belief that Johnson supports specific issues relative to McKinsey—we do not find statistically significant differences ($p < .05$) between respondents with racial linked fate and those without racial linked fate across treatment conditions. These findings are consistent with Hochschild and Weaver (2007) and Lerman et al. (2015). In sum, the salience of different skin tones and hairstyles does not activate racial linked fate differences among Black voters.

Race-Gender Linked Fate

To assess our third possible outcome, we interacted race-gender linked fate by treatment condition separately for men and women. Because we are interested in differences among men and women, rather than differences between men and women, we used separate models. Again, we are focused on how Black voters rate Johnson relative to McKinsey and whether individuals with race-gender linked fate are more likely than those without race-gender linked fate to rate Johnson a particular way relative to McKinsey by treatment condition. As with racial linked fate, we find minimal evidence that differences in evaluations of Black women candidates exist among Black men and women who differ in their sense of race-gender linked fate.[1] Table 8.1 summarizes the statistically significant findings. As this table shows, women with race-gender linked fate are more likely to say Johnson will win the election when Johnson is presented as Light Curly. By contrast, men with race-gender linked fate are less likely to say Johnson will win the election, relative to McKinsey, when Johnson is presented as Dark Curly. When Johnson is presented as Light Locs, women with race-gender linked fate tend to be less likely to say Johnson is very close to Black people relative to saying McKinsey is very close to Black people. Men with race-gender linked fate are also less likely to assign Johnson a higher score than McKinsey on resilience, uncontrolled, and self-reliant when Johnson is presented in the Dark Straight and Dark Curly conditions. In other words, among men, McKinsey performs better on those trait assessments. Men are also less likely to select affordable housing as an issue Johnson supports, relative to selecting it for

Table 8.1 Race-Gender Linked Fate and Evaluations of Johnson Relative to McKinsey

	Women	Men
Who Wins?[2] (1=Johnson, 0=McKinsey)		
Light Curly	.32, p=.049	
Dark Curly		−.32, p=.041
Close to Black People[3]		
Light Locs	−2.82, p = .028	
Traits[4]		
Intelligent *Dark Locs*	.78, p = .011	
Resilient *Dark Straight*	.62, p = .016	−.48, p = .015
Uncontrolled *Dark Curly*		−.53, p = .023
Self-reliant *Dark Curly*		−.58, p = .007
Issues[5]		
Housing *Light Locs*		−.48, p = .002

McKinsey. When Johnson is shown as Dark Locs and Dark Straight, women with race-gender linked fate are more likely to assign Johnson a higher score than McKinsey on intelligence and resilience. In other words, women in these treatment conditions with race-gender linked fate give Johnson more favorable ratings on these traits.

Discussion and Conclusion

While Stacey Abrams did not win the gubernatorial race for governor of Georgia in 2018, she received overwhelming support from Black voters (93%). Still, despite widespread support from Black voters, Abrams suffered a 9 percentage point penalty from Black men (88%), who lagged behind Black women's support for Abrams (97%).[6] Our findings lend insight to the differences in support for Abrams among Black men and women. We find minimal evidence that there is heterogeneity among Black voters by either racial linked fate or race-gender linked fate. When we do find heterogeneity, it is mostly among men. Black men with a sense of race-gender linked fate are more likely to say McKinsey will win and are also less likely to assign Johnson a higher score than McKinsey on trait evaluations in some treatment conditions. Applying these findings to the Abrams election, it is possible that Black men with a sense of race-gender linked fate did not believe Abrams could win the governor's seat. By contrast, women with a sense of race-gender linked fate in the conditions that present Johnson as darker-skinned tend to be more likely to give Johnson a higher rating than McKinsey on intelligence and resilience. These findings suggest that exposure to a particular kind of Black woman candidate—one with darker skin—may activate a sense of race-gender linked fate that results in a favorable view of that candidate. In other words, these findings show that race-gender linked fate is a political shortcut (Dawson 1994) to selecting a darker-skinned Black woman candidate when she runs against a lighter-skinned Black woman. As this study was restricted to Black Democrats, these findings also suggest that among Black Democrats, when two Black women run against each other, a Black woman candidate's skin tone and hairstyle do not consistently operate as a heuristic for a candidate's leadership competencies or her closeness to Black people. In other words, skin tone and hairstyle do not consistently split Black voters who have racial linked fate or race-gender linked fate (e.g., Hochschild and Weaver 2007).

We suggest two possible explanations for these findings. First, both racial linked fate and race-gender linked fate may not differentiate how Black voters assess Black women candidates because race was not salient in either experiment (e.g., Weaver 2012). In the first experiment, a single candidate was running, and in the second, two Black women were running against each other. Thus, there may be no need for "race as a heuristic" in the absence of a non-Black candidate (Dawson 1994). The second reason racial linked fate and race-gender linked fate may not differentiate Black Democratic voters is that Black candidates are not a monolith. For instance, the fact that a candidate is Black does not mean that candidate has a record of substantively representing Black Americans (e.g., Wamble 2018). As such, even if individual Black voters strongly identify with their racial group or their race-gender group, neither heuristic may be relevant in contests where little information is given about candidates' specific issue stances, policy plans, or history of working with Black communities (e.g., Wamble 2018; McConnaughy et al. 2010). While Black voters rate Black women candidates differently as they deviate from a lighter-skinned, straight-haired Eurocentric prototype, we do not find strong evidence that voter responses to Black women candidates who vary in appearance differ by the presence of either form of linked fate.

9

Conclusion

> That bill happened because of these people here. People are listening
> and I think that's why it's important to have events like Curlfest be-
> cause the world listens, legislation listens, politicians listen. That's
> why we're so happy it happened because we know we're a part of that.
>   —Melody Henderson, co-founder of Curlfest
>   and Curly Girl Collective

Curly Girl Collective, started in 2010 by a group of friends who had recently gone natural, went into business together in 2014. This business is dedicated to making those with Afro-textured hair feel seen, beautiful, and appreciated. The group's purpose is to "flip the false narrative around unruly brown beauty, and create one that accurately showcases the glory of our crowns, the richness of our skin, and the joy of our culture. Our hope is that the next generation of women and girls grow up knowing that whether fair-skinned or dark, straight-haired or kinky, beauty has many faces, including theirs."[1] The natural hair commu-nity has embraced the events that the Curly Girl Collective has hosted around New York City, including Curlfest, which has grown to a must-attend summer event. Today, Curlfest is the largest natural beauty festival in the United States. It attracts over 75,000 attendees and is 100% Black women owned.

"Oh, yes! It's a whole vibe, chill. Just a good time of folx celebrating natural hair and the culture. It's intergenerational, too. Just bring your blanket and sit outside all day; and connect with good folx," said Rose, an attendee of the 2019 Randall's Island Curlfest (Personal interview, May 30, 2020). Rose described the event as a welcoming and supportive environment that fostered commu-nity building among naturalistas. She continued, "At first, I didn't know if there would be things there for people with locs like me, or just loose nat-ural hair. But there was. From the vendors, musicians, artists, to food trucks, there was something for everyone." Rose pointed out that Curlfest was not just about connecting with other naturalistas and celebrating the culture, but

Sister Style. Nadia E. Brown and Danielle Casarez Lemi, Oxford University Press (2021). © Oxford University Press.
DOI: 10.1093/oso/9780197540572.003.0009

that the event was also attended by politicians and local organizers, although Rose mainly spent time with her friends during Curlfest and did not engage elected officials.

Curlfest 2019 coincided with the New York state legislature passing the CROWN Act. Assemblywoman Tremaine Wright (D-Bedford-Stuyvesant), the lead sponsor of the bill, noted that "as a Black woman who prioritizes equity, and has worn my natural hair for 17 years, this bill is deeply personal to me" (Rankine 2019). Indeed, as Henderson's notes in this chapter's epigraph, politicians are paying attention. The natural movement, a shift toward embracing and affirming Black women's bodies, is ubiquitous. This movement has touched the lives of Black women from all walks of life, from everyday women like Rose to elected officials like Asw. Wright and Curlfest co-organizer Melody Henderson. Naturalistas are making others listen and pay attention. Black women are claiming space for themselves, space that challenges Eurocentric beauty norms and anti-Blackness ideals. The collective, the natural hair movement, and spaces like Curlfest led to the passage of the CROWN Act in New York and have showcased the political power of naturalistas who want politicians in other states to propose this legislation.

The confluence of the natural hair movement and national politics is a display of the power of Black Girl Magic. It is also a challenge to pervasive anti-Blackness, respectability politics, and Eurocentric beauty norms. Certainly, this moment in history is made possible by Black women—as both voters and elected officials—who are playing by the rules of American democracy to gain political recognition (Gillespie and Brown 2019; Hardy-Fanta et al 2016). Black women cast ballots and run for office at disproportionate rates (Kaba 2011; Orey and Brown 2014). Now, they are attempting to bring their full and authentic selves into government.

In the research we have presented in this book, we sought to reveal how Black women's appearances impact electoral politics and the political experiences of Black women office seekers. Through the lens of embodiment, our research revealed Black women political elites' personhood, voice, and agency, as well as their disruption or reinforcement of European depictions of female beauty and the role that plays in electoral politics. Indeed, the stories that the politicians tell about their appearance and others' perceptions of them are influenced by what is valued by our culture (Patterson and Renwick Monroe 1998). Listening closely to Black women political elites and voters, we find that this group of political actors is keenly aware that appearance matters. There is no one-size-fits-all model of how Black women successfully traverse the politics of appearance.

Although the United States has witnessed an increase in the number of Black women elected officials, little is known about the impact of these candidates' race-gender identity on their campaigns and elections. Current research on women's under-representation in elective office almost exclusively centers on White women's initial decisions to run for office (Lawless and Fox 2005, 2010). The analysis of women or minority candidates within this literature has provided limited findings for how racialized women candidates experience both race and gender in the American context. As a result, this scholarship fails to demonstrate how Black women's identities, visual representations, and raced-gendered experiences inform their candidacies for public office.

Through the use of original qualitative and quantitative data, we argued that due to their embodiment of race and gender as seen in their hair texture/style and skin tone, Black women political elites are assessed on their appearance. Indeed, the corporeal markers of both race and gender are bound together in the physical personhood of Black women candidates. Thus, these candidates are keenly aware of (a) how their bodies and corporeal experiences are racialized/gendered, (b) how their bodies fall outside the hegemonic constructions of beauty and femininity, and (c) the impact of race/gender-based perceptions on voters' decisions. This study's findings illustrate the importance of an intersectional approach to Black feminist research on politics that pays attention to embodiment, American political culture, gender and racialized performance, and Black women's stereotypes.

Substantively, political scientists have used studies of women *or* racial/ethnic candidates to demonstrate how Black women candidates are viewed by voters (Fox and Lawless 2010; Seltzer and Smith 1991; Terkildsen 1993; Weaver 2012). However, such examinations provides only a partial picture of Black women's candidacies. To understand Black women's subject positions, we need to ask a different set of questions about their experiences of running for office. Scholars should ask whether a focus on Black women's appearances provides a more complex and nuanced understanding of how their raced-gendered identities impact their political experiences. Our study has shown that Black women's hair texture/style and skin tone produce experiences that both challenge and provide opportunities for their candidacies.

Review of Findings

The first part of the book relies on interpretivist methods to make sense of how and why Black women's hair, skin color, and representation styles are culturally constructed and mediated. In Chapter 2, we provided the reader with a primer on Afro-textured hair. This background was necessary for those who are less familiar with this texture of hair and with the different care and maintenance regimens it requires. From there, we turned to a historical overview of how Afro-textured hair has been politicized, denigrated, and then later reclaimed and celebrated. This section is a foundational component of the book as it explains why Afro-texture hair matters in meaningful ways for Blacks and non-Blacks alike. Through a case study of New Jersey's CROWN Act, we highlighted the rationale for hair discrimination legislation. This analysis centered on two New Jersey state lawmakers who connected their personal experiences as Black women and the needs of their majority-minority constituency to create legislation as part of the CROWN Coalition. Linking descriptive and substantive representation, we showed that good public policy is made when Black women lawmakers translate a legislative need to a broader audience. However, in convincing their legislative colleagues that the CROWN Act was necessary for New Jersey residents, Asw. McKnight and Sen. Cunningham had help from a viral video of New Jersey high school wrestler Andrew Johnson, whose dreadlocks were forcibly cut prior to a championship match, an incident that elicited outrage and a call for public action.

Our analysis proceeded with one-on-one interviews with Black women political elites in Chapter 3. Through the narratives of Black women office seekers and elected officials, we demonstrated that their hair is a salient issue within electoral politics, particularly on the campaign trail. This finding is ubiquitous for Black women regardless of their generational cohort, geographic location, partisanship, motherhood status, or incumbency. We showed that while hair matters in meaningful and important ways for all the Black women in our study, its significance to individuals varies in intensity. Most of the women presented in this chapter engaged directly with respectability politics. The chapter highlights Black women's agency in styling choices and self-presentation by demonstrating the politics of refusal in their resistance to prescribed beauty norms. Still, the political nature of their decision about how to present themselves to voters and constituents reveals the strategic fluidity within which Black women decide how to wear their hair.

Furthermore, Chapter 3 pointedly combines issues of skin tone and hair texture for Black women political elites. In their narratives, the women do not divorce lived experiences with colorism from hair texture. Both skin tone and hair texture are visible markers of race that have different implications for women than for men, that have historical roots in enslavement, and that continue to animate Black women's experiences in American culture and politics. In sum, we showed that Black women politicians are not passive subjects who are complicit in the raced-gendered practices that dehumanize them. They are active participants in challenging or rearticulating aesthetic norms that impact their electoral chances.

In Chapter 4, we examined innovative focus group data from Black women elected officials and candidates. We partnered with the Black Women's Political Action Committee of Texas (BWPAC TX) to discuss the politics of appearance in a more conversational and interactive discussion. We observed how Black women political elites interacted with one another, how they described their experiences with aesthetics in a group setting, and how they responded to others' experiences. Our focus group quickly revealed generational cleavages in how Black women adhere to or challenge respectability politics. The data also showed a collective will among Black women elites to push back against Eurocentric beauty ideals. Our findings also documented the ability for Black women political elites to see themselves as a sisterhood, regardless of past or present disagreements, and to come together to create affirming spaces for one another.

One of the main points of contention during our focus group in Chapter 4 was between Millennial and Boomer/Silent Generation Black women political elites. These groups of women have markedly different ideals about the proper or acceptable way for Black women to present themselves to constituents and voters. While the majority of the women in the room had natural hairstyles, they disagreed on how to style Afro-textured hair while seeking electoral office or representing their constituents. The Millennial women had similar opinions on a majority of styling issues, ranging from makeup to hair styling to clothing choices. Overall, these younger women were less conservative in their preferred aesthetic, but they still valued some aspects of a traditional professional look.

The book proceeds with an analysis of likely Black women voters. In Chapter 5, we centered the voices of members of Delta Sigma Theta Sorority, Inc., a women's Black Greek Letter Organization (BGLO), to learn how these women assess Black women candidates and the role that appearance may play in their evaluation of such candidates. This data enabled us to make connections between beauty politics and candidate preference among a group of politically engaged Black women. The benefits of holding this focus group with members of Delta Sigma Theta are twofold. First, Deltas are heirs to a long legacy of politically active Black women. For over a century, members of Black sororities have been pledging to uplift Black communities and Black women specifically. These organizations promote raced-gendered civic engagement. Second, Black sororities have been critiqued for prioritizing Eurocentric beauty standards and holding restrictive views of gendered norms and femininity. Thus, members of BGLOs are possibly the best group with whom to assess respectability politics for Black women. Our findings revealed that the Deltas who participated in our study all preferred Black women candidates regardless of the candidates' appearance. The Deltas entered into a conversation about Black women's electability, their chief concern, via a conversation about appropriate appearance.

While participants were uniform in their preference for Black women candidates and their association of positive traits with this population of office seekers, we saw a pattern of generational differences similar to that found in earlier chapters. Indeed, generational cleavages were a consistent part of our findings throughout the interpretivist and qualitative chapters in the book. The Millennials and Generation Xers in the focus group were more likely than older generations to challenge preferences of Eurocentric beauty norms for Black women candidates. They believed that a Black woman should not alter her authentic self—whatever form that may take, but most specifically represented by the wearing of Afro-textured hair—in order to appeal to voters. The sorority sisters were cognizant of the common stereotypes of Black women, and of the significance these stereotypes play in electoral politics.

We now turn to a review of the positivist and quantitative section of the book. Chapters 6 to 8 build upon the preceding chapters to measure voters' perceptions of Black women candidates. The theoretical foundation of the first half of the book informs the hypotheses and analyses of the second half. Here, we draw from novel visual data and experimental data to access the roles of colorism, gender, and linked fate in voter evaluations of Black women candidates based on phenotype.

In Chapter 6, we presented findings from an original dataset on the appearances of Black women candidates who sought office in 2018. Consistent with prior research on colorism and representation, Chapter 6 presents data that shows that the pool of Black women candidates skews lighter-skinned with straightened hair, and that candidates who wear braids or locs styles may disproportionately lose their contests. These findings suggest that Black women who seek local-level offices with natural styles like locs may find it difficult to enter political office and rise to higher levels of office. More research should be done on a larger scale to assess this trend.

In Chapter 7, we presented findings from two experiments that examined the effect of variation in Black women's appearances on Black voter behavior. In the first experiment, we asked whether a single Black woman candidate's appearance may influence Black voters' evaluations of her, and our findings showed evidence of this effect. In the second experiment, we modeled an election between two Black women Democrats in a special election, as this scenario may be realistic for Black women candidates running in majority-minority districts (e.g., Philpot and Walton 2007). Focusing on Black Democrats, we found that changing the appearance of one candidate pushes voters to evaluate both candidates differently. This suggests that when appearances are made salient (e.g., Weaver 2012), Black Democrats view co-partisan Black woman candidates differently, perhaps because of differences in political ideology (Lerman et al. 2015).

In Chapter 8, our last empirical chapter, we considered whether there was heterogeneity by racial linked fate and race-gender linked fate among Black voters and their evaluations of Black women candidates who vary in appearance. Overall, we found little evidence that Black voters evaluate Black women candidates differently based on the presence of either form of linked fate. However, when two Black women Democrats run against each other and one has darker skin and naturally curly hair, Black men with race-gender linked fate tend to doubt a candidate's likelihood of winning relative to her opponent. These findings highlight the nuanced ways in which political behavior intersects with gender for Black Democrats. Indeed, as White and Laird (2020) find, Blacks are "steadfast Democrats" who identify with this political party even when their ideological self-identification may not closely align with Democratic policy positions. This enduring partisan unity, based on racialized social constraint (White and Laird 2020), demonstrates that Black voters understand and internalize their political groupness. Black women, perhaps, are most likely to view solidarity politics as a key strategy for making political gains. As our focus group data with members of Delta Sigma Theta Sorority, Inc., documented, Black women draw from organizational ties and develop in-group networks that maintain racialized social pressure to support the Democratic Party.

Throughout this book, we have presented a systematic and holistic analysis of how the politics of appearance impact Black women political elites' styling choices and voters' assessment of these candidates. Through a mixed-method approach we have used novel data to show a realistic, yet nuanced, view of how Black women themselves think about their appearance and its impact on electoral politics. Our comprehensive analyses offer a deeper understanding of the differences in how and why Black women vary in their political experiences as well as preferences.

Implications

Our study has several theoretical, normative, methodological, and substantive implications. Theoretically, we have expanded traditional intersectional studies on Black women beyond the holy trinity of race, class, and gender (Brown 2014, Romero 2017). Intersectional theory encompasses multiple sites of oppression and privilege such as age, ableism, ethnicity, citizenship, nativity, and sexual orientation, and has moved beyond the United States to examine the interconnectedness of colonialism, immigration, imperialism, and conquest (Nash 2018). Multidimensional approaches to examining social inequalities have failed to include the physical embodiment of social categories among group members in their intersectional analysis. Our study adds phenotype or appearance to intersectional projects on Black women political elites. Recognizing the diversity in political experiences based on a Black woman's appearance thus reveals another salient social identity. Gender and race are performed (Johnson 2003; West and Zimmerman 1987). Thus, the process by which gender and race—along with other identities such as sexual orientation—are created and recreated through interpersonal performances is continually shaped through both positive and negative social reinforcements. In sum, how African American women candidates include performances of race and gender in their styling practices reveals how political leaders shape their race-gender identities.

Turning to normative democratic theory, we move beyond descriptive representation by ascribed race (Mansbridge 1999) to show that individuals' literal descriptive representation has political implications. Hair, and specifically hairstyle and hair texture, can signal a specific set of political ideologies (Mercer 20005). Campaign managers and strategists know the importance of hair and the impact it can have on a candidate evaluation. This is true for White women, as illustrated by the example of Hillary Clinton's Yale University commencement speech, in which she warned, with tongue in cheek, "The most important thing I have to say to you today is that hair matters. . . . This is a life lesson my family did not teach me [and] Wellesley or Yale failed to instill in me. Your hair will send significant messages to those around you. It will tell people what you stand for—what hopes and dreams you have for the world, and especially what hopes and dreams you have for your hair. . . . Pay attention to your hair, because everyone else will" (Zernike, 2001).

Though Clinton's tone here is clearly ironic, her account demonstrates the serious fact that women's hairstyles impact how they are perceived, and that they thus play an important role in their gendered experience as politicians. However, scholars have had little understanding as to how hair texture/style in combination with skin tone may influence political experiences and electoral success. In the case of Black women, in particular those who disrupt Eurocentric depictions of female beauty, the role that body politics plays in defining political experiences was previously unknown. We have shown that the bodily markers of both race and gender are bound together in the physical personhood of Black women legislators.

Methodologically, our work illustrates the power of focus groups. Rarely do political scientists use focus groups to build theory or study race relations (e.g., Wilkinson 2015). One of the key contributions of this work is our use of the focus group method with elites—to our knowledge, this is the first time this has been done. In our focus groups, participants created their ideal Black woman candidate for political office in their own words (Stewart and Shamdasani 1990). By gathering data in this manner, we collected data that was richer than it would have been had we solely relied on data collected through one-on-one interviews, because the use of focus groups allowed us to observe intergenerational dynamics in the group setting that we would have missed had we used only individual interviews (Onwuegbuzie et al. 2009). Furthermore, the focus groups revealed that at both the elite and the voter level, constructions of beauty and femininity, as well as race- and gender-based stereotypes, impact elites' and voters' decisions. This finding is crucial, because so little theoretical and empirical work guides our current understanding of how voters perceive Black women candidates and how Black women elites identify themselves.

Substantively, we show that the self-presentations of political elites are carefully constructed personas that reflect social and cultural norms. These personas, either directly or indirectly, provide voters with a glimpse of these candidates' personalities, political ideologies, and sense of self. While political self-presentations are often depicted as strategic (e.g., McIlwain and Caliendo 2011), this research shows that styling choices are deeply personal, and that individuals' manipulation of their self-presentation is not always done lightly or solely in service of political ambition.

Practically, this research offers key insights for prospective candidates and campaign advisers. Campaign advisers may be quick to tell candidates to aim for the styles that make them as attractive as possible within Eurocentric beauty standards (e.g., Laustsen 2014). Current strategies to address race and gender in a campaign may be selected without a nuanced understanding of how race/gender, colorism, and Eurocentrism constrain and facilitate opportunities for different Black women candidates (e.g., McIlwain and Caliendo 2011; Bauer 2019). Given the key role of campaign consultants in contemporary politics (Dulio 2004; Panagopoulos 2006; Johnson 2001; Thurber 1998; Grossman 2009), we urge consultants to take heed before advising a Black woman client to straighten her hair and present herself with an image that is closer to that of a White woman candidate. Our data shows that this advice may amount to telling her to change an aspect of her appearance that informs her sense of self (Tajfel and Turner 1986).

Moving Forward

Public office, either in state legislatures or in county courts, is the workplace of Black women political elites. Our study adds another layer to the conversation on race and the institutional climate for representatives of color (e.g., Fraga et al. 2006; Brown 2014; Tyson 2016; Lemi 2018). Within the next three decades, the United States will become the first major postindustrial society to witness a population move from a White majority to a White minority. This change in demographics poses many challenges and opportunities for the study of politics and political actors. As Melody Henderson notes in this chapter's epigraph, the natural hair movement is causing politicians to pay attention to issues associated with having Afro-textured hair. Henderson further noted that society has come a long way in acknowledging race-based hair discrimination, but that there is still room for improvement (Spencer et al., 2019). While the demographic change alone will not bring about policy shifts in favor of ethno-racial minority group interests, it may signal that concerns that were previously uncrystallized are now becoming part of the political conversation, a change due in large part to Black women political elites and voters who are advancing these issues.

Prospective candidates may be reading this book and wondering, "What now?" In some ways, our findings may seem discouraging. Colorism exists. Voters respond to Black women's hairstyles in sometimes negative ways. However, we hope that these findings will influence those considering running for office, as well as those seeking to recruit Black women to run for office and mentor Black women leaders, to realize that part of genuinely supporting Black women means respecting their autonomy as individuals and extending access to resources irrespective of appearances. Because Black women are most likely to run as Democrats, Democratic Party leaders should pay attention to their candidacies and offer authentic support. Ultimately, we hope this research empowers prospective candidates with knowledge to exercise agency over their self-presentations as they seek political office.

Thus, our work seeks to reconceptualize how Black women political elites are thought about, assessed, measured, and evaluated. Scholars may take interest in further disaggregating beyond race and gender in their analysis of Black women's political experiences. Furthermore, Black women political elites themselves may be challenged to rethink professional norms that have stifled their preferred professional expression. Voters should also consider how their implicit and explicit biases about Black women's bodies impact their evaluation of these candidates. Lastly, a broader discussion should continue within Black communities about acceptable appearances for Black women political elites. The focus of this book is on Black communities; however, White and non-Black voters should also reconsider how they evaluate Black women political elites and how they use candidates' bodies as a political heuristic in their vote choice.

It is our hope that this book causes readers—scholars, politicos, and the general public alike—to ask more questions about the salience of Black women's bodies in American politics. This book should be the starting point for a deeper conversation about how race, gender, generation, and class status meet markers of femininity, social norms, and racialized performances of identity. The multiplicity of ways in which social structures, identities, cultural norms, and politics interact with one another provokes further questions rather than offering a clear answer to our query, What should a Black woman political elite look like?

Notes

Chapter 1

1. https://apnews.com/a814ba9fa30a4d6182d80d77b2d16071
2. https://www.cawp.rutgers.edu/fact-sheets-women-color
3. https://cawp.rutgers.edu/election-analysis/black-women-candidates-2020
4. https://www.cnn.com/2020/08/04/opinions/black-women-biden-vice-president-jones/index.html
5. https://www.npr.org/sections/itsallpolitics/2011/12/22/144139845/michelle-obama-gets-apology-from-sensenbrenner-for-big-butt-remark
6. https://www.cnbc.com/2018/05/29/roseanne-apologizes-for-planet-of-the-apes-tweet-about-obama-aide-jarrett.html
7. https://www.essence.com/entertainment/solange-dont-touch-my-hair-moments/
8. In his 1994 essay "Black to the Future," Mark Dery coined the term "Afro-futurism" to refer to how speculative fiction treats African American themes by using technoculture to address twentieth-century African American concerns. The term applies to the development of a Black prosthetically enhanced future through the use of technology.

Chapter 2

1. https://nj.gov/state/elections/index.shtml
2. https://ballotpedia.org/Sandra_Cunningham
3. https://www.njsendems.org/senators/sandra-cunningham/
4. https://www.njleg.state.nj.us/members/bio.asp?Leg=383
5. https://rbscp.lib.rochester.edu/4398

Chapter 3

1. The Mammy stereotype positions Black women as a content and loyal maternal figure who takes care of Whites but often treats her own family with disdain. She is desexualized and often portrayed as dark skinned and obese. Conversely, the Jezebel stereotype depicts Black women as both promiscuous and predatory—as lascivious, lewd, seductive, and tempting. The Jezebel is hypersexual, and as such, embodies the idea that black women are naturally wanton. Lastly, the Sapphire stereotype portrays Black women as loud, stubborn, rude, and overbearing. An angry Black woman who is emasculating and has malicious tendencies, the Sapphire is often abusive and mean-spirited. Her wrath is often directed toward Black men—as captured in Sapphire

Stevens, a character on the "Amos 'n' Andy" minstrel show—whom she dominates in an aggressive manner. This shrill, nagging and often indignant woman is the foil to the coon caricature of Black men.

2. https://aapf.org/2014/06/woc-letter-mbk/
3. See Hakeem Jefferson, (2020) "Punishment and the Politics of Respectability among Black Americans. [White Paper] https://politicalscience.stanford.edu/people/hakeem-jefferson"
4. The larger interview protocol asked questions about the woman's political priorities, how her appearance may or may not impact her political experiences, and her understanding of how race/gender influences her political behavior.

Chapter 4

1. https://factfinder.census.gov/faces/tableservices/jsf/pages/productview.xhtml?src=CF
2. https://www.ozy.com/flashback/the-black-texas-congresswoman-who-took-on-nixon/87679/
3. https://tshaonline.org/handbook/online/articles/pwwzj
4. https://www.teenvogue.com/story/beto-orourke-won-texas-black-women-still-moral-compass-united-states-politics
5. https://www.cnn.com/election/2018/exit-polls/texas/governor
6. https://time.com/5290985/lupe-valdez-governor-texas-democratic-candidate/
7. https://www.cnn.com/2019/01/01/us/harris-county-judges-texas-houston-black-women-trnd/index.html
8. https://www.census.gov/quickfacts/fact/table/dallascitytexas/PST045218

Chapter 5

1. Joyce Beatty D-OH), Yvette Clark (D-NY), Val Demings (D-FL), Marcia Fudge (D-OH), Brenda Lawrence (D-MI), and Lucy McBath (D-GA). Non-voting Delegate Stacey E. Plaskett (D-VI) is also a member of Delta Sigma Theta.
2. https://www.nps.gov/articles/woman-suffrage-procession1913.htm
3. https://www.washingtonpost.com/graphics/2020/local/history/suffrage-racism-black-deltas-parade-washington/?hpid=hp_hp-banner-low_deltas-715am%3Ahomepage%2Fstory-ans&itid=hp_hp-banner-low_deltas-715am%3Ahomepage%2Fstory-ans
4. http://circuitous.org/scraps/combahee.html
5. As described on the Delta Sigma Theta Sorority, Inc Madison Alumnae Chapter website, "Delta D.E.A.R.S. (Dedicated, Energetic, Active, Respected Sorors) are members of Delta Sigma Theta's sisterhood who have been blessed to reach the golden age of 62 years. Dedicated to upholding the ideals and traditions of their sorority, Delta D.E.A.R.S. set a standard of excellence in service, scholarship". http://madisonalumnaedst.org/delta-dears/4594218657
6. https://www.deltasigmatheta.org/political.php

Chapter 6

1. We distinguish between natural-looking curls and curls created by first straightening hair and then using a barreled curling iron.

Chapter 7

1. In Lemi and Brown (2019), we tested the interaction of skin tone and hairstyle. The findings were suggestive of an interaction but were not conclusive. We now believe that what matters for evaluations of Black women candidates is their deviation from a lighter-skinned, straightened-hair prototype, as this is the "preferred" Black woman in numerous sectors of American society. Rather than the effect of skin tone depending on the value of hairstyle, we believe that the deviation from White beauty norms is what sets off attitudes associated with colorism. As such, we report our findings for the two experiments using the Light Straight condition as the reference group.
2. We processed our data using linear regression (OLS) with robust standard errors (Gerber and Green 2012), using Light Straight as the baseline category.
3. In Lemi and Brown (2019), we tested the interaction of skin tone and hairstyle. The findings were suggestive of an interaction but were not conclusive. We now believe that what matters for evaluations of Black women candidates is their deviation from a lighter-skinned, straightened-hair prototype, as this is the "preferred" Black woman in numerous sectors of American society. Rather than the effect of skin tone depending on the value of hairstyle, we believe that the deviation from White beauty norms is what sets off attitudes associated with colorism. As such, we report our findings for the two experiments using the Light Straight condition as the reference group.

Chapter 8

1. For closeness to White people, the sample size was not large enough for women and race-gender linked fate.
2. OLS with robust standard errors.
3. Logit with robust standard errors.
4. OLS with robust standard errors.
5. OLS with robust standard errors.
6. https://www.cnn.com/election/2018/results/georgia/governor.

Chapter 9

1. https://www.curlfest.com/our-story

References

Abramson, Paul R., 1976. "Generational change and the decline of party identification in America: 1952-1974." *The American Political Science Review* 70 (2): 469–78.

Abramson, Paul R., and Ronald Inglehart. 1987. "Generational replacement and the future of post-materialist values." *The Journal of Politics* 49 (1): 231–41.

Adida, Claire L., Lauren D. Davenport, and Gwyneth McClendon. 2016. "Ethnic Cueing across Minorities: A Survey Experiment on Candidate Evaluation in the United States." *Public Opinion Quarterly* 80 (4): 815–36.

Ahler, Douglas J., Jack Citrin, Michael C. Dougal, and Gabriel S. Lenz. 2017. "Face Value? Experimental Evidence that Candidate Appearance Influences Electoral Choice." *Political Behavior* 39 (1): 77–102.

Ahuja, Amit, Susan L. Ostermann, and Aashish Mehta. 2016. "Is Only Fair Lovely in Indian Politics? Consequences of Skin Color in a Survey Experiment in Delhi." *Journal of Race, Ethnicity, and Politics* 1 (2): 227–52.

Alba, Richard, and Victor Nee. 1997. "Rethinking Assimilation Theory for a New Era of Immigration." *International Migration Review* 31 (4): 826–74. Special Issue: "Immigrant Adaptation and Native-Born Responses in the Making of Americans."

Alexander, Deborah, and Kristi Andersen. 1993. "Gender as a Factor in the Attribution of Leadership Traits." *Political Research Quarterly* 46 (3): 527–45.

Alex-Assensoh, Yvette, and Karin Stanford. 1997. "Gender, Participation, and the Black Urban Underclass." In *Women Transforming Politics: An Alternative Reader*, edited by Cathy J. Cohen, Kathleen B. Jones, and Joan C. Tronto, 398–411. New York, NY: New York University Press.

Allen, Maya. 2019. "The Fascinating History of Braids You Never Knew About." *Byrdie* (blog). October 24. https://www.byrdie.com/history-of-braids

Almond, Gabriela A., and Sidney Verba. 1965. *The Civic Culture*. Boston, MA: Little, Brown and Company.

Arnesen, Eric. 2006. *Encyclopedia of US Labor and Working-Class History*. New York: Routledge.

Arnold, Laura W., Rebecca E. Deen, and Samuel C. Patterson. 2000. "Friendship and Votes: The Impact of Interpersonal Ties on Legislative Decision Making." *State and Local Government Review* 32 (2): 142–47.

Ashforth, Blake E., and Fred Mael. 1989. "Social Identity Theory and the Organization." *The Academy of Management Review* 14 (1): 20–39.

Ashmore, R., and F.K. Del Boca. 1981. "Conceptual Approaches to Stereotypes and Stereotyping." In *Cognitive Processes*, edited by D. Hamilton, 1–36. Hillsdale, NJ: Erlbaum.

Bailey, Moya, and Trudy. 2018. "On Misogynoir: Citation, Erasure, and Plagiarism." *Feminist Media Studies* 18 (4): 762–68.

Baldwin, Davarian L. 2007. *Chicago's New Negroes: Modernity, the Great Migration, & Black Urban Life*. Chapel Hill, NC: University of North Carolina Press.

Banducci, Susan A., Jeffrey A. Karp, Michael Thrasher, and Colin Rallings. 2008. "Ballot Photographs as Cues in Low-Information Elections." *Political Psychology* 29 (6): 903–17.

Banks, Ingrid. 2000. *Hair Matters: Beauty, Power and Black Women's Consciousness.* New York: New York University Press.

Bauer, Nichole M., and Colleen Carpinella. 2018. "Visual Information and Candidate Evaluations: The Influence of Feminine and Masculine Images on Support for Female Candidates." *Politically Research Quarterly* 71 (2): 395–407.

Bauer, Nichole M. 2015. "Who Stereotypes Female Candidates? Identifying Individual Differences in Feminine Stereotype Reliance." *Politics, Groups, and Identities* 3 (1): 94–110.

Bauer, Nichole M. 2019. "A Feminine Advantage? Delineating the Effects of Feminine Trait and Feminine Issues Messages on Evaluations of Female Candidates." *Politics & Gender* 16 (3): 660–80. https://doi.org/10.1017/S1743923X19000084

BBC Trending. 2016. "The Women Saying No, 'Afropuff' Hair Is Not Unruly." *BBC News.* February 18. https://www.bbc.com/news/blogs-trending-35596018

Bejarano, Christina E. 2013. *The Latina Advantage: Gender, Race, and Political Success.* Austin, TX: University of Texas Press.

Berinsky, Adam J., Gregory A. Huber, and Gabriel S. Lenz. 2012. "Evaluating Online Labor Markets for Experimental Research: Amazon.com's Mechanical Turk." *Political Analysis* 20 (3): 351–68.

Betancourt, Bianca. 2020. "Kamala Harris Honors Black Women as the 'Backbone of Our Democracy' in Her VP Victory Speech." *Harper's Bazar.* https://www.harpersbazaar. com/culture/politics/a34608098/kamala-harris-vice-president-victory-speech/ Accessed on November 9, 2020.

Bey, Jamila. 2011. "'Going Natural' Requires Lots of Help." *New York Times.* June 8. https:// www.nytimes.com/2011/06/09/fashion/hair-care-for-african-americans.html

Bey, Jamila. 2012. "For African-Americans, 'Going Natural' Can Require Help." *The New York Times,* 8 June 2011. Web. Nov. 4, 2012.

Bhaskar, Roy. 1989. *The Possibility of Naturalism: A Philosophical Critique of the Contemporary Human Sciences.* 3rd ed. London: Routledge.

Bischof, Daniel. 2015. "New Graphic Schemes for Stata: Plotplain & Plottig." *Stata Journal* 17 (3): 748–59.

Blackwelder, Julia Kirk. 2003. *Styling Jim Crow: African American Beauty Training During Segregation.* College Station, TX: Texas A&M University Press.

Bobo, Lawrence, and Frank D. Giliam. 1990. "Race, Sociopolitical Participation, and Black Empowerment." *American Political Science Review* 84: 377–94.

Bonilla-Silva, Eduardo. 2014. *Racism without Racists: Color-Blind Racism and the Persistence of Racial Inequality in the United States.* 4th ed. Lanham, MD: Rowman & Littlefield.

Brazile, Donna, Yolanda Caraway, Leah Daughtry, Minyon Moore, and Veronica Chambers. 2018. *For Colored Girls Who Have Considered Politics.* New York, NY: St. Martin's Press.

Branigin, Anne. 2018. "Black Hair Matters: The Affirmative Power of Politicians Like Ayanna Pressley and Stacey Abrams." *The Root.* December 3. https://theglowup. theroot.com/black-hair-matters-the-affirmative-power-of-politician-1830750951

Breakfast Club Power 105.1 FM. 2018. "Stacey Abrams on Why Skin Color Plays a Role in the Georgia Primary Election." YouTube. Video, 2:49. https://www.youtube.com/ watch?v=bgM4_pOu3ys

Brown, Nadia E. and Sarah Allen Gershon. 2016. "Intersectional Presentations: An Exploratory Study of Minority Congresswomen's Websites' Biographies." *Du Bois Review* 13 (1): 85–108.

Brown, Nadia, and Kira Hudson Banks. 2014. "Black Women's Agenda Setting in the Maryland State Legislature." *Journal of African American Studies* 81 (2): 1–17.

Brown, Nadia. 2012. "Negotiating the Insider/Outsider Status: Black Feminist Ethnography and Legislative Studies." *Journal of Feminist Scholarship* 3: 19–39.

Brown, Nadia. 2014. "'It's More Than Hair . . . That's Why You Should Care': The Politics of Appearance for Black Women State Legislators." *Politics, Groups, and Identities* 2 (3): 295–312.

Brown, Nadia. 2018. "What's Hair Got to Do with It? Black Women's Bodies and the Traditional Look of Success in American Politics." Scholars Strategy Network. June 12. https://scholars.org/brief/whats-hair-got-do-it-black-womens-bodies-and-traditional-look-success-american-politics

Brown, Nadia E, and Sarah Allen Gershon. 2020. "Glass Half Full: Cautious Optimism and the Future of Black Women Political Elites in America." *The Journal of Race, Ethnicity, and Politics*: 1–13. https://www.cambridge.org/core/article/glass-half-full-cautious-optimism-and-the-future-of-black-women-political-elites-in-america/1186B095B4CE6046C02FD1429D081BB7.

Brown, Tamara L., Gregory S. Parks, and Clarenda M. Phillips. 2012. *African American Fraternities and Sororities: The Legacy and the Vision.* Lexington, KY: University Press of Kentucky.

Burge, Camille, Julian J. Wamble, and Rachel Cuomo. 2020. "A Certain Type of Descriptive Representative?: Understanding How the Skin Tone and Gender of Candidates Influences Black Politics." *Journal of Politics* 82 (4): 1596–1601. https://www.journals.uchicago.edu/doi/10.1086/708778

Burke, Anabel. 2020. "Eddie Bernice Johnson." *Waco History.* https://wacohistory.org/items/show/199

Burns, Nancy, Kay Lehman Schlozman, and Sidney Verba. 2001. *The Private Roots of Public Action: Gender, Equality, and Political Participation.* Cambridge, MA: Harvard University Press.

Burrell, Barbara. 1994. *A Woman's Place Is in the House.* Ann Arbor, MI: University of Michigan Press.

Butler, David E., and Donald Stokes. 1969. *Political Change in Britain.* New York, NY: St. Martin's Press.

Byrd, Ayana D., and Lori L. Tharps. 2001. *Hair Story: Untangling the Roots of Black Hair in America.* New York: St. Martin's Griffin.

Caldeira, Gregory A., and Samuel C. Patterson. 1987. "Political Friendship in the Legislature." *Journal of Politics* 49 (4): 953–75.

Caldeira, Gregory A., and Samuel C. Patterson. 1988. "Contours of Friendship and Respect in the Legislature." *American Politics Research* 16 (4): 466–85.

Calhoun-Brown, Allison. 1996. "African American Churches and Political Mobilization: The Psychological Impact of Organizational Resources." *Journal of Politics* 58 (4): 935–53.

Campbell, Mary E., Verna M. Keith, Vanessa Gonlin, and Adrienne R. Carter-Sowell. 2020. "Is a Picture Worth a Thousand Words? An Experiment Comparing Observer-Based Skin Tone Measures." *Race and Social Problems* 12: 266–78. https://link.springer.com/article/10.1007%2Fs12552-020-09294-0.

Candelario, Ginetta E.B. 2007. *Black Behind the Ears: Dominican Racial Identity from Museums to Beauty Shops*. Durham, NC: Duke University Press.

Carr, Glynda S, and Kimberly Peeler-Allen. 2018. "2018 Is the Year Black Women Are Taking Power." *CNN*. May 25. https://www.cnn.com/2018/05/25/opinions/2018-is-the-year-black-women-are-taking-power-carr-peeler-allen/index.html

Carroll, Noel. 2000. "Ethnicity, Race, and Monstrosity: The Rhetorics of Horror and Humor." In *Beauty Matters*, edited by Peggy Zeglin Brand, 37–56. Bloomington, IN: Indiana University Press.

Carroll, Susan J. 1994. *Women as Candidates in American Politics*. 2nd ed. Bloomington, IN: Indiana University Press.

Carroll, Susan J., and Kira Sanbonmatsu. 2013. *More Women Can Run: Gender and Pathways to the State Legislatures*. New York: Oxford University Press.

Casellas, Jason P. 2011. *Latino Representation in State Houses and Congress*. New York: Cambridge University Press.

Cash, Thomas F., and Timothy A. Brown. 1989. "Gender and Body Images: Stereotypes and Realities." *Sex Roles* 21 (5–6): 361–73.

Cassandre. 2014. "Shocking History: Why Women of Color in the 1800s Were Banned From Wearing Their Hair in Public." *BGLH Marketplace*. July 7. https://bglh-marketplace.com/2014/07/shocking-history-why-women-of-color-in-the-1800s-were-banned-from-wearing-their-hair-in-public/ .

Cassese, Erin C. and Mirya R. Holman. 2016. Religious Beliefs, Gender Consciousness, and Women's Political Participation. *Sex Roles* 75 (9–10): 514–27.

Chambers, Alli D. 2017. "The Failure of the Black Greek-Letter Organization." *Journal of Black Studies* 48 (6): 610–21.

Citrin, Jack, Donald Philip Green, and David O. Sears. 1990. "White Reactions to Black Candidates: When Does Race Matter?" *Public Opinion Quarterly* 54 (1): 74–96.

Clarke, Chris. 2009. "Paths between Positivism and Interpretivism: An Appraisal of Hay's via Media." *Politics* 29 (1): 28–36.

Clifford, Scott, Ryan M. Jewell, and Philip D. Wagonner. 2015. "Are Samples Drawn From Mechanical Turk Valid for Research on Political Ideology?" *Research and Politics* 2 (4): 1–9.

Cohen, Cathy J. 2010. *Democracy Remixed: Black Youth and the Future of American Politics*. New York: Oxford University Press.

Cohen, Rachel M. and Ryan Grim. 2019. "How Morgan Harper's Ohio Primary Challenge Explains the House Democratic Meltdown." *The Intercept*. July 16. https://theintercept.com/2019/07/16/morgan-harper-congressional-black-caucus-primary/

Cole, Elizabeth R., and Abigail J. Stewart. 1996. "Meanings of Political Participation among Black and White Women: Political Identity and Social Responsibility." *Journal of Personality and Social Psychology* 71 (1): 130.

Collet, Christian. 2008. "Minority Candidates, Alternative Media, and Multiethnic America: Deracializion or Toggling?" *Perspectives on Politics* 6 (4): 707–28.

Collins, Patricia Hill. 1990. *Black Feminist Thought: Knowledge, Consciousness and Politics of Empowerment*. New York: Routledge.

Collins, P. H. 2000. *Black Feminist Thought: Knowledge, Consciousness, and the Politics of Empowerment*. 2nd edition. New York: NY Routledge.

Cooper, Brittany. 2017. *Beyond Respectability: The Intersectional Thought of Race Women*. Urbana-Champaign, IL: University of Illinois Press.

Copeland, M Shawn. 2010. *Enfleshing Freedom: Body, Race, and Human Being.* Minneapolis, MN: Fortress Press.

Craig, Maxine Leeds. 2006. "Race, Beauty, and the Tangled Knot of a Guilty Pleasure." *Feminist Theory* 7 (2): 159–77.

Creswell, John W. and Vicki L. Plano Clark. 2017. *Designing and Conducting Mixed Methods Research.* Los Angeles, CA: SAGE Publications. Kindle version.

Crosley Coker, Hillary. 2014. "Alpha Kappa Alpha Revises Position on Members Protesting in Letters." *Jezebel.* https://jezebel.com/alpha-kappa-alpha-revises-position-on-members-protestin-1669839633.

Darcy, R., Charles D. Hadley, and Jason F. Kirksey. 1993. "Election Systems and the Representation of Black Women in American State Legislatures." *Women & Politics* 13 (2): 73–89.

Davis, Angela Y. 1994. "Afro Images: Politics, Fashion, and Nostalgia." *Critical Inquiry* 21 (1): 37–45. http://www.jstor.org/stable/1343885.

Dawson, Michael C. 1994. *Behind the Mule: Race and Class in African-American Politics.* Princeton, NJ: Princeton University Press.

Dawson, Michael C. 2001. *Black Visions: The Roots of Contemporary African-American Political Ideologies.* Chicago: University of Chicago Press.

DeSante, Christopher D., and Candis Watts Smith. 2020. "Less Is More: A Cross-Generational Analysis of the Nature and Role of Racial Attitudes in the Twenty-First Century." *Journal of Politics* 82 (3): 967–80. https://doi.org/10.1086/707490.

Dimock, Michael. 2019. "Defining Generations: Where Millennials End and Generation Z Begins." *Pew Research Center.* January 17. https://www.pewresearch.org/fact-tank/2019/01/17/where-millennials-end-and-generation-z-begins/

Dolan, Kathleen. 1996. "Support for Women Political Candidates: An Examination of the Role of Family." *Women & Politics* 16 (2): 45–60.

Dolan, Kathleen. 2004. *Voting for Women: How the Public Evaluates Women Candidates.* Boulder, CO: Westview Press.

Dolan, Kathleen. 2014a. "Gender Stereotypes, Candidate Evaluations, and Voting for Women Candidates: What Really Matters?" *Political Research Quarterly* 67 (1): 96–107.

Dolan, Kathleen. 2014b. *When Does Gender Matter?: Women Candidates and Gender Stereotypes in American Elections.* New York: Oxford University Press.

Drake, Saint C., and Horace R. Cayton. 1970. *Black Metropolis: A Study of Negro Life in a Northern City.* Chicago: University of Chicago Press.

Du Bois, William Edward Burghardt. 1903. *The talented tenth.* New York, NY: James Pott and Company.

Due Billing, Y., & Alvesson, M. (2000). "Questioning the Notion of Feminine Leadership: A Critical Perspective on the Gender Labelling of Leadership." *Gender, Work & Organization, 7* (3), 144–57.

Dulio, David A. 2004. *For Better or Worse?: How Political Consultants Are Changing Elections in the United States.* Albany, NY: SUNY Press.

Durkheim, Emile. 1982. *The Rules of Sociological Method and Selected Texts on Sociology and Its Method,* Basingstoke, UK: Macmillan.

Ettinger, Zoe. 2020. "8 Times Kids Stood Up for Their Natural Hair." *Insider.* April 24. https://www.insider.com/children-who-stood-up-for-natural-hair-2020-4

Evans, Stephanie Y. 2004. "Black Greek-Lettered Organizations and Civic Responsibility. (Last Word)." *Black Issues in Higher Education* 21 (17): 98.

Farris, Emily M., and Mirya R. Holman. 2014. "Social Capital and Solving the Puzzle of Black Women's Political Participation." *Politics, Groups, and Identities* 2 (3): 331–49.

Farris, Emily M. and Heather Silber Mohamed. 2018. "Picturing Immigration: How the Media Criminalizes Immigrants." *Politics, Groups, and Identities* 6 (4): 814–24.

Faul, Franz, Edgar Erdfelder, Albert-Georg Lang, and Axel Buchner. 2007. "G*Power 3: A Flexible Statistical Power Analysis Program for the Social, Behavioral, and Biomedical Sciences." *Behavior Research Methods* 39 (2): 175–91. http://www.gpower.hhu.de/fileadmin/redaktion/Fakultaeten/Mathematisch-Naturwissenschaftliche_Fakultaet/Psychologie/AAP/gpower/GPower3-BRM-Paper.pdf.

Feldman, Kate. 2020. "Texas Teen Who Refused to Cut Dreadlocks Attends Oscars with 'Hair Love' Team." *NY Daily News*. February 9. https://www.nydailynews.com/snyde/ny-texas-dreadlocks-oscars-hair-love-20200209-yi675gw3efcxbkdeksu3y27r6m-story.html

Fenno, Jr., Richard F. 1978. *Home Style: House Members in Their Districts*. 2003. New York: Pearson, Addison-Wesley Publishers, Inc. .

Fisher, Dana R. 2019. *American Resistance: From the Women's March to the Blue Wave*. New York: Columbia University Press.

Fisher, Patrick. 2018. "A political outlier: The distinct politics of the millennial generation." *Society* 55 (1): 35–40.

Fisher, Patrick. 2020. "Generational Replacement and the Impending Transformation of the American Electorate." *Politics & Policy* 48 (1): 38–68.

Fiske, Susan T., and Shelley E. Taylor. 1991. *Social Cognition*. New York: McGraw Hill.

Ford, Tanisha. 2015. *Liberated Threads: Black Women, Style, and the Global Politics of Soul*. Durham, NC: University of North Carolina Press.

Fraga, Luis, Valerie Martinez Ebers, Linda Lopez, and Ricardo Ramirez. 2006. "Gender and Ethnicity: Patterns of Electoral Success and Legislative Advocacy among Latina and Latino State Officials in Four States." *Journal of Women, Politics & Policy* 28 (3/4): 121–45.

Fraga, Bernard L. and Hans J.G. Hassell. 2020. "Are Minority and Women Candidates Penalized by Party Politics? Race, Gender, and Access to Party Support." *Political Research Quarterly*. https://doi.org/10.1177/1065912920913326

Fraga, Bernard, Eric Gonzalez Juenke, and Paru Shah. 2019. "Candidates' Characteristics Cooperative Database, 2018 State Legislative Elections." Version 2. September 12. (in our work and release notes we will be listing all of the collaborators who participated in this collection).

Fraga, Luis Ricardo, Linda Lopez, Valerie Martinez-Ebers, and Ricardo Ramirez. 2006. "Gender and Ethnicity: Patterns of Electoral Success and Legislative Advocacy Among Latina and Latino State Officials in Four States." *Journal of Women, Politics & Policy* 28 (3–4): 121–45.

Frazier, E. F. 1957. Black Bourgeoisie: The Rise of a New Class in the United States. The Free Press & The Falcon's Wing Press.

Gaines, Kevin K. 2012. *Uplifting the Race: Black Leadership, Politics, and Culture in the Twentieth Century*. Chapel Hill, NC: University of North Carolina Press.

Garza, Alicia. 2014. "A Herstory of The# BlackLivesMatter Movement." *The Feminist Wire*. October 7. https://thefeministwire.com/2014/10/blacklivesmatter-2/

Gatewood, W.B. Jr. 1988. "Aristocrats of Color: South and North, the Black Elite." *Journal of Southern History* 54: 3–20.

Gay, Claudine, Jennifer Hochschild, and Ariel White. 2016. "Americans' Belief in Linked Fate: Does the Measure Capture the Concept?" *Journal of Race, Ethnicity, and Politics* 1: 117–44.

Gay, Claudine, and Katherine Tate. 1998. "Doubly Bound: The Impact of Gender and Race on the Politics of Black Women." *Political Psychology* 19 (1): 169–84.

Gerber, Alan S. and Donald P. Green. 2012. *Field Experiments: Design, Analysis, and Interpretation*. New York: W.W. Norton.

Gershon, Sarah Allen, Celeste Montoya, Christina Bejarano, and Nadia Brown. 2019. "Intersectional Linked Fate and Representation." *Politics, Groups, and Identities* 7 (3): 642–53.

Giddings, Paula. 1984. *When and Where I Enter: The Impact of Black Women on Race and Sex in America*. New York: Amistad Publishing.

Giddings, Paula J. 2009. *In Search of Sisterhood: Delta Sigma Theta and the Challenge of the Black Sorority Movement*. New York, NY: Harper Collins.

Gill, Tiffany. 2010. *Beauty Shop Politics*. Urbana-Champaign: University of Illinois Press.

Gillespie, Andra. 2010. Judged by His Actions: How President Obama Addressed Race in the First Six Months of His Administration. *Journal of Race & Policy* 6 (1): 9–23.

Gillespie, Andra, ed. 2010. Whose Black politics? Cases in Post-Racial Black Leadership. New York, NY: Routledge.

Gillespie, Andra, and Nadia E Brown. 2019. "# BlackGirlMagic Demystified." *Phylon (1960-)* 56 (2): 37–58.

Gilman, Sander. 1985. *Difference and Pathology*. Ithaca, NY: Cornell University Press.

Githens, Marianne, and Jewell Prestage. 1977. *A Portrait of Marginality: The Political Behavior of the American Woman*. Boston, MA: Addison-Wesley Longman Ltd.

Gittens, Sandra. 2002. *African-Caribbean Hairdressing*. Boston, MA: Cengage Learning.

Goering, J.M. 1971. "Changing Perceptions and Evaluations of Physical Characteristics among Blacks." *Phylon (1960-)* 33: 231–41.

Gollancz, Victor. 2019. "Race Uplift." In *The World of Jim Crow America: A Daily Life Encyclopedia* [2 volumes]: 251 edited by Steven A. Reich. Santa Barbara, CA: ABC-CLIO.

Gordon, Milton. 1961. "Assimilation in America: Theory and Reality." *Daedalus* 90 (2): 263–85.

Graham, Lawrence Otis. 1999. *Inside America's Black Upper Class: Our Kind of People"* New York: Routledge.

Griffin, Chante'. 2019. "How Natural Black Hair at Work Became a Civil Rights Issue." *JSTOR Daily*. July 13. https://daily.jstor.org/how-natural-black-hair-at-work-became-a-civil-rights-issue/

Grigsby Bates, Karen. (2014). "Black Fraternities and Sororities Split on Protest Policy." *NPR*. December 13. https://www.npr.org/sections/codeswitch/2014/12/13/370427539/black-fraternities-and-sororities-split-on-protest-policy

Grose, Christian. 2011. *Congress in Black and White: Race and Representation in Washington and at Home*. Ebook. New York: Cambridge University Press.

Grossman, Matt. 2009. "Going Pro? Political Campaign Consulting and the Professional Model." *Journal of Political Marketing* 8 (2): 81–104.

Guest, Greg, Emily Namey, Jamilah Taylor, Natalie Eley, and Kevin McKenna. 2017. "Comparing Focus Groups and Individual Interviews: Findings from a Randomized Study." *International Journal of Social Research Methodology*, 20 (6): 693–708.

Gutherie, R.D. 1976. *Body Hotspots*. New York: Van Nostrand Reinhold.

Hajnal, Zoltan L., and Taeku Lee. 2011. *Why Americans Don't Join the Party: Race, Immigration, and the Failure (of Political Parties) to Engage the Electorate*. Princeton, NJ: Princeton University Press.

Halliday, Aria S., and Brown, Nadia E. 2018. "The power of Black girl magic anthems: Nicki Minaj, Beyoncé, and 'feeling myself' as political empowerment." *Souls* 20 (2): 222–38.

Hancock, Ange-Marie. 2007. "When Multiplication Doesn't Equal Quick Addition: Examining Intersectionality as a Research Paradigm." *Perspectives on Politics* 5 (1): 63–79.

Hancock, Jeffrey T., and Catalina Toma. 2009. "Putting Your Best Face Forward: The Accuracy of Online Dating Photographs." *Journal of Communication* 59: 367–86.

Hardy-Fanta, Carol, Dianne Pinderhughes, and Christine Marie Sierra. 2016. *Contested Transformation*. Cambridge, UK: Cambridge University Press.

Harris, Angela. 2009. "Foreword: Economics of Color." In *Shades of Difference*, edited by Evelyn Glenn, 1–5. Stanford, CA: Stanford University Press.

Harris, Duchess. 2009. *Black Feminist Politics from Kennedy to Clinton*. New York, NY: Palgrave Macmillan.

Harris, Fredrick. 2012. *The Price of the Ticket: Barack Obama and Rise and Decline of Black Politics*. New York: Oxford University Press.

Harris, Fredrick C. 2014. "The Rise of Respectability Politics." *Dissent* 61 (1): 33–37.

Harris, Kamala. 2019. *The Truths We Hold: An American Journey*. New York: Penguin.

Harrison, Maxine. 2018. "The Natural Hair Movement May Have Improved Afro Hair Acceptance, but Films Like *Nappily Ever After* Are Still Needed More than Ever." *Independent*. October 1. https://www.independent.co.uk/voices/natural-hair-movement-nappily-ever-after-afro-hair-acceptance-sanaa-lathan-a8562026.html

Harris-Perry, Melissa. 2011. *Sister Citizen: Shame, Stereotypes and Black Women in America*. New Haven, CT: Yale University Press.

Harris-Perry, Melissa. 2013. "Black Female Voices: Who Is Listening—A Public Dialogue between bell hooks + Melissa Harris-Perry." *The New School*. November 8.

Hawkesworth, Mary. 2003. "Congressional Enactments of Race-Gender: Toward at Theory of Race-Gendered Institutions." *American Political Science Review* 97 (4): 529–50.

Hernandez, Marcia D. 2011. "Challenging Controlling Images: Appearance Enforcement within Black Sororities." In *Black Greek-Letter Organizations 2.0: New Directions in the Study of African American Fraternities and Sororities*, edited by Matthew W. Hughey and Gregory S. Parks, 212–29. Jackson, MS: University Press of Mississippi.

Hero, Rodney E. and Robert R. Preuhs 2013. *Black-Latino Relations in U.S. National Politics: Beyond Conflict or Cooperation*. Cambridge, UK: Cambridge University Press.

Herring, Cedric. 2004. "Skin Deep: Race and Complexion Matter in the "Color-Blind" Era." In *Skin Deep: How Race and Complexion Matter in the "Color-Blind" Era*, edited by Cedric Herring, Verna Keith, and Hayward Derrick Horton, . Chicago: University of Illinois Press, 1–21.

Hicks, Heather. 2017. "Intersectional Stereotyping and Support for Black Women Candidates." Paper presented at the American Political Science Association Annual Meeting, San Francisco, CA, August 31–September 2.

Higginbotham, Evelyn Brooks. 1993. *Righteous Discontent: The Women's Movement in the Black Baptist Church 1180–1920*. Cambridge, MA: Harvard University Press.

Hill, Mark E. 2000. "Color Differences in the Socioeconomic Status of African American Men: Results of a Longitudinal Study." *Social Forces* 78 (4): 1437–60.

Hill Collins, Patricia. 1991. *Black Feminist Thought*. New York: Routledge.

Hine, Darlene Clark. 1997. *Hine Sight: Black Women and the Re-Construction of American History*. Bloomington, IN: Indiana University Press.

Hobson, Janell. 2003. "The 'Batty' Politic: Toward an Aesthetic of the Black Female Body." *Hypatia* 18 (4): 87–105.

Hochschild, Jennifer, and Vesla Weaver. 2007. "The Skin Color Paradox and the American Racial Order." *Social Forces* 86 (2): 643–70.

Hochschild, Jennifer, Vesla Weaver, and Traci Burch. 2012. *Creating a New Racial Order: How Immigration, Multiracialism, Genomics, and the Young Can Remake Race in America*. Princeton, NJ: Princeton University Press.

Hoff, Victoria Dawson. 2015. "Zendaya Speaks Out After Her Dreadlocks Are Criticized At Oscars." *Elle*. February 25. https://www.elle.com/culture/celebrities/news/a26962/zendaya-dreadlocks-criticism.

hooks, bell. 1995. *Killing Rage*. New York: H. Holt & Company.

Huddy, Leonie. 1994. "The Political Significance of Voters' Gender Stereotypes." In *Research in Micopolitics*, edited by M.D. Carpini, L. Huddy, and R.Y. Shapiro, 169–93. Greenwich, CT: JAT Press.

Huddy, Leonie. 2001. "From Social to Political Identity: A Critical Examination of Social Identity Theory." *Political Psychology* 22: 127–56.

Huddy, Leonie, and Nayda Terkildsen. 1993a. "Gender Stereotypes and the Perception of Male and Female Candidates." *American Journal of Political Science* 37 (1): 119–47.

Huddy, Leonie, and Nayda Terkildsen. 1993b. "The Consequences of Gender Stereotypes for Women Candidates at Different Levels and Types of Office." *Political Research Quarterly* 46 (3): 503–25.

Hudgins v. Wright, 11 Va. 134 (1 Hen. & M.) (Sup. Ct. App. 1806).

Huff, Connor and Dustin Tingley. 2015. "'Who Are These People' Evaluating the Demographic Characteristics and Political Preferences of MTurk Survey Respondents." *Research & Politics* 2 (3): 1–12.

Hughes, Michael, and Bradley R. Hertel. 1990. "The Significance of Color Remains: A Study of Life Chances, Mate Selection, and Ethnic Consciousness." *Social Forces* 68 (4): 1105–20.

Hughey, Matthew W., Gregory S. Parks, and Theda Skocpol. 2011. *Black Greek-Letter Organizations 2.0 : New Directions in the Study of African American Fraternities and Sororities*. Jackson, MS: University Press of Mississippi. http://ebookcentral.proquest.com/lib/purdue/detail.action?docID=683905

Hunter, Margaret L. 1998. "Colorstruck: Skin Color Stratification in the Lives of African American Women." *Sociological Inquiry* 68 (4): 517–35.

Hunter, Margaret L. 2005. *Race, Gender, and the Politics of Skin Tone*. New York: Routledge.

Hunter, Margaret L. 2007. "The Persistent Problem of Colorism: Skin Tone, Status, and Inequality." *Sociology Compass* 1 (1): 237–54.

Inglehart, R., 1977. "Values, Objective Needs, and Subjective Satisfaction among Western Publics." *Comparative Political Studies* 9 (4): 429–58.

Jackson, John L., Jr. 2008. *Racial Paranoia: The Unintended Consequences of Political Correctness*. New York: Basic Civitas.

Jamyra, Perry. 2020. "Black Women Learn How to Braid While Social Distancing." *Philadelphia Tribune*. April 4. https://www.phillytrib.com/lifestyle/black-women-learn-how-to-braid-while-social-distancing/article_e3655765-45f7-5dff-911e-c7977ff6b62a.html#/questions

Jann, Ben. 2005. "Making Regression Tables from Stored Estimates." *Stata Journal* 5 (3): 288–308.

Jann, Ben. 2007. "Making Regression Tables Simplified." *Stata Journal* 7 (2): 227–44.

Jefferson, Hakeem. 2018. "Policing Norms: Punishment and the Politics of Respectability among Black Americans." Working paper.

Jefferson, Hakeem. 2019. *Policing Norms: Punishment and the Politics of Respectability Among Black Americans.* University of Michigan, Ann Arbor. Dissertation.

Jenkins, Richard. 1996. *Social Identity.* London: Routledge.

Johnson Carew, Jessica D. 2012. *"Lifting as We Climb?" The Role of Stereotypes in the Evaluations of Political Candidates at the Intersection of Race and Gender.* Dissertation, Duke University.

Johnson Carew, Jessica D. 2016. "How Do You See Me? Stereotyping of Black Women and How It Affects Them in an Electoral Context." In *Distinct Identities: Minority Women in U.S. Politics,* edited by Nadia E. Brown and Sarah Allen Gershon Brown, 111–31. New York: Routledge.

Johnson, Alexis McGill, Rachel D. Godsil, Jessica MacFarlane, Linda R. Tropp, and Phillip Atiba Goff. 2017. "The 'Good Hair' Study: Explicit and Implicit Attitudes toward Black Women's Hair." *Perception Institute.* https://perception.org/ wp-content/uploads/2017/ 01/TheGood-HairStudyFindingsReport.pdf

Johnson, Dennis W. 2001. *No Place for Amateurs: How Political Consultants are Reshaping American Democracy.* New York: Routledge.

Johnson, Elizabeth. 2013. *Resistance and Empowerment in Black Women's Hair Styling.* New York: Routledge.

Johnson, Patrick. 2003. *Appropriating Blackness: Performance and the Politics of Authenticity.* Durham, NC: Duke University Press.

Jones, M. S. 2020. *Vanguard: How Black Women Broke Barriers, Won the Vote, and Insisted on Equality for All.* Basic Books.

Joo, Jungseock, and Zachary C. Steinert-Threlkeld. 2018. "Image as Data: Automated Visual Content Analysis for Political Science." https://arxiv.org/abs/1810.01544

Joseph-Salisbury, Remi, and Laura Connelly. 2018. "'If Your Hair Is Relaxed, White People Are Relaxed. If Your Hair Is Nappy, They're Not Happy': Black Hair as a Site of 'Post-Racial' Social Control in English Schools." *Social Sciences* 7 (11): 219. https://doaj.org/ article/56fb3ada79f54d0f81341216279b3949.

Junn, Jane. 1997. "Assimilating or Coloring Participation? Gender, Race, and Democratic Political Participation." In *Women Transforming Politics,* edited by Cathy Cohen, Kathleen B. Jones, and Joan C. Tronto, 387–97. New York: New York University Press.

Junn, Jane. 2017. "The Trump Majority: White Womanhood and the Making of Female Voters in the U.S." *Politics, Groups, and Identities* 5 (2): 343–52.

Junn, Jane and Natalie Masuoka. 2008. "Asian American Identity: Shared Racial Status and Political Context." *Perspectives on Politics* 6 (4): 729–40.

Kaba, Amadu Jacky. 2011. "African American Women Voters." *Review of Black Political Economy* 38 (3): 183–203.

Kahn, Kim Fridkin. 1994. "Does Gender Make a Difference? An Experimental Examination of Sex Stereotypes and Press Patterns in Statewide Campaigns." *American Journal of Political Science* 38 (1): 162–95.

Kahn, Kim Fridkin. 1996. *The Political Consequences of Being a Woman.* New York: Columbia University Press.

Kant, Immanuel. 1997. *Critique of Judgement*, edited by. J. C. Meredity. New York, NY: Oxford University.

Kantamneni, Abhilash, Richelle L. Winkler, and Kirby Calvert. 2019. "Incorporating Community: Opportunities and Challenges in Community-Engaged Research." In *A Research Agenda for Environmental Management*, edited by Halvorsen, Kathleen E., Chelsea Schelly, Robert M. Handler, Erin C. Pischke, and Jessie L. Knowlton, 64–78. Cheltenham: Edward Elgar Publishing.

Kérchy, Anna. 2005. "The Female Grotesque in Contemporary American Culture." *Atenea* 25 (2): 173–86.

King, Deborah. 1988. "Multiple Jeopardy, Multiple Consciousness: The Context of Black Feminist Ideology." *Signs: Journal of Women in Culture and Society* 14 (1): 88–111.

Kitchin, Rob, and Nicholas Tate. 2000. *Conducting Research into Human Geography*. Harlow, UK: Prentice Hall.

Klarner, Carl. 2018. "State Legislative Election Returns, 1967–2016." 2018 update. Harvard Dataverse. https://doi.org/10.7910/DVN/3WZFK9

Koch, Jeffrey W. 2000. "Do Citizens Apply Gender Stereotypes to Infer Candidates' Ideological Orientations?." *Journal of Politics* 62 (2): 414–29.

Krcmaric, Daniel, Stephen C. Nelson, and Andrew Roberts. 2020. Studying Leaders and Elites: The Personal Biography Approach. *Annual Review of Political Science* 23 (8): 1–19.

Krueger, Richard A. and Marry Anne Casey. 2014. Focus Groups: *A Practical Guide for Applied Research*. 5th ed.. Kindle Edition. SAGE Publications, Inc.

Lambert, Briana. 2020. "When Non-Black Minorities Adopt Black Style, Is It Still Appropriation?" *Huffington Post*. October 14. https://www.huffpost.com/entry/non-black-minorities-appropriation_l_5d974be7e4b0f5bf797372ba

Laustsen, Lasse. 2014. "Decomposing the Relationship Between Candidates' Facial Appearance and Electoral Success." *Political Behavior* 36, 777–91.

Lavariega Monforti, Jessica, and Gabriel R. Sanchez. 2010. "The Politics of Perception: An Investigation of the Presence and Sources of Perceptions of Internal Discrimination among Latinos." *Social Science Quarterly* 91 (1): 245–65.

Lawless, Jennifer L. 2004a. "Politics of Presence? Congresswomen and Symbolic Representation." *Political Research Quarterly* 57 (1): 81–99.

Lawless, Jennifer. 2004b. "Women, War, and Winning Elections: Gender Stereotyping in the Post–September 11th Era." *Political Research Quarterly* 57 (3): 479–90.

Lawless, Jennifer, and Richard Fox. 2005. *It Takes a Candidate: Why Women Don't Run for Office*. New York, NY: Cambridge University Press.

Lawless, Jennifer L., and Richard L. Fox. 2010. *It Takes a Candidate: Why Women Don't Run for Office*. New York: Cambridge University Press.

Lawless, Jennifer L. and Richard L. Fox. 2018. "A Trump Effect? Women and the 2018 Midterm Elections." *The Forum* 16 (4). https://www.degruyter.com/view/journals/for/16/4/article-p665.xml.

Lee, Free. 2012. *Relaxed or Natural: You Can Have Beautiful, Black, Healthy Hair. Comprehensive Guide to Growing Longer, Stronger, Healthier Hair*. Scotts Valley, CA: CreateSpace Independent Publishing Platform.

Lee, Taeku. 2008. "Race, Immigration, and the Identity-to-Politics Link." *Annual Review of Political Science* 11: 457–78.

Lemi, Danielle Casarez. "Do Voters Prefer Just Any Descriptive Representative? The Case of Multiracial Candidates." *Perspectives on Politics*: 1–21.

Lemi, Danielle Casarez. 2018. "Identity and Coalitions in a Multiracial Era: How State Legislators Navigate Race and Ethnicity." *Politics, Groups, and Identities* 6 (4): 725–42. https://www.tandfonline.com/doi/abs/10.1080/21565503.2017.1288144.

Lemi, Danielle Casarez, and Nadia E. Brown. 2020. "The Political Implications of Colorism Are Gendered." *PS: Political Science & Politics* 53 (4): 669–73.

Lerman, Amy E., Katherine T. McCabe, and Meredith L. Sadin. 2015. "Political Ideology, Skin Tone, and the Psychology of Candidate Evaluations." *Public Opinion Quarterly* 79 (1): 53–90.

Lerman, Amy E., and Meredith L. Sadin. 2016. "Stereotyping or Projection? How White and Black Voters Estimate Black Candidates' Ideology." *Political Psychology* 37 (2): 147–63. https://onlinelibrary.wiley.com/doi/abs/10.1111/pops.12235.

Lerner, Gerda. "Early Community Work of Black Club Women." *Journal of Negro History* 59 (2) (1974): 158–67

Lester, Neal A. 2000 "Nappy Edges and Goldy Locks: African-American Daughters and the Politics of Hair." *The Lion and the Unicorn* 24: 201–24.

Lincoln, Yvonna S., and Norman K. Denzin, eds. 2003. *Turning points in qualitative research: Tying knots in a handkerchief (Vol. 2)*. Walnut Creek, CA: Altamira Press.

Lindsey, Treva. 2015. "Post-Ferguson: A 'Herstorical' Approach to Black Violability." *Feminist Studies* 41 (1): 232–37.

Lindsey, Treva. 2017. *Colored No More: Reinventing Black Womanhood in Washington, DC*. Urbana-Champaign, IL: University of Illinois Press.

Loc Artist. 2016. "The History of Locs (an Excerpt from *The Art & Science of Locs*)." *Medium*. January 7. https://medium.com/@loc_artist/the-history-of-locs-an-excerpt-from-the-art-science-of-locs-78fbc2e5b052.

Logan, Casey S., Jesse Chandler, Adam Seth Levine, and Dara Z. Strolovitch. 2017. "Intertemporal Differences among MTurk Workers: Time-Based Sample Variations and Implications for Online Data Collection." *SAGE Open* 7 (2): 1–15.

Longhurst, Robyn. 2003. "Semi-Structured Interviews and Focus Groups." *Key Methods in Geography* 3 (2): 143–56.

Lopez, I. F. H. 1994. The Social Construction of Race: Some Observations on Illusion, Fabrication, and Choice. *Harvard Civil Rights–Civil Liberties Law Review* 29 191–203.

Maddox, Keith B., and Stephanie A. Gray. 2002. "Cognitive Representations of Black Americans: Reexploring the Role of Skin Tone." *Personality and Social Psychology Bulletin* 28 (2): 250–59.

Mannheim, Karl. 1972. "The Problem of Generations." In *The New Pilgrims*, edited by Philip G. Altbach and Robert S. Laufer. New York: David McKay (originally published in 1928).

Mansbridge, Jane. 1999. "Should Blacks Represent Blacks and Women Represent Women? A Contingent 'Yes." *Journal of Politics* 61 (3): 628–57.

Mansbridge, Jane, and Katherine Tate. 1992. "Race Trumps Gender: The Thomas Nomination in the Black Community." *PS: Political Science and Politics* 25 (3): 488–92.

Mariani, Mack D. 2008. "A Gendered Pipeline? The Advancement of State Legislators to Congress in Five States." *Politics & Gender* 4 (2): 285–308.

Mason, Lilliana and Julie Wronsi. 2018. "One Tribe to Bind Them All: How Our Social Group Attachments Strengthen Partisanship." *Political Psychology* 39 (S1), Supplement: Advances in Political Psychology, 257–77.

Massey, Douglas S., and Jennifer A. Martin. 2003. *The NIS Skin Color Scale*. Princeton: Princeton University Press.

Masuoka, Natalie. 2006. Together They Become One: Examining the Predictors of Panethnic Group Consciousness among Asian Americans and Latinos. *Social Science Quarterly* 87 (5): 993–1011.

Masuoka, Natalie, and Jane Junn. 2013. *The Politics of Belonging: Race, Public Opinion and Immigration.* Chicago: University of Chicago Press.

Matthews, Donald R., and James Warren Prothro. 1966. *Negroes and the New Southern Politics.* San Diego, CA: Harcourt, Brace & World.

Mayes, Ernest M. 1997. "Chapter 5: As Soft as Straight Gets: African American Women and Mainstream Beauty Standards in Haircare Advertising." *Counterpoints* 54: 85–108. http://www.jstor.org/stable/42975205.

McCall, Leslie. 2005. "The Complexity of Intersectionality." *Signs: Journal of Women in Culture and Society* 30 (3): 1771–800.

McClain, Paula D., Jessica D. Johnson Carew, Eugene Walton, Jr., and Candis S. Watts. 2009. "Group Membership, Group Identity, and Group Consciousness: Measures of Racial Identity in American Politics?" *Annual Review of Political Science* 12: 471–85.

McConnaughy, Corrine M., Ismail K. White, David L. Leal, and Jason P. Casellas. 2010. "A Latino on the Ballot: Explaining Coethnic Voting among Latinos and the Response of White Americans." *Journal of Politics* 72 (4): 1199–211.

McCourt, Kathleen. 1977. *Working-Class Women and Grass-Roots Politics.* Bloomington, IN: Indiana University Press.

McDermott, Monika. 1998. "Race and Gender Cues in Low-Information Elections." *Political Research Quarterly* 51 (4): 895–918.

McGill Johnson, Alexis, Rachel D. Godsil, Jessica MacFarlane, Linda R. Tropp, and Phillip Goff Atiba. 2017. *The "Good Hair" Study: Explicit and Implicit Attitudes Toward Black Women's Hair.* Washington, D.C.: Perception Institute.

McIlwain, Charlton D., and Stephen D. Caliendo. 2011. *Race Appeal: How Candidates Invoke Race in US Political Campaigns.* Philadelphia: Temple University Press.

McKenna, Katelyn Y.A., and John A. Bargh. 1998. "Coming Out in the Age of the Internet: Identity De-Marginalization from Virtual Group Participation." *Journal of Personality and Social Psychology* 75 (3): 681–94.

Mercer, Kobena. 1994. *Welcome to the Jungle: New Positions in Black Cultural Studies.* New York: Routledge.

Mercer, Kobena. 2005. "Black Hair/Style Politics." In *The Subcultures Reader,* edited by Ken Gelder, 420–35. London: Routledge.

Merolla, Jennifer L., Abbylin H. Sellers, and Danielle Casarez Lemi. 2017. "Does the Presence of Women on the Ballot Increase Female Empowerment?" Paper presented at the American Political Science Association Annual Meeting, San Francisco, CA, August 31–September 2.

Mikesell, Lisa, Elizabeth Bromley, and Dmitry Khodyakov. 2013. "Ethical Community-Engaged Research: A Literature Review." *American Journal of Public Health* 103 (12): e7–e14.

Miller, Warren E. 1992. "Generational changes and party identification." *Political Behavior* 14 (3): 333–52.

Minta, Michael D. 2019. "Diversity and Minority Interest Group Advocacy in Congress." *Political Research Quarterly* 73 (1): 208–20. https://doi.org/10.1177/1065912919885024.

Minta, Michael D. and Nadia E. Brown. 2014. "Intersecting Interests: Gender, Race, and Congressional Attention to Women's Issues." *Du Bois Review: Social Science Research on Race* 11 (2): 253–72.

Minta, Michael D. and Valeria Sinclair-Chapman. 2013. "Diversity in Political Institutions and Congressional Responsiveness to Minority Interests." *Political Research Quarterly* 66 (1): 127–40.

Mitchell, Toya. 2019. *US Black Haircare Market Report*. Mintel Reports. https://reports.mintel.com/display/919874/

Mohdin, Aamna. 2018. "There's Now a Searchable Database of the Black Women Running for Office in 2018." *Quartz*. January 24. https://qz.com/1187950/the-searchable-database-of-the-black-women-running-for-office-in-2018/

Mokoena, Hlonipha. 2016. "From Slavery to Colonialism and School Rules: A History of Myths about Black Hair." *The Conversation*. https://theconversation.com/from-slavery-to-colonialism-and-school-rules-a-history-of-myths-about-black-hair-64676

Montell, Frances. 1999. Focus Group Interviews: A New Feminist Method. *NWSA Journal* 11 (1): 44–71.

Mora, G. Cristina. 2014. *Making Hispanics: How Activists, Bureaucrats, and Media Constructed a New American*. Chicago: University of Chicago Press.

Morin, Jason L., Yoshira Macias Mejia, and Gabriel R. Sanchez. 2020. "Is the Bridge Broken? Increasing Ethnic Attachments and Declining Party Influence among Latino Voters." *Political Research Quarterly*. https://doi.org/10.1177/1065912919888577

Morioka, K. 2005. *Hair follicle: Differentiation under the Electron Microscope—An Atlas*. Japan: Springer Japan.

Moskowitz, David, and Patrick Stroh. 1994. "Psychological Sources of Electoral Racism." *Political Psychology* 15 (2): 307–29.

Moulite, Jessica. 2020. "Exclusive: Rep. Ayanna Pressley Reveals Beautiful Bald Head and Discusses Alopecia for the First Time." *The Root*. January 16. https://theglowup.theroot.com/exclusive-rep-ayanna-pressley-reveals-beautiful-bald-1841039847

Mutnick, Ally, Heather Caygle, and Sarah Ferris. 2020. Black Caucus seeks to squash liberal insurgents. *Politico*. April 28. https://www.politico.com/news/2020/04/28/black-caucus-squash-liberal-insurgents-211969

Nash, Jennifer C. 2008. "Re-thinking Intersectionality." *Feminist Review* 89 (1): 1–15.

Nash, Jennifer C. 2018. *Black Feminism Reimagined: After Intersectionality*. Durham, NC: Duke University Press.

Ndichu, Edna G, and Shikha Upadhyaya. 2019. "'Going Natural': Black Women's Identity Project Shifts in Hair Care Practices." *Consumption Markets & Culture* 22 (1): 44–67. https://doi.org/10.1080/10253866.2018.1456427.

Neal, Angela, and Midge Wilson. 1989. "The Role of Skin Color and Features in the Black Community: Implications for Black Women and Therapy." *Clinical Psychology Review* 9 (3): 323–33.

Nelson, Camille A. 2006. "Of Eggshells and Thin-Skulls: A Consideration of Racism-Related Mental Illness Impacting Black Women." *International Journal of Law and Psychiatry* 29 (2): 112–36.

Newman, Benjamin J., Jennifer Merolla, Sono Shah, Danielle Casarez Lemi, and Karthick Ramakrishnan. n.d. "The Trump Effect: An Experimental Investigation of the Emboldening Effect of Racially Inflammatory Elite Communication." Working Paper.

Noble, Safiya Umoja. 2018. *Algorithms of Oppression: How Search Engines Reinforce Racism*. New York: New York University Press.

North, Anna. 2020. "Joe Biden Breaks Record for Most Votes Ever in a Presidential Election." *Vox*. Accessed on November 9, 2020. https://www.vox.com/2020/11/4/21550081/joe-biden-record-votes-2020-election-trump.

O'Grady, Lorraine. 1992. "Olympia's Maid: Reclaiming Black Female Subjectivity." *Afterimage* 20 (1): 14–20.

Okazawa-Rey, Margo, Tracy Robinson, and Janie Victoria Ward. 1987. "Black Women and the Politics of Skin Color and Hair." *Women & Therapy* 6 (1–2): 89–102.

Onwuegbuzie, Anthony J., Wendy B. Dickinson, Nancy L. Leech, and Annmarie G. Zoran. 2009. "A Qualitative Framework for Collecting and Analyzing Data in Focus Group Research." *International Institute for Qualitative Methodology* 8 (3): 1–21. https://doi.org/10.1177%2F160940690900800301.

Opie, Tina R., and Katherine W. Phillips. 2015. "Hair Penalties: The Negative Influence of Afrocentric Hair on Ratings of Black Women's Dominance and Professionalism." *Frontiers in Psychology* 6 (131): 1–14.

Orey, Byron D'Andra, and Nadia E. Brown. 2014. "Black Women State Legislators: Electoral Trend Data 1995–2011." *National Political Science Review* 16: 143–47.

Orey, D'Andrea, Wendy Smooth, Kimberly Adams, and Kish Harris-Clark. 2006. "Race and Gender Matter: Refining Models of Legislative Policy Making in State Legislatures." *Journal of Women, Politics, & Policy* 28 (3/4): 97–119.

Orey, Byron D'Andra and Yu Zhang. 2019. Melanted Millennials and the Politics of Black Hair. *Social Science Quarterly* 100 (6): 2458–76.

Oyedemi, Toks. 2016. "Beauty as Violence: 'Beautiful' Hair and the Cultural Violence of Identity Erasure." *Social Identities* 22 (5): 537–53. http://www.tandfonline.com/doi/abs/10.1080/13504630.2016.1157465.

Packnett, Brittany. 2017. "Black Women Kept Roy Moore Out of Office. Here's How to Actually Thank Them." *The Cut*. December 13. https://www.thecut.com/2017/12/black-women-turnout-roy-moore-doug-jones.html

Panagopoulos, Costas. 2006. "Political Consultants, Campaign Professionalization, and Media Attention." *PS: Political Science & Politics* 39 (4): 867–69.

Parks, Gregory. 2008. *Black Greek-Letter Organizations in the Twenty-First Century: Our Fight Has Just Begun*. Lexington, KY: University Press of Kentucky.

Patterson, Molly, and Kristin Renwick Monroe. 1998. "Narrative in Political Science." *Annual Review of Political Science* 1: 315–31.

Payne, Charles. 1990. "Men Led, but Women Organized: Movement Participation of Women in the Mississippi Delta." In *Women and Social Protest*, edited by Vicki L. Crawford, Jacqueline Anne Rouse, and Barbara Woods, 156–65. Brooklyn, NY: Carlson.

Pellegrino, Greg, Sally D'Amato, and Anne Weisberg. 2010. *Paths to Power: Advancing Women in Government*. Deloitte Touche Tohmatsu.

Perry, Huey L. 1991. Deracialization as an Analytical Construct in American Urban Politics. *Urban Affairs Review* 27 (2): 181–91.

Pew Research Center. 2010. "Millennials: Confident, Connected, Open to Change." Pew Research Center, Washington, DC. https://www.pewsocialtrends.org/2010/02/24/millennials-confident-connected-open-to-change/

Philpot, Tasha S., and Hanes Walton Jr. 2007. "One of Our Own: Black Female Candidates and the Voters Who Support Them." *American Journal of Political Science* 51 (1): 49–62. http://www.jstor.org/stable/4122905.

Portes, Alejandro, and Min Zhou. 1993. "The Second Generation: Segmented Assimilation and Its Variants." *Annals of the American Academy of Political and Social Science* 530: 74–96.

Price, Kimala. 2010. "What Is Reproductive Justice? How Women of Color Activists Are Redefining the Pro-Choice Paradigm." *Meridians* 10 (2): 42–65.

Purdie-Vaughns, Valerie, and Richard P. Eibach. 2008. "Intersectional Invisibility: The Distinctive Advantages and Disadvantages of Multiple Subordinate-Group Identities." *Sex Roles* 59 (5–6): 377–91.

Puwar, Nirmal. 2004. *Space Invaders: Race, Gender and Bodies out of Place*. New York: Berg.

Pyke, Karen, and Tran Dang. 2003. "'FOB' and 'Whitewashed': Identity and Internalized Racism Among Second Generation Asian Americans." *Qualitative Sociology* 26 (2): 147–72.

Quaresma, Maria Victoria, Maria Abril Martinez Velasco, and Antonella Tosti. 2015. "Hair Breakage in Patients of African Descent: Role of Dermoscopy." *Skin Appendage Discord* 1 (2): 99–10.

Ramakrishnan, Karthick, Jane Junn, Taeku Lee, and Janelle Wong. 2012. National Asian American Survey. Version V2. Resource Center for Minority Data. July 19. doi:–10.3886/ICPSR31481.v2

Randle, Brenda A. 2015. "I Am Not My Hair." *Race, Gender & Class* 22 (1–2): 114–21. http://www.jstor.org/stable/26505328.

Rankine, Louric. "Wright's Natural Hair Act Passes as CURLFEST Comes To NYC." *Kings County Politics*. Accessed on November 5, 2020 https://www.kingscountypolitics.com/wrights-natural-hair-act-passes-as-curlfest-comes-to-nyc/

Reich, Steven A. 2019. *The World of Jim Crow America: A Daily Life Encyclopedia* [2 volumes]. Santa Barbara, CA: ABC-CLIO.

Roberts, Deborah, Ignacio Torres, and Jasmine Brown. 2016. "As Natural Hair Goes Mainstream, One High School's Natural Hair Ban Sparks Firestorm." *ABC News*. September 15. https://abcnews.go.com/US/natural-hair-mainstream-high-schools-policy-sparks-firestorm/story?id=42100267

Robinson, Cynthia L. 2011. "Hair as Race: Why 'Good Hair' May Be Bad for Black Females." *Howard Journal of Communications* 22 (4): 358–76.

Robinson, Eugene. 2018. "If There Is a 'Blue Wave,' Democrats Would Have Black Women to Thank." *Washington Post*. October 22. https://www.washingtonpost.com/opinions/if-there-is-a-blue-wave-democrats-would-have-black-women-to-thank/2018/10/22/d72dbede-d63d-11e8-aeb7-ddcad4a0a54e_story.html

Robinson-Moore, Cynthia L. 2008. "Beauty Standards Reflect Eurocentric Paradigms—So What? Skin Color, Identity, and Black Female Beauty." *Journal of Race & Policy* 4 (1): 66–85.

Robnett, Belinda. 2000. *How Long How Long? African American Women in the Struggle for Civil Rights*. Oxford: Oxford University Press.

Romero, Mary. 2017. *Introducing Intersectionality*. Hoboken, NJ: John Wiley & Sons.

Rooks, Noliwe M. 1996. *Hair Raising: Beauty, Culture, and African American Women*. New Brunswick, NJ: Rutgers University Press.

Rosenthal, Cindy Simon. 1995. "The Role of Gender in Descriptive Representation." *Political Research Quarterly* 48: 599–611.

Rouse, Stella M. 2013,2016. *Latinos in the Legislative Process: Interests and Influence*. New York: Cambridge University Press. First paperback edition.

Rouse, Stella M., and Ashley D. Ross. 2018. *The Politics of Millennials: Political Beliefs and Policy Preferences of America's Most Diverse Generation*. Ann Arbor, MI: University of Michigan Press.

Rudman, Laurie A., and Meghan C. McLean. 2016. "The Role of Appearance Stigma in Implicit Racial In-Group Bias." *Group Processes and Intergroup Relations* 19 (3): 374–93.

Sanbonmatsu, Kira. 2002. "Gender Stereotypes and Vote Choice." *American Journal of Political Science* 46 (1): 20–34.

Sanbonmatsu, Kira. 2003. "Gender-Related Political Knowledge and the Descriptive Representation of Women." *Political Behavior* 25 (4): 367–88.

Sapiro, Virginia. 1980. "News from the front: Intersex and intergenerational conflict over the status of women." *Western Political Quarterly* 33 (2): 260–77.

Sanchez, Gabriel R., and Natalie Masuoka. 2010. "Brown-Utility Heuristic? The Presence of Contributing Factors of Latino Linked Fate." *Hispanic Journal of Behavioral Sciences* 32 (4): 519–31.

Sanchez, Gabriel R., and Edward D. Vargas. 2016. "Taking a Closer Look at Group Identity: The Link Between Theory and Measurement of Group Consciousness and Linked Fate." *Political Research Quarterly* 60 (1): 160–74.

Saperstein, Aliya. 2012. Capturing Complexity in the United States: Which Aspects of Race Matter and When? *Ethnic and Racial Studies* 35 (8): 1484–502.

Saro-Wiwa, Zina. 2012. "Black Women's Transitions to Natural Hair." *New York Times*. May 31. http://www.nytimes.com/2012/06/01/opinion/ black-women-and-natural-hair.html?_r=0.

Schaverien, Anna. 2019. "There Is a Huge Gap in the Hair Care Market. Afrocenchix Is Filling It." *Forbes*. January 14. https://www.forbes.com/sites/annaschaverien/2019/01/14/afrocenchix-natural-afro-hair-care/#6c7c98a92d6c.

Schildkraut, Deborah J. 2013. "Which Birds of a Feather Flock Together? Assessing Attitudes about Descriptive Representation among Latinos and Asian Americans." *American Politics Research* 41 (4): 699–729.

Schildkraut, Deborah J. 2017. "White Attitudes about Descriptive Representation in the U.S.: The Roles of Identity, Discrimination, and Linked Fate." *Politics, Groups, and Identities* 5 (1): 84–106.

Schmidt, Samantha. 2020. "The Gender Gap Was Expected to Be Historic. Instead, Women Voted Much as They Always Have." *The Washington Post*. Accessed on November 9 2020. https://www.washingtonpost.com/dc-md-va/2020/11/06/election-2020-gender-gap-women/.

Schneider, Andrew. 2019. "Meet 'Black Girl Magic,' The 19 African-American Women Elected as Judges in Texas." *National Public Radio*. January 16. https://www.npr.org/2019/01/16/685815783/meet-black-girl-magic-the-19-african-american-women-elected-as-judges-in-texas

Schneider, Monica C., and Angela L. Bos. 2011. "An Exploration of the Content of Stereotypes of Black Politicians." *Political Psychology* 32 (2): 205–33.

Schuman, Howard, Charlotte Steeh, Lawrence Bobo, and Maria Krysan. 1997. *Racial Attitudes in America: Trends and Interpretations*. Cambridge, MA: Harvard University Press.

Schutze, Jim. 1986. *The Accommodation: The Politics of Race in an American City*. New York, NY: Citadel Press.

Scott, Eugene. 2017. "The Democratic Party Owes Black Female Voters a Big 'Thank You.'" *Washington Post*. November 9. https://www.washingtonpost.com/news/the-fix/wp/2017/11/09/the-democratic-party-owes-black-women-voters-a-big-thank-you/

Scott, Rachel, MaryAlice Parks, and Brittany Berkowitz. 2018. "Registered Nurse Lauren Underwood Wants to Become the First Black Woman to Represent Her District." *Good Morning America*. October 26. https://www.goodmorningamerica.com/news/story/registered-nurse-lauren-underwood-black-woman-represent-district-58582936

Sellers, Regina E. 2003. "The Kink Factor: A Womanist Discourse Analysis of African-American Mother/daughter Perspectives on Negotiating Black Hair/body Politics." In *Understanding African American Rhetoric: Classical Origins to Contemporary Innovations*, edited by R.L. Jackson and E.B. Richardson, 223–43. New York: Routledge.

Seltzer, Richard, and Robert C. Smith. 1991. "Color Differences in the Afro-American Community and the Differences They Make." *Journal of Black Studies* 21: 279–86.

Sen, Maya and Omar Wasow. 2016. "Race as a Bundle of Sticks: Designs That Estimate Effects of Seemingly Immutable Characteristics." *Annual Review of Political Science* 19: 499–522.

Shaw, Andrea Elizabeth. 2006. *The Embodiment of Disobedience: Fat Black Women's Unruly Political Bodies*. Lanham, MD: Lexington Books.

Shelby Rosette, Ashleigh, and Tracy L. Dumas. 2007. "The Hair Dilemma: Conform to Mainstream Expectations or Emphasize Racial Identity." *Duke Journal of Gender Law & Policy* 14: 407–22.

Sigelman, Carol K., Lee Sigelman, Barbara J. Walkosz, and Michael Nitz. 1995. "Black Candidates, White Voters: Understanding Racial Bias in Political Perceptions." *American Journal of Political Science* 39 (1): 243–65.

Silva, Andrea and Carrie Skulley. 2019. "Always Running: Candidate Emergence Among Women of Color over Time." *Political Research Quarterly* 72 (2): 342–59.

Simien, Evelyn M. 2005. "Race, Gender, and Linked Fate." *Journal of Black Studies* 35 (5): 529–50.

Simien, Evelyn M. 2006. *Black Feminist Voices in Politics*. Albany, NY: State University of New York Press.

Simien, Evelyn M., and Rosalie A. Clawson. 2004. "The Intersection of Race and Gender: An Examination of Black Feminist Consciousness, Race Consciousness, and Policy Attitudes." *Social Science Quarterly* 85 (3): 793–810.

Sims, Jennifer Patrice, Whitney Laster Pirtle, and Iris Johnson-Arnold. 2020. "Doing Hair, Doing Race: The Influence of Hairstyle on Racial Perception across the U.S." *Ethnic and Racial Studies* 43 (12): 2099–119. https://www.tandfonline.com/doi/abs/10.1080/01419870.2019.1700296

Sims, Naomi. 1982. *All About Hair Care for the Black Woman*. New York: Doubleday and Company.

Simpson, Andrea Y. 1998. *The Tie That Binds: Identity and Political Attitudes in the Post–Civil Rights Generation*. New York: New York University Press.

Simpson, Andrea Y. 2014. "Public Hazard, Personal Peril: The Impact of Non-Governmental Organizations in the Environmental Justice Movement." *Richmond Journal of Law and the Public Interest* 18: 515.

Smithson, Janet. 2000. "Using and Analysing Focus Groups: Limitations and Possibilities." *International Journal of Social Research Methodology* 3 (2): 103–19.

Smooth, Wendy G. 2001. "Perceptions of Influence in State Legislatures: A Focus on the Experiences of African American Women in State Legislatures." PhD diss., University of Maryland.

Smooth, W.G. 2006. "Intersectionality in Electoral Politics: A Mess Worth Making." *Politics and Gender* 2 (3): 400–14.

Smooth, W.G. 2006. "Intersectionality and Politics: Recent Research on Gender, Race, and Political Representation in the United States." *Gender and Politics* 2 (3): 400–14.

Spellers, R.E. 2003. "The Kink Factor: A Womanist Discourse Analysis of African-American Mother/Daughter Perspectives on Negotiating Black Hair/Body Politics." In *Classical Origins to Contemporary Innovations*, edited by R.L. Jackson and E. B. Richardson, 223–243. New York: Routledge.

Spellers, Regina E. 2002. "Happy to Be Nappy! Embracing an Afrocentric Aesthetic for Beauty." In *Readings in Intercultural Communication*, edited by J.N. Martin, T. K. Nakayama and L.A. Flores, 52–60. New York: McGraw Hill.

Spelman, Elizabeth. 1988. *Inessential Woman: Problems of Exclusion in Feminist Thought*. Boston, MA: Beacon Press.

Spencer, Tallie, Marquis Hughes, and Elisa Tang. 2019. "At Curlfest, Women (and Men) Share What Their Natural Hair Means to Them." *Good Morning America*. July 29. https://www.goodmorningamerica.com/style/story/curlfest-women-share-natural-hair-means-64584381

Springer, Kimberly. 2005. *Living for the Revolution: Black Feminist Organizations 1968–1980*. New York: Routledge.

St. Jean, Yanick, and Joe R. Feagin. 1997. "Racial Masques: Black Women and Subtle Gendered Racism." In *Subtle Sexism: Current Practice and Prospects for Change*, edited by Nijole V. Benokraitis, 179–200. Thousand Oaks, CA: SAGE Publications.

Story, Kaila Adia. 2010. "Racing Sex—Sexing Race." In *Imagining the Black Female Body*, edited by Carol E. Henderson, 23–43. New York, NY: Palgrave Macmillan.

Story, Kalia Adia. 2017. "Fear of a Black Femme: The Existential Conundrum of Embodying a Black Femme Identity While Being a Professor of Black, Queer, and Feminist Studies." *Journal of Lesbian Studies* 21 (4): 407–19. DOI: 10.1080/10894160.2016.1165043

Stout, Christopher T., Kelsy Kretschmer, and Leah Ruppanner. 2017. "Gender Linked Fate, Race/Ethnicity, and the Marriage Gap in American Politics." *Political Research Quarterly* 70 (3): 509–22.

Swain, Carol M. 1993. *Black Faces, Black Interests: The Representation of African Americans in Congress*. Cambridge, MA: Harvard University Press.

Tajfel, Henri. 1974. "Social Identity and Intergroup Behavior." *Social Science Information* 13 (2): 65–93.

Tajfel, Henri. 1981. *Human Groups and Social Categories*. Cambridge, UK: Cambridge University Press.

Tajfel, Henri, and John C. Turner. 1986. "The Social Identity Theory of Intergroup Behavior." In *Psychology of Intergroup Relations*, edited by Stephen Worchel and William G. Austin, 7–24. Chicago: Nelson-Hall Inc..

Tate, Katherine. 2001. "The Political Representation of Blacks in Congress: Does Race Matter?" *Legislative Studies Quarterly* 26 (4): 623–38.

Terborg-Penn, Rosalyn, and Sharon Harley. 1978. *The Afro-American Woman: Struggles and Images*. Port Washington, NY: Kennikat Press.

Terkildsen, Nayda. 1993. "When White Voters Evaluate Black Candidates: The Processing Implications of Candidate Skin Color, Prejudice, and Self-Monitoring." *American Journal of Political Science* 37 (4): 1032–53. http://www.jstor.org/stable/2111542.

Terracol, Antoine. 2001. "SUTEX: Stata Module to LaTex Code for Summary Statistics Tables." Statistical Software Components, Boston College Department of Economics.

Thomas, Kyle A., and Scott Clifford. 2017. "Validity and Mechanical Turk: An Assessment of Exclusion Methods and Interactive Experiments." *Computers in Human Behavior* 77: 184–97.

Thompson, Cheryl. 2014. "Black Beauty Products: Why Women's Hair Needs Safer Care." *Herizons* 28 (1): 20.

Thomson, Rosemarie Garland. 1997. *Extraordinary Bodies: Figuring Disability in American Culture and Literature.* New York: Columbia University Press.

Thurber, James A.1998. The Study of Campaign Consultants: A Subfield in Search of Theory. *PS: Political Science & Politics.* 31 (2): 145–49.

Tillman, Linda C. 2002. Culturally Sensitive Research Approaches: An African-American Perspective. *Educational Researcher* 31 (9): 3–12.

Travis, Julie. 1999. "Exploring the Constructs of Evaluative Criteria for Interpretivist Research." In *Proceedings of the 10th Australasian Conference on Information Systems,* 1037–49. CiteseerX.

Trent, Sydney. 2020. "The Black Sorority That Faced Racism in the Suffrage Movement but Refused to Walk Away." *Washington Post.* August 8. https://www.washingtonpost.com/graphics/2020/local/history/suffrage-racism-black-deltas-parade-washington/

Treviño, A. Javier, Michelle A. Harris, and Derron Wallace. 2008. "What's So Critical about Critical Race Theory?" *Contemporary Justice Review* 11 (1): 7–10.

Trüeb, Ralph M. 2017. From Hair in India to Hair India. *International Journal of Trichology* 9 (1): 1–6.

Tyson, Vanessa C. 2016. *Twists of Fate: Multiracial Coalitions and Minority Representation in the US House of Representatives.* New York: Oxford University Press.

Uzogara, Ekeoma E., and James S. Jackson. 2016. "Perceived Skin Tone Discrimination Across Contexts: African American Women's Reports." *Race and Social Problems* 8 (2): 147–59.

Valentine, Gill. 2005. "Tell Me About . . .: Using Interviews as a Research Methodology." *Methods in Human Geography: A Guide for Students Doing a Research Project* 2: 110–27.

van Leeuwen, Esther, van Knippenberg, Daan, and Naomi Ellemers. 2003. "Continuing and Changing Group Identities: The Effects of Merging on Social Identification and Ingroup Bias." *Personality and Social Psychology Bulletin* 29 (6): 679–90.

Verba, Sidney, Kay Lehman Schlozman, and Henry E. Brady. 1995. *Voice and Equality: Civic Voluntarism in American Politics.* Cambridge, MA: Harvard University Press.

Walker, Andre. 1997. *Andre Talks Hair.* New York: Simon & Schuster.

Walker, Susannah. 2007. *Style and Status: Selling Beauty to African American Women, 1920–1975.* Lexington, KY: University Press of Kentucky.

Wamble, Julian. 2018. "Show Us that You Care: How Community Commitment Signals Affect Black Political Considerations." Ph.D diss., University of Maryland.

Weaver, Vesa M. 2012. "The Electoral Consequences of Skin Color: The "Hidden" Side of Race in Politics." *Political Behavior* 34 (1): 159–92.

Welch, Susan, and Lee Sigelman. 1982. "Changes in Public Attitudes toward Women in Politics." *Social Science Quarterly* 63 (2): 312–22.

West, Candace, and Don H. Zimmerman. 1987. "Doing Gender." *Gender and Society* 1 (2): 125–51.

Whaley, Deborah Elizabeth. 2010. *Disciplining Women: Alpha Kappa Alpha, Black Counterpublics, and the Cultural Politics of Black Sororities.* Albany, NY: SUNY Press.

White, Deborah Gray. 1993. "The Cost of Club Work, the Price of Black Feminism." In *Visible Women: New Essays on American Activism*, edited by Nancy A. Hewitt and Suzanne Lebsock, 247–69. Urbana, IL: University of Illinois Press.

White, Ismail K., and Cheryl N. Laird. 2020. *Steadfast Democrats: How Social Forces Shape Black Political Behavior*. Princeton, NJ: Princeton University Press.

White, Shane, and Graham White. 1995. "Slave Hair and African American Culture in the Eighteenth and Nineteenth Centuries." *Journal of Southern History*, 61 (1): 45–76.

Wilkinson, Betina Cutaia. 2015. *Partners or Rivals? Power and Latino, Black, and White Relations in the Twenty-First Century*. Charlottesville, VA: University of Virginia Press.

Williams, Linda Faye. 2001. "The Civil Rights-Black Power Legacy: Black Women Elected Officials at the Local, State, and National Levels." In *Sisters in the Struggle: African American Women in the Civil Rights-Black Power Movement*, edited by Bettye Collier and V. P. Franklin, 306–32. New York: New York University Press.

Williams, Tasha. 2019. "Democrats Need Black Women Voters Now More Than Ever." *Yes Magazine*. November 21. https://www.yesmagazine.org/democracy/2019/11/21/voting-black-women-democrats/

Williams, Tia. 2014. "What You Said: Transitioning vs. 'The Big Chop.'" *Essence*. May 8. https://www.essence.com/hair/transitioning/what-you-said-transitioning-vs-big-chop/

Wise, Tim. 2009. *Between Barack and a hard place: Racism and white denial in the age of Obama*. San Francisco, CA: City Lights Books.

Woolford, Susan J., Carole J. Woolford-Hunt, Areej Sami, Natalie Blake, and David R. Williams. 2016. "No Sweat: African American Adolescent Girls' Opinions of Hairstyle Choices and Physical Activity." *BMC Obesity* 3 (1): 31–38.

Zernike, Kate. 2001. "Commencements; At Yale, Mrs. Clinton Ponders Hair and Politics." *New York Times*. May 21. https://www.nytimes.com/2001/05/21/nyregion/commencements-at-yale-mrs-clinton-ponders-hair-and-politics.html

Zinn, Maxine Baca. 1979. "Field Research in Minority Communities: Ethical, Methodological and Political Observations by an Insider." *Social Problems* 27 (2): 209–19. http://www.jstor.org/stable/800369.

Index

For the benefit of digital users, indexed terms that span two pages (e.g., 52–53) may, on occasion, appear on only one of those pages.

Figures and tables are indicated by *f* and *t* following the page number.